AF506289

Cultural region

Cultural region
North east England
1945–2000

Natasha Vall

Manchester University Press

Manchester and New York

distributed in the United States exclusively

by Palgrave Macmillan

Copyright © Natasha Vall 2011

The right of Natasha Vall to be identified as the author of this work has been asserted by her in accordance with the Copyright, Designs and Patents Act 1988.

Published by Manchester University Press
Oxford Road, Manchester M13 9NR, UK
and Room 400, 175 Fifth Avenue, New York, NY 10010, USA
www.manchesteruniversitypress.co.uk

Distributed in the United States exclusively by
Palgrave Macmillan, 175 Fifth Avenue, New York,
NY 10010, USA

Distributed in Canada exclusively by
UBC Press, University of British Columbia, 2029 West Mall,
Vancouver, BC, Canada V6T 1Z2

British Library Cataloguing-in-Publication Data
A catalogue record for this book is available from the British Library

Library of Congress Cataloging-in-Publication Data applied for

ISBN   978 0 7190 8228 3   hardback

First published 2011

The publisher has no responsibility for the persistence or accuracy of URLs for any external or third-party internet websites referred to in this book, and does not guarantee that any content on such websites is, or will remain, accurate or appropriate.

Typeset in 10.5/12.5pt Garamond
by Graphicraft Limited, Hong Kong
Printed in Great Britain
by TJ International Ltd, Padstow

Contents

List of figures

List of tables

Acknowledgements

For help during the researching and writing of this book I would like to express my thanks to librarians and archivists in north east England, in particular Newcastle City Libraries, Tyne and Wear Archive Service, Gateshead Library and Durham University Library, as well as to the BBC Written Archive Centre, Caversham. The book would not have been possible without the reminiscences of a number of indidividuals who have given their time generously. Particular thanks are extended to the late Leonard Barras and Alan Plater, who are sorely missed. Thanks are also extended to Tom, Connie and Catherine Pickard, Anna Pepperall, Peter Stark, Val McLane, Michael Mould, Heather Ging and David Whetstone for invaluable insights. I would further like to thank the members of the AHRC Centre for North East England History 2000–5 who helpfully read and commented upon several early drafts; in particular the late Bill Griffiths and Rob Lee, whose generous influences can be detected in many parts of this book. Finally thanks must go to Rosalind and Kenneth Vall, Bill, Madeleine and Wilfrid Lancaster Vall, for tireless support and patience, especially during their summer holidays.

1

Cultural region: 1945–2000

The region, stretching from beyond the Tees in the south to well beyond the Tyne in the north is a region with a culture, a tradition and a way of life entirely of its own.[1]

Writing to celebrate the launch of Tyne Tees Television in 1959, the show business brothers George and Alfred Black reminded their readers of the north east's distinctive and coherent qualities. Joint directors of the new station, the Blacks were members of a long-established family of north east theatrical impresarios and had spent much of 1958 visiting workingmen's clubs and cinemas in the region to gauge popular taste in planning their programmes, finding that good local humour was the key, 'down to earth stuff … a little music, but nothing too highbrow'.[2] Meanwhile Labour politician and fellow board member of Tyne Tees Television, T. Dan Smith, had begun preparations for the 'Blaydon Races Centenary Celebration' in the same year. Smith was keen to articulate the region's cultural tradition and to harness it to a vision of the modern region. The importance of the area's particular characteristics had been emphasised by the Blacks in their proposal to secure the franchise for the first commercial television station in the region, and initially the local integrity of their projected programme format had persuaded the licensing authority that this team surpassed its competitors.

Tyne Tees' regional focus was timely. The 1954 Television Act had stipulated that commercial broadcasting was to develop a regional as opposed to national structure as distinct from the BBC as a national organisation. But the projection of vernacular culture in commercial broadcasting and local politics was not universally embraced and competing versions of the cultural region were emerging at the same time. When the first Arts Council of Great Britain regional boards were established during the 1960s, metropolitan arts officials referred to the north east as a 'cultural desert'. This unfortunate predicament was to be alleviated by the new 'Northern Arts' through a range of initiatives that would establish orchestras, theatres, art galleries and museums, in a concerted effort to modify the image of the area as being peopled by former miners and 'hearty barbarians rolling their "rs" and blowing crude pipes'.[3] Thus began the campaign to promote the region as a site of connoisseur metropolitan culture. The ensuing tension between this imperative and the contrasting celebration of vernacular culture is a central concern for this study.

The importance of managing the presentation of culture and history continues to be as pertinent to the process of regional projection at the beginning of the twenty-first century as it evidently was during the 1960s. By the 1990s academics, journalists and commentators began enthusiastically promoting this area's cultural renaissance and its role in the transformation from an industrial region to a post-industrial society with 'flagship' cultural institutions. The national and regional press added to the sense of a dramatic and triumphant transformation with headlines that described rising phoenixes and boundless cultural achievements such as 'YES IT's NEWCASTLE: from coal hole to city of palaces' and 'Birth place of the cultural revolution'.[4]

This book examines the evolution of regional cultural policy since 1945. For our purposes the term 'cultural policy' refers to arts and cultural management by local and national government, the growing number of semi-independent agencies charged with a cultural remit, as well as regional public and commercial broadcasting. The discussion extends the usual parameters of the term cultural policy beyond arts policy to incorporate both commercial broadcasting and the BBC because these media had an important part to play in both shaping and representing regional culture. In addition, their regional structure, relationship to the government and designated remit also warrant comparison. The development of BBC radio during the inter-war years was influenced by the Reithian imperative to improve popular taste. This found echoes in national arts policy with the transition from voluntarism to the state-led management of cultural patronage after the Second World War.[5] These national institutional developments, and the creation of associated regional organisations, provide a point of departure for an investigation of the relationship between cultural policy and vernacular practices. The following chapters will trace a converging political, economic and arts policy and broadcasting agenda in the promotion of the region as a cultural entity after 1945, which reached a high point by the beginning of the 1970s. After examining the evolution of this process, we analyse how the cultural region responded to the urban regeneration of the 1980s and 1990s. We consider the point that by the 1990s regions assumed a more central role in the wake of the declining significance of national cultures.[6]

An important aspect of this historical assessment of cultural policy revolves around the response of institutions, such as the regional arts boards and the media, to a vibrant and deeply rooted vernacular popular culture. Did these new regional cultural structures help to overcome the divisions between 'metropolitan' and 'provincial' culture or did they reinforce them? Such questions are crucial in order to understand the history of regional cultural policy in England and this book will offer the first historical assessment of the evolution of regional cultural policy after 1945. Whilst national studies have focused upon the transition from voluntaristic to state-led cultural policy after 1945, regional perspectives are largely contemporary and argue for the contribution of cultural management to urban and regional regeneration.[7] Theoretical approaches, on the other hand, have related cultural policy to questions of national public governance whilst there has also been a growing debate on the efficacy of 'culture-led regeneration'.[8] By focusing upon the history of cultural policy through the lens of a regional setting this book will show how national imperatives were enacted or rejected. The focus upon the history of cultural policy also places this work in the context of national and international studies of arts policy and cultural management including the critical evaluation of the economic benefits of the cultural sector, alongside those who have championed increased public resourcing of cultural regeneration.[9] The north east is a fruitful site to explore this continuing debate. With its historic combination of cultural infrastructural deficit and tenacious vernacular traditions the region is a significant 'ideal type' for assessing the efficacy of cultural policy initiatives since 1945. During the 1980s and 1990s Northern Arts helped to secure funding for the now well-known national markers of cultural regeneration such as the globally recognised *Angel of the North*. Whilst these initiatives provide evidence for the rising prominence of 'place marketing' in urban regeneration, such developments have not occurred in a historical vacuum. This book will bring the historical record to bear upon this process, asking whether cultural regeneration since the 1980s really represented a distinct break with past initiatives in regional cultural projection.[10]

As well as reflecting upon the role of cultural policy within the process of regional projection it must be noted that this book is also a history of north east England that stands alongside recent works on northern regional culture.[11] With its unique dialect and memorable urban industrial landscape the north east has often been described as England's most distinctive region.[12] This book builds upon those who have explored the history of a self-conscious north east whilst acknowledging the recent challenge to the *longue durée* of north east identity.[13] The region's contested history serves as a reminder that academic knowledge production has consequences for the legitimisation, representation and emasculation of territories.[14] In seeking to avoid the pitfalls of essentialist history the following analysis understands 'region' as a type of identity formation that deploys a territorial dimension, and following this approach the term 'cultural region' is deployed principally as a discursive concept.[15] Despite the popular tenacity of the culturally coherent north east what follows does not hope to discover the origins of the 'cultural region' in historically specific vernacular traditions.[16] But equally, in the palpable contemporary absence of regional political or economic coherence, the idea of the north east as a cultural space is probably the most important site of regional projection. Bringing a historical perspective to bear upon the contemporary process of cultural regeneration may provide a timely reflection upon the wider debate over territorial affiliation, which has yet to fully consider the role of culture as a carrier of regional identity. However, as Russell and many others have demonstrated, the wider 'north', and the associated idea of northernness as delineated space, is a modern social and cultural construct. In turn the north east, located within that imagined north, is also viewed as a fluctuating, shifting and contingent creation.[17] Some historians have yoked the idea of the 'north east' to the emergence of economic organisations and institutions during the late nineteenth century. Milne, for example, draws attention to engineers and industrialists employing the term 'north east coast' from the late nineteenth century when referring to the location of shipbuilding and heavy engineering. Similarly, McCord has emphasised the role of the North East Railway Company as helping to delineate the region.[18] But there is little evidence that the term had a wider currency, and 'the north' remained the popular descriptor for all northern counties well into the twentieth century. The government mining inspectorate which controlled the region's largest industry was established in the 1850s into 'districts' including the 'North' which comprised Durham, Northumberland, Cumberland and Westmorland. The profession of mining engineers adopted the same geographical region when they established their headquarters in Newcastle in 1852.[19] The North East Railway Company had operations across a large geographical area and its headquarters were in the city of York.

What remains interesting for our discussion is not whether there is a 'regional identity' corresponding to the various geographical delineations of the north east, rather that an awareness of, and reaction to, the notion of a distinctive culture has been present at all. Moreover perhaps the process of locating the contested cultural region is less troublesome for contemporary historians than those of past centuries, thanks to the existence of institutions that were created for the express purpose of resourcing and administering culture in the north east. As Lancaster has shown, the regional descriptor was a demonstrable reality only from the inter-war years. The North East Coast Shipbuilders and Engineering Institute exhibition of 1929 was designed to attract business to the region's faltering economy. The publicity created by the exhibition and the growing economic crisis served to link the term 'north east' with the depressed industrial areas of Northumberland and Durham. The 'north east' was subsequently adopted by government literature and the press and media covering events such as the Jarrow march.[20] The geographical area covered by this book, in respect of the sensible observation that it is important to know what one is talking about when referring to the 'north east's' contribution to art, literature or music, will often be confined to the counties of Northumberland and Durham, but also extends to incorporate parts of Westmoreland, Cumberland, Teesside and the North Riding of Yorkshire. Given the focus on cultural policy the research materials are primarily held in, and relevant to, the major conurbations, but the book also details the history of regional cultural institutions such as Northern Arts that selected Newcastle as their 'regional capital' and adopted boundaries approximating to the geographic designation of a 'North Country' by Professor Fawcett at the beginning of the twentieth century.[21] One of Fawcett's criteria was that this area possessed a shared culture and a 'readily identifiable capital'.[22]

Newcastle has dominated the region culturally and economically since the Norman period. Recently an OECD international survey of 'city regions' concluded that more than 60% of the region's economic and social life was linked to Newcastle.[23] Many elsewhere in the region may feel uncomfortable with Newcastle's dominant position, but clearly little has changed since Fawcett first drafted his map. The work of this geographer has undoubtedly been reinforced by the historiography that acknowledges the importance of the industrial legacy to the creation of regional identity. Fawcett's evidence for shared culture was the coalfield and the associated economic and social connections with Cumberland and Westmoreland.[24] Successive government departments and cultural and planning institutions have adopted Fawcett's map and this common geography allows us to examine the relationship between institution building and regional consciousness as well as providing a regional setting for the development of cultural policy. Much of the ensuing discussion focuses upon the relationship between institutions and cultural practices in delineating, making and remaking the contours of the late-modern cultural region. Therefore it might be helpful to keep in mind a distinction between 'regional consciousness' as referring directly to people's lives and experiences and the 'identity of the region' – an expression of institutions (in the widest sense) incorporating the notion that where territorial consciousness coincides with regional institution building the awareness of the regional space will be strong.[25]

Equally important a rationale for this book is the evidence for the role of individuals in the active projection of the north east as a discrete cultural entity after 1945. The manner of its projection varied according to the architects and audiences for this process. In some cases there were clear attempts to accentuate vernacular particularisms such as dialect, perceived to be at odds with English national culture, but for others the promotion of the north east as a cultural space was concerned to present the area as integral to national culture. Therefore it is important to understand the waxing and waning of regional projection and to appreciate its relationship to the era's major cultural shifts, such as the expansion of broadcasting, state-led cultural policy as well as the growth of commercial popular culture.

The representation of regions in media, including radio and television, is also salient. These communicative processes have been understood in the national setting, but there is still much to learn about the impact of such media upon regional cultures. The need to understand the cultural region in relation to wider developments is heightened by the emergence during the twentieth century of the 'creative industries' as economic forces in their own right. As has been well documented, the emergence of the autonomous cultural sector has produced a new generation of managers and bureaucrats intervening in and shaping the representation of culture.[26] To what extent did this twentieth-century shift involve a territorial dimension corresponding to the region? What was the role of these new 'cultural go-betweens' in the north east and who were they?

Exploring the emergence of a new generation of cultural bureaucrats also allows the role of the past in shaping the cultural region to be revealed. As others have shown, the industrial cultural legacy informed the various revivals of vernacular authenticity after 1945, especially folk music and music hall, which in turn cast their gaze back to a past during the late nineteenth century, equally characterised by revivalist fervour. For our purposes the influence of historical consciousness across a range of practices is read as an attempt to negotiate the conditions of the present. This work does not represent a search for the 'roots' of the cultural region, a quest that would be complicated by the competing and contested layers of revivals that continue to inform our reading of the north east's history. The real history of the cultural region is not privileged or distinguished from the imagined, and what follows attempts to understand the part played by historical consciousness in shaping the cultural region since 1945.

The preoccupation with arts and cultural policy might strike some readers as peculiar and perhaps warrants further explanation. As well as the popular perception of the north east as sustaining a strong working-class culture, several audits of the north east's cultural life have confirmed that middle-class cultural spaces such as theatres, orchestras, museums and art galleries have historically played a small part in the region's cultural landscape. As a corollary a strong and vibrantly patronised working-class culture that during the twentieth century nourished a disproportionate number of pubs, workingmen's clubs, allotment associations and pigeon crees has provided a rich resource for successive social historians.[27] Sport deserves special mention as the practice that provided a forum for the alleged fusion of class and territorial affiliation. However, what follows is not a 'survey' of popular culture, nor does it represent a broader 'cultural history' of the area. Wider trends in leisure, particularly sport, fall outside the scope of this book. This is not through disregard for these themes as important factors in the north east as a cultural region, but these aspects of the region's cultural landscape are already well served.[28] Equally, what follows might address the complaint that the history of the north east has too often been equivalent to the lives of 'working-class men'.[29] In the discussion of theatre and broadcasting the role of women as contributors to making the cultural region has often been decisive. But the focus upon the role of the cultural go-between, the editors, politicians and curators of the twentieth-century cultural region, still draws attention to the question of class. The problem of representing working-class culture was a pivotal preoccupation for the institutions featured in this discussion, notably

Northern Arts, the Northern Sinfonia, Tyne Tees Television, the BBC, Beamish Museum, the Amber Film Collective as well many smaller cultural organisations. The emphasis of this discussion is upon the tension between the celebration of working-class culture and the continuing pressure to erase its presence from the public image of the region.

The empirical investigation begins by examining the emergence of regional broadcasting during the twentieth century. English cultural regions emerged as an institutional reality during the twentieth century. After 1945 developments in broadcasting and cultural policy were central features of this process. In 1975 Asa Briggs went so far as to predict that the new broadcasting regions would redefine England's regional map.[30] But we have no clear understanding of how these national policies and programmes were played out in their regional settings. Did they mobilise an awareness of the region as a cultural space or did they simply reveal the limits of the area's cultural coherence?

The discussion focuses upon the development of regional radio during the inter-war years. The implementation of the BBC's 'Regional Scheme' provides a point of departure for an exploration of the ascendancy of the 'broadcasting north' with its headquarters in Manchester, and the impact of broadcasting region-alisation upon listeners and producers in the north east. The tension between the Reithian cultural commitment to public service broadcasting as an arbiter of public taste, and the emergence of a new generation of broadcasters deter-mined to bring vernacular authenticity to their listeners, is pivotal.[31] For despite the ongoing emphasis on the primacy of a national service, after 1945 the BBC's boost to the regional presence in radio resulted in a renaissance of vernacular material across the nation's airwaves. Programme makers in the north east cap-italised on acknowledged cultural particularities, such as popular song and dialect, and it appears that these media may have allowed a new regionally rooted cul-ture to flourish. There was a surge in the popularity of dialect drama and humour and nowhere more so than in the north east, where programmes such as *Wot Cheor, Geordie!* and *Vox Pop* achieved record listening figures and audience ratings by the early 1960s. Such developments are explored drawing upon a series of interviews with scriptwriters including Alan Plater and Leonard Barras. We ask how the new media influenced existing cultural practice, and whether the experience of 'hearing itself' may have helped to affirm the north east as a cultural entity.

The advent of television was eagerly awaited in the last English region with-out a transmitter and echoing the developments in arts policy the deficit of cul-tural institutions once again became an important factor in sharpening the focus upon the boundaries of the cultural region. During the 1950s the campaign for regional television facilities mobilised political representatives from across the spectrum in the north east who successfully petitioned parliament on this issue. But by this time the BBC had an already established broadcasting northern region, incorporating the north east, with headquarters in Manchester. Within the BBC there was a growing feeling that the north east was punching above its cultural (and licence numbers) weight: in a sour note on the opening of the north east's discrete BBC station at Pontop Pike, D. Stephenson, controller of the BBC North Region, referred tersely to 'the teeming millions of the north east ... and their noisy press'. Despite its auspicious beginnings the triumph of vernacular was not to be harnessed in the development of commercial television and as we shall see 'Tyne Tees' struggled to realise the aspiration to broadcast more programmes of regional interest than the BBC. Programmes that led the visual representation of north-eastern culture during the 1960s, such as *The Likely Lads*, were made by rival stations with a clear metropolitan imprint. Whilst the imagery and topography of the industrial north east inspired Le Frenais and Clements, the first series of *The Likely Lads* was filmed in London, close to Television Centre, and was broadcast on the new BBC2 years before it was available to viewers in the north east.

The difficulty of representing vernacular culture in broadcasting is a theme that continues in the discussion of individual artists and impresarios. Having sold 100,000 copies to readers including Harold Wilson and workers in Vladivostock by 1975, *Larn Yersel Geordie*, published by Frank Graham and written by the Northumberland-born bohemian Scott Dobson, once a fine art teacher at Manchester Grammar School, did much to shore up the impression of tribal fervour stirring in the north east. Despite the efforts of the regional arts boards to erase the legacy of industrial culture, the tenacity of the 'regional impresarios', including Dobson, would ensure that the vernacular cultural region was sustained.

Here the dynamic partnership between Dobson the writer and publicist and Graham the publisher provides an insight into the wider phenomenon of north-eastern revival during the 1960s. This study of regional pastiche acknowledges work that has revealed how dialect is furnished to evidence both the coherent and fragmented characteristics of the cultural region. The origins of a north east dialect as it has survived to the present can be traced to Old English, and the boundaries of the dialect region correspond to the areas that escaped Viking presence. Importantly, this is one way in which we can define the region as a cultural space and be reasonably confident about its southern boundaries.[32] But equally Griffiths has shown us the parallels between the dialect revival of the 1960s and the nineteenth century's first folk revival which likewise sought to emphasise accent particularism *within* the north east. For instance, nineteenth-century Weardale dialect writers emphasised their accent's distinguishing features against the accents of Newcastle, industrial Durham and rural Cleveland, because that was a time 'when Weardale was aware of, and had a need to assert, its own identity: almost desperately' in response to the decline of lead mining as the area's most important source of employment.[33]

Griffiths's notion of regional projection as a means of negotiating the present is an important and recurring theme. The impresarios of events such as the Blaydon Races Centenary Celebrations, including the infamous T. Dan Smith, the creators of the Beamish Open Air Museum, and Frank Graham's publishing initiatives, were connected by the shared celebration of the industrial cultural heritage. But their reasons for celebrating this version of the past could be very different. Smith was promoting a vision that was modern and outward looking; the creators of Beamish, the region's most important site for the public history of industrial material culture, took their cue from a Scandinavian open air museum developed at the beginning of the twentieth century.

Although such evidence sounds a note of caution against the familiar view of revival as a celebration of a disappearing world, at the core of the rediscovery were nineteenth- and early twentieth-century songs, materials and artefacts celebrating male work culture. Likewise Graham's Geordie Beuks promoted a distinctly muscular industrial inheritance and we also explore how far this and other examples of revival during the 1960s can be read as a crisis of masculinity. The view that deindustrialisation, together with the arrival of 'the sixties', mobilised concerted efforts to celebrate a fast disappearing world of industrial masculine certainties resonates with the development of a 'Scouse' revival in Liverpool at the same time.

In contrast to the often nostalgic regional pastiche of the 1960s, the 1970s witnessed the emergence of vernacular culture with clearer political overtones that also played an important part in shaping the contours of the region's cultural landscape. Like Scott Dobson, Val McLane was a school teacher and together with Geoff Gillham founded Live Theatre in Newcastle in 1973. The early years of the theatre's existence provide an interesting counterpoint to the 1960s impresarios of north east revival. Live Theatre was rooted in left politics and was influenced by Joan Littlewood's Theatre Workshop project. A community project in origin, Live Theatre began by touring the region's workingmen's clubs and schools bringing the work of playwrights like C. P. Taylor to new audiences. The contribution of the 1970s cultural left to shaping the cultural region was equally important, but this discussion makes a distinction between the radical inheritance of the 1970s, as expressed in the regional theatre movement, and the nostalgic vernacularism of the 1960s.

The subsequent discussion returns to the question of institutions and details the history of Northern Arts, the Arts Council of Great Britain's regional board that was to become the blueprint for regional cultural policy nationally. It considers whether the fledgling arts council offered an alternative account of the cultural region to the one promoted by artists and impresarios or the media. Did they embrace these developments? Were they rejected or simply ignored? As with broadcasting the context for Northern Arts was the development of new national cultural institutions after the Second World War. After 1945 a number of European nations extended the scope of the welfare state to foster equality and democracy in culture and the arts. British and European cultural policy was structured around a shared humanist discourse predicated upon a definition of 'Culture' anchored in the 'great European tradition', which had also influenced Reithian thinking on the role of the BBC as a leader of national culture.[34] A central ambition of the post-1945 era of cultural policy was to enhance individual benefit from, and access to, this tradition.[35] The British government incorporated cultural policy into its post-war settlement agenda for a number of reasons. The democratic impulse for inclusion and the overcoming of barriers to wider participation was a major consideration which also built upon earlier labour movement cultural initiatives. These developments could also resonate with the disdain that some on the left felt towards modern forms of popular culture and mass entertainment. After 1945 these strategies were influenced by a growing concern that the appetite of ordinary people for commercial entertainment was militating against the success of the cultural policy project. Thus a range of measures, including public subsidy of the arts and educational reform, were deployed with the aim of both protecting the arts and encouraging participation, beginning with creation of the British Arts Council in 1946. Like the BBC the Arts Council of Great Britain shared the status of being in the public sector but formally independent of direct government control.

The history of this process in specific cities or regions has yet to receive comprehensive attention and, as has been noted recently, the field of international cultural policy research would benefit from both local and historical perspectives.[36] Drawing upon evidence from north east England we explore how a national agenda was enacted in the regional setting. The impetus for the development of regional arts boards during the late 1950s came from the centre in response to complaints that the metropolitan bias of the Arts Council was deepening the intractable problem of widening participation. But in the north east the response to this agenda proved to be highly distinctive.

Although it was not the first of such cultural 'branch plants', the North East Association for the Arts (established in 1961) appears to have been the only regional arts council to maintain links with the local political and economic establishment, including trade unions, local authorities and the Northern Economic Planning Council. In 1960 Ted Fletcher, a prominent Newcastle councillor, veteran of the Spanish Civil War, chairman of the Labour Party in Newcastle during the 1950s, and the Labour MP for Darlington after 1964, submitted a memorandum on 'the case for a regional arts council'. Tyneside was proposed as the initial area, and shortly afterwards collaboration over funding for the arts was extended to Teesside and Wearside.[37] Northern Arts' regional imprint quickly came to the attention of the Arts Council of Great Britain. In 1964, the arts association was asked by the Arts Council to extend their administration to coincide with the boundaries of the Northern Economic

Planning Council.[38] This administrative development was highly significant as for the first time northern culture was given implicit geographical definition based upon pre-existing government regional boundaries.

In addressing the apparently unique mobilisation of local political interest in regional arts policy, this discussion examines the role of individual politicians. Arthur Blenkinsop, Northern Arts' first acting secretary and Labour MP for Newcastle East between 1945 and 1951, and other notable figures, including T. Dan Smith, brought their earlier experience of cultural radicalism, voluntarism and the workers' theatre movement to the ambition to construct new cultural facilities in the north east. The same men joined politicians, bureaucrats and businessmen in occupying central positions on the regional economic development council and this crossover allows our analysis to reveal the overlapping rhetoric of economic modernisation and cultural improvement. Northern Arts shared personnel with the development council, but was also distinguished by the new role afforded to women, as senior executives, bureaucrats and subsidised artists.

Against the evidence for the distinctive characteristics of the north east's cultural policy the discussion also reveals that regional arts officers were rarely less than traditional in their approach to cultural improvement. Rather they endorsed the Arts Council ambition to 'offer a cultural corrective to the uniformity of mass culture' and therefore perpetuated the tension between the vernacular and metropolitan.[39] This discussion then considers how far the post-war era's new cultural patrons were able to improve or manage popular sensibilities. Was there an engagement with the arts and music agenda beyond a small minority? Who were the principal recipients of subsidy? Were the regional arts council activities largely confined to the industrial conurbations or were rural areas equally represented? Can the regional arts council be said to have contributed to cohesion in cultural activities, or were these institutional overtures an anachronism in a protean and varied territorial culture?

As we move from the developments of the 1960s and 1970s Chapter 6 details another phase of cultural policy that brought impetus to the process of shaping the cultural region. New amongst the factors that contributed to the development of a cultural region during the 1980s was the arrival of private and public initiatives that fostered intra-regional as well as international competition for resources to fund culture and art. By the last decades of the twentieth century the idea that art could deliver economic rewards had been extended to a belief in its benefits for urban regeneration. By this time the north east appeared to be meeting the criteria for successful culture-led regeneration.

During the 1980s and 1990s Northern Arts helped to secure funding for the now well-known markers of cultural regeneration: Millennium Bridge, Baltic and the Sage Music Centre in Gateshead. The Newcastle/Gateshead site has generated significant national and international attention, particularly in the wake of the failed Capital of Culture bid, but there have been equally important developments on the banks of the Wear and Tees, such as the Sunderland Glass Centre and new riverside university campus, and Teesside's audacious 'Middlehaven' project, a plan for a new riverside urban centre. The analysis explores the history of, and motivation for, the new focus upon riverside cultural development. It asks how far the growing preoccupation with reinvigorating the industrial rivers was a local motivation whilst considering the evidence that the great emphasis upon waterfront developments was largely imported. The new urban development corporations were central government initiatives and the regeneration of an urban riverside area had been tested in London before it was developed in the north east. But were there local interventions or specific responses to this new form of urban management? And to what extent did the regeneration of the riverside orchestrated since 1987 reflect the growing popularity of regeneration models imported from the USA?

This discussion explores the continuities and discontinuities in this new phase of cultural policy. In addressing this question it examines the relationship between Northern Arts, the local government and the urban development corporations as the regeneration of the urban riversides was rolled out. The discussion centres upon the experience of arts officers and directors of Northern Arts whose work in arts policy and urban regeneration spanned the 1980s and 1990s. This focus reveals how the tension between imported 'flagship' projects and local knowledge and culture was managed. The personal histories of cultural workers involved with the regeneration and rebranding of areas such as Gateshead Quays, who witnessed first-hand the transition from arts policy as a state-led cultural corrective, to the emergence of the market-oriented 'cultural sector', will be central.

Drawing upon interviews with key figures involved in the physical and cultural regeneration of the north east's urban riverside areas we seek to understand how far developments during the 1980s were distinguishable from the efforts to create a cultural region after 1945. Some features were unprecedented. Prior to the remodelling of Gateshead Quays the town had long been in the shadow of the regional capital. Similar to developments in Salford and Walsall, it appears that the process of competing for cultural resources provided an opportunity to question the inherited cultural geography of the north east. But whilst the physical transformation of the region's cultural spaces was equally palpable, with new galleries, music venues and theatres visibly changing the region's urban skyline, the underlying idea that economic benefits could accrue from cultural improvement had been present amongst politicians and industrialists in the north east since the 1960s. It is perhaps unsurprising that many of those involved in strategic regional policy during the 1960s made the transition readily to a free-market urban regeneration and found new positions on the urban development corporations of the 1990s. The north east has been described by one critic as 'the land of a hundred quangos' and perhaps the increasingly centralised approach to institutional development was accepted readily in a region where local control over cultural institutions had historically been weak.[40] Even Northern Arts has lost much of its regional jurisdiction following the Arts Council's recent restructuring, which saw the disappearance of the last vestiges of local autonomy. This is far removed from the regional arts policy as envisaged by Blenkinsop and Fletcher, with their background in grassroots Labour politics and the workers' theatre movement, who pioneered this institutional development after the Second World War. Did the proliferation of centralised institutions contribute to the alienation of local artists and communities? Did the popularity of new transnational models for place marketing diminish the need for an identifiable regional cultural? Or was the celebration of vernacular culture a salient feature of the new cultural policy?

The question of 'cultural policy' is a developing field of enquiry amongst historians. This book reveals the importance of cultural policy to the process of regional projection after 1945. The findings of this study demonstrate that after 1945 a weak inheritance of public cultural institutions created space and opportunity for regional protagonists in the north east to map the cultural region. Since 1945 this process was informed by the interconnection of several factors including the emergence of national and regional arts policy, the growth of regional broadcasting, the influence of 1960s counterculture, the regional revival movement and recently transnational influences in cultural regeneration. The evolution of regional cultural policy was not confined to the sphere of public arts funding and management and its influence was felt by individuals, both as consumers and producers of art and music in particular, in broadcasting as well as in regional economic policy. Thus this book suggests that the complex 'cultural sector' is not without historical precedent and also argues for the application of the term 'cultural policy' beyond the parameters of arts policy. In reaching this conclusion this study's findings can be connected to the growing critical evaluation of cultural policy. Perspectives developed within the cultural policy field assessing the use of culture in urban space, as well as the critical appraisal of the use of art in alleviating social exclusion, will be especially relevant. Equally urban policy's assessment of the merits of cultural regeneration and the burgeoning historical perspectives upon urban place marketing provide crucial reference points. Drawing upon this growing and cross-disciplinary debate this book brings a much needed historical focus to the experience of culture-led regeneration.

Notes

1 *The Viewer*, 1 (1959), p. 3.

2 G. Philips, *Tyne Tees Television* (Durham: G. P. Electronic Service, 1998), p. 18.

3 Northern Arts, *Northern Arts annual report* (Newcastle, 1974); the preface noted that 'Northern Arts has stimulated interest in the arts to such an extent that this region is no longer the "cultural wilderness" it once was'.

4 M. A. Sighart, 'Grim up North? It's an urban myth from Leeds to Glasgow', *The Times* (26 May 2005); R. Christiansen, 'Birthplace of a cultural revolution', *Daily Telegraph* (2 Jan. 2006); S. Steward, 'YES … IT'S NEWCASTLE!: from coal hole to city of palaces', *Daily Telegraph* (10 May 2003).

5 R. Weight, 'Building a new British culture: the Arts Centre movement 1943–53', in R. Weight and A. Beach (eds), *The right to belong: citizenship and national identity in Britain 1930–1960* (London: I. B. Tauris, 1998), p. 158; for critical perspectives on the post-war settlement and literary culture see A. Croft, 'Betrayed spring: the Labour government and British literary culture', in J. Fyrth (ed.), *Labour's promised land: culture and society in Labour Britain 1945–51* (London: Lawrence and Wishart, 1995), pp. 218–219.

6 B. Charlton, 'Post modernity and regional culture', *Northern Review* 1 (1995), pp. 3–9.

7 Weight, 'Building a new British culture'; F. Bianchini and M. Parkinson (eds), *Cultural policy and urban regeneration: the West European experience* (Manchester: Manchester University Press, 1996).

8 E. Belfiore and O. Bennett, 'Rethinking the social impact of the arts', *International Journal of Cultural Policy* 13: 2 (2007), pp. 135–151.

9 J. Myerscough, *The economic importance of the arts in Britain* (London: Policy Studies Institute, 1988); B. Casey, R. Dunlop and S. Selwood, *Culture as commodity? The economics of the arts and the built heritage in the UK* (London: Policy Studies Institute, 1996).

10 G. Kearns and C. Philo (eds), *Selling places: the city as cultural capital past and present* (London: Pergamon, 1993).

11 D. Russell, *Looking North: Northern England in the national imagination* (Manchester: Manchester University Press, 2004); J. Belchem, *Merseypride: essays in Liverpool exceptionalism* (Liverpool: Liverpool University Press, 2000); N. Kirk (ed.), *Northern identities: historical interpretations of the north and northerness* (Farnham: Ashgate, 2000); Christopher Ehland (ed.), *Thinking northern: textures of identity in the north of England* (Amsterdam and New York: Rodopi, 2007).

12 B. Lancaster, 'The north east, England's most distinctive region?', in B. Lancaster, D. Newton and N. Vall (eds), *An agenda for regional history* (Newcastle: Northumbria University Press, 2007), p. 23; P. Payton, '"A Duchy in every respect un-English": discourses of identity in late-modern Cornwall', in Lancaster, Newton and Vall, *Agenda*, p. 321.

13 R. Colls and B. Lancaster (eds), *Geordies: roots of regionalism* (Edinburgh: Edinburgh University Press, 1992); Lancaster, 'The north east'; A. Green and A. Pollard (eds), *Regional identities in North East England 1300–2000* (Woodbridge: Boydell and Brewer, 2007).

14 P. Aronsson, 'The old cultural regionalism and the new', in Lancaster, Newton and Vall, *Agenda*, p. 253.

15 Aronsson suggests that in such an analysis the often artificial separation between 'region', 'locality' and 'nation' may be avoided.

16 Aronsson, 'The old cultural regionalism', p. 253; A. Paasi, 'Region and place: regional identity in question', *Progress in Human Geography* 4 (2003), pp. 239–256.

17 J. Walton, 'Imagining regions in comparative perspective: the strange birth of North West England', in Lancaster, Newton and Vall, *Agenda*, pp. 289–303.

18 G. Milne, *North-East England 1850–1914: the dynamics of a maritime-industrial region* (Woodbridge: Boydell Press, 2006), pp. 6–8, 71–73; N. McCord, 'The regional identity of north-east England in the nineteenth and early twentieth centuries', in E. Royle (ed.), *Issues of regional identity* (Manchester: Manchester University Press, 1998), pp. 102–118.

19 North of England Institute of Mining and Mechanical Engineers, *The mining institute renaissance 1852–2002* (Newcastle upon Tyne: North of England Institute of Mining and Mechanical Engineers, 2002). The miners themselves, however, continued to organise their unions along county lines similar to miners elsewhere in Britain.

20 Lancaster, 'The north east', p. 27.

21 Russell, *Looking North*, p. 14; Colls and Lancaster, *Geordies*, p. ix.

22 Lancaster, 'The north east', p. 28.

23 *Newcastle in the North East United Kingdom* (Paris: OECD, 2006).

24 C. B. Fawcett, *Provinces of England: a study of geographical aspects of devolution* (London: Hutchinson, 1961) ch. 6 passim.

25 P. Aronsson, *Regionernas roll i Sveriges historia* (Fritzes: ERU rapport, 1995), pp. 209–213.

26 K. Snell, 'The regional novel: themes for inter-disciplinary research', in K. Snell (ed.), *The regional novel in Britain and Ireland 1880–1990* (Cambridge: Cambridge University Press, 1998), pp. 1–54.

27 B. Bennison, 'Drink in Newcastle', in R. Colls and B. Lancaster (eds), *Newcastle: a modern history* (Chichester: Philimore and Co. Ltd., 2001), pp. 176–190; B. Lancaster, 'Sociability in the city', in Colls and Lancaster, *Newcastle*, pp. 319–341.

28 D. Holt and R. Physick, 'Sport on Tyneside', in Colls and Lancaster, *Newcastle*, pp. 193–213; K. Gregson, 'The media, regional culture and the Great North Run: Big Bren's human race', *Culture, Sport and Society* 4: 1 (2001), pp. 31–48; A. Metcalf, *Leisure and recreation in a Victorian mining community: the social economy of leisure in north-east England 1820–1940* (London: Routledge, 2005).

29 D. Russell, 'Culture and the formation of northern English identities from c. 1850', in Lancaster, Newton and Vall, *Agenda*, pp. 289–303.

30 A. Briggs, 'Local and regional in northern sound broadcasting', *Northern History* 10 (1975), p. 180.

31 P. Scannell and D. Cardiff (eds), *A social history of British broadcasting volume 1: 1922–1939. Serving the nation* (Oxford: Oxford University Press, 1991), p. 10.

32 Russell notes the difficulties of locating the southern boundary of 'the north', Russell, *Looking North*, p. xii.

33 B. Griffiths, 'Mrs Podkin and Mrs Brown', *Northern Review* 15 (2005), pp. 17–27; K. Wales, *Northern English: a social and cultural history* (Cambridge: Cambridge University Press, 2006).

34 N. Vall, 'Bringing art to the "man in the backstreet": regional and historical perspectives of labour and the evolution of cultural policy in Europe 1945–75', *Labour History Review* 75: 1 (2010), pp. 30–31.

35 E. Belfiora, 'The methodological challenge of cross-national research: comparing cultural policy in Britain and Italy', Centre for Cultural Policy Studies, University of Warwick, Research Paper 8 (2004), p. 33. www2.warwick.ac.uk/fac/arts/theatre_s/cp/publications/centrepubs. Accessed 17 February 2009.

36 A. Lindgren, 'Varför inrätta kulturnämnd? Lokal kulturpolitik i två kommuner', *Historisk Tidskrift* 128: 2 (2008), p. 179.

37 Tyne and Wear Archive Service (hereafter TWAS) MD/NC/94/22, Special Committee for the Encouragement of Cultural Activities, Corporation of Newcastle upon Tyne, General Minute Book, 27 July 1960, pp. 294–297, 320–322, 353–354, 376–385, 442.

38 TWAS, D. 4347, Northern Arts Records, North East Arts Association, Annual Report, 1964–5.

39 TWAS, D. 4347, Northern Arts Records, Bound Volumes, Minutes of the 5th Annual General Meeting, 1965.

40 Office of the Deputy Prime Minister: Housing, Planning, Local Government and The Regions – Written Evidence. Memorandum by Councillor Chris Foote-Wood, Vice Chair, North East Assembly (RG 21), 6 March 2006.

2

'Radio Days': sound broadcasting in the north east

For much of the twentieth century radio broadcasting remained faithful to its public service origins. From its inception during the 1920s radio was defined by the state as a national service to operate in the public interest. This brief was given expression in the measures taken to inhibit commercial development and legislatively through the licence system.[1] These parameters were interpreted initially by Lord Reith as requiring a unified service of the highest standards to provide leadership in public taste. Radio broadcasting gave fresh impetus to the Victorian reforming ideal and created a new bureaucracy of improving officials intent on using the technologies of radio to engender social and national unity. This was uppermost amongst protagonists of the BBC's monopoly which provided the means of making 'the nation as one man'.[2] On the other hand, progressive intellectuals saw in this new medium the potential to create a more egalitarian society. As John Grierson wrote, 'we turned to the new wide-reaching instruments of radio and cinema as necessary instruments both in the practice of government and the enjoyment of citizenship'.[3]

The Reithian legacy does not readily invite regional analysis, but this discussion seeks to understand the impact of an externally imposed framework, in the form of the BBC's monopoly in sound broadcasting, on regional culture. It examines institutional developments such as the transition from 'local' to 'regional' radio under the aegis of the BBC's Regional Scheme from 1929 which led to the 'accession of Newcastle' to the 'broadcasting north' with its new headquarters in Manchester.[4] Whilst Scannell and Cardiff's comprehensive analysis of radio during the 1930s has shed light on the emergence of the 'broadcasting north', the question of how the north east, or 'the old north', responded to and was represented by the region as a technological construct provides the focus here. The return of regional broadcasting after the Second World War, and particularly the emergence in the north east of programmes such as *Wot Cheor, Geordie!* and *Vox Pop*, takes our discussion into the second half of the twentieth century.[5] For despite the BBC's ongoing emphasis on the primacy of a national service, the 1950s appear to have been a brief 'golden age' for north-eastern radio. The strong cultural tradition of popular song and dialect was utilised by radio producers in the north east and there are indications that radio provided a new venue in which a regional culture could flourish.

Following the formation of the BBC in 1922, the country was divided into nine areas in which one or more broadcasting stations would be permitted. Along with eight other British cities, Newcastle was designated for a broadcasting station in the north east and 5NO went on air five weeks after the London station. Tom Payne, the owner of Payne and Hornsby's wireless shop in Gallowgate, was the first Newcastle station director. The inaugural broadcast came from the stables of the Co-op warehouse in Blandford Street where Marconi had constructed the Newcastle transmitter. New premises were an early priority and in 1925 5NO moved to 54 New Bridge Street, described in one memoir as 'just about the most unsuitable premises for their purposes it was possible to imagine'. The island site, facing the Laing Art Gallery, remained the home of the Newcastle BBC for the next sixty-three years.[6] Formerly a maternity hospital, the new premises of the Newcastle station elicited many complaints. In 1934 there was official praise for the refurbishment; the prestige architect and designer Wells Coats had been enlisted for the job. Although the site was just about large enough to accommodate brass bands – 'so popular in this area' – generally the studios were unsuitable for modern broadcasting and the number of items broadcast from Newcastle was limited.[7]

With awkward and expensive studios, the range of the transmitter in Newcastle barely covering the Tyneside area and poor reception from the north of England regional transmitter in Huddersfield, it is no surprise that the attraction of the new media was restricted to a small group of 'enthusiasts'. G. L. Marshall, station director of Newcastle from 1928, was an early protagonist. Previously a journalist and 'colonial university' lecturer, Marshall was also on the executive of the North of England Musical Tournament, and in an interview with the Newcastle *Journal* shortly after his appointment he noted that radio could help children to 'acquire a command of good spoken English'.[8] Similar views were expressed by school teachers: in 1933 the headmaster of the South Shields High School reflected that 'the introduction occasionally of references to Northern weaknesses in speech' would be beneficial to school children in the area. He further noted that the corporation's didactic ambitions were sometimes difficult to realise, conceding that the 'expert' use of 'London speech ... before the microphone' tended to amuse rather than instruct his own pupils.[9] In the early years radio held demonstrable appeal for the educated middle classes. Prompted by Lettice Jowitt (warden of Bensham and Seaham settlements) members of the Newcastle Literary and Philosophical Society wrote to the Newcastle station director requesting the loan of a BBC wireless for their fledgling listening groups. Marshall was evidently anxious to extend the social base of listening and thought it imprudent to 'lend a set to a society which has ample funds and cannot be compared with miners' institutes, working men's clubs etc'.[10]

Jowitt later secured the loan of a wireless for use by the unemployed miners in Seaham, but the appeal of radio was, as yet, not widespread.

The lack of popular enthusiasm for radio was also reflected in the response to the proposed Regional Scheme. Prompted by the international hunt for new wavelengths, this resulted in the closure of Newcastle as an independent broadcasting station and secured its operation as a subsidiary of Manchester from 1929. The boundaries of the new broadcasting regions were also shaped by the range of the corporation's transmitters and only parts of the north east could receive the broadcasts from Huddersfield. An initial report by the corporation engineer had proposed facilities for a separate 'north eastern region', autonomous from the northern region, to address the problems with reception.[11] But this was never realised and the 'accession of Newcastle' to Manchester was completed with little opposition other than from 'a small group of local enthusiasts' clamouring for the right to make programmes in the north east.

Most north-eastern listeners were apparently more concerned to secure improved reception for national programmes produced in London.[12] In 1926 the *Northern Echo* published demands for 'national radio only on Christmas Day' and complaints about the 'quality of Newcastle orchestra … the cause of many a listener buying a gramophone'. Likewise, when the *Newcastle Chronicle* ran a series of reports in 1927 on the BBC's music policy, this elicited no demands for more local items, only a tirade from the vicar of Heaton about the corrupting influences of jazz. William Noble of the Newcastle Chamber of Commerce was an apparently lone voice in demanding more local news bulletins whilst there were further letters to the *Chronicle* in 1932 demanding more 'national programmes'.[13] The weak response to the closure of the Newcastle station contrasts sharply to the situation in Sheffield, where Scannell has described the siege of the BBC by angry Sheffield civic authorities as 'a unique case of official resistance to the scrapping of the original local service'.[14]

Representatives of the Newcastle station were nevertheless vocal in their opposition to the cut in the number of broadcasting orchestras.[15] Further, Marshall fought a lengthy and successful battle to secure the reading of local news on the 'Daventry waveband' on the grounds that the Huddersfield transmitter was unable to reach most north-eastern listeners.[16] Whilst there were only three broadcasts from Newcastle in the BBC calendar in 1935 (the Newcastle Bach Choir, a microphone tour of Newcastle and excerpts from Northern Command Tattoo), Marshall used the campaign over local news to secure other local broadcasts, a strategy which programme directors in Manchester were quick to discourage.[17] Edward Liveing, corporation director of the north region, had responded smartly: 'in my opinion listeners in Newcastle ought to look for their news to the Regional News Bulletin broadcast on the North Regional wavelength'.[18] Station director of Manchester from 1926, Liveing presided over the transition to the Regional Scheme. He emphasised that the north was ripe territory for this new medium, but his vision of the north's cultural assets was dominated by his appreciation of Lancashire and Yorkshire. St Hilda's Colliery Band was the only north-eastern organisation to be included in his review of resources available for broadcasting, a long list that included Yorkshire and Manchester's flourishing repertory movement, the Leeds Symphony Orchestra, Manchester's Hallé and Sir Thomas Beecham's Manchester Operatic Society.[19] So whilst the closure of the Newcastle station never roused official resistance, local listeners' demands for more 'national' programmes reflected unease over the growing influence of Manchester and the north west: in 1932 one local newspaper published a letter demanding more national programmes and referring to the 'tin can' northern regional orchestra.[20]

Although Marshall secured some concessions for 'the old North', disenchantment with the Regional Scheme was clearly compounded by the poor reception from both local and regional transmitters.[21] In 1936 70% of households in Northumberland, where transmission from the Newcastle station was good, held radio licences, a figure not exceeded anywhere else in the northern region. In County Durham only 34% of households held licences, the lowest figure in England.[22] This area was poorly served by both the local transmitter in Newcastle and the north region transmitter in Huddersfield, but the low listening levels also attest to the correlation between low rates of income and listening prior to introduction of the cheaper 'utility set' in 1944. Equally these figures need to be offset by evidence that the north east coast had some of the highest levels of listening by relay, which was cheaper, provided better reception and brought the gain of listening to overseas broadcasts.[23]

The problem of poor reception and low levels of listening in County Durham is interesting given that the area was the location for some of the most innovative programmes to be made in the north east during the inter-war years. Although the imposition of a Manchester-led 'broadcasting north' irked radio enthusiasts in the north east, such as they were, the representatives of the Regional Scheme were part of a new breed of broadcasters who took seriously the task of reflecting regional authenticity and variety to listeners. The foregrounding of the lives of ordinary working people in radio was pioneered in Manchester under the leadership of programme directors such as E. Harding. For Scannell and Cardiff this era changed the face of British broadcasting by 'establishing a relationship with the audience that was radically different to that between the national programme in London and its nationwide audience' and prepared the ground for the development of popular radio nationally after the Second World War.[24] Whilst programme directors such as Harding may have helped to realise this new style of broadcasting in the north, it is likely that the writers and performers he recruited drew on influences beyond northern England. This was, after all, a cultural milieu in which the working classes were beginning to be represented by other agencies. As Stead notes, the American development of the feature film and its preoccupation with tackling 'social problems' was a stimulant to the grow-ing artistic fascination with working-class life in Britain.[25]

The programmes made in this period that had north east settings played an important role in the external representation of vernacular culture. Two of the Manchester station's most memorable programme makers, Geoffrey Bridson and Olive Shapley, frequently based their programmes on the everyday lives of 'northerners' in the north east. Bridson, a poet and writer from Manchester, enjoyed a distinguished career in the BBC as a writer and producer for radio. His first work was *Harry Hopeful*, which starred Frank Nicholls as the imagi-nary out-of-work glass blower and detailed his trek across the north west in search of employment. The programme featured interviews with people they met on their travels, which were later scripted and broadcast from the Manchester studios. The show was popular and one of the first to make serious use of dialect. It was also an expression of Bridson's desire to communicate an 'aesthetically significant' vision of the industrial north.[26] This desire was articulated in his four big industrial features: *Steel, Cotton, Wool* and *Coal.* Bridson was later criticised for over exerting his creative license in *Steel,* presented as a symphony that moved from a pastiche of moors and peaks on the periphery of Sheffield, to dawn in the town and the arrival of workers at the factory gates. These creative extravagances prompted the local press to complain that the programme lacked integrity.[27]

Bridson took these complaints to heart and in his final feature, *Coal,* he strove to ensure that the desired impact was achieved without compromising actuality:

> I was talking to P.D yesterday about the *Coal* programme … There are various difficul-ties in this and first of all the choice of mine. I, personally, think that the mine should be chosen from the Durham or Northumberland coalfield in order to get the North-Eastern accent as a change from a Lancashire and Yorkshire … and also to tap into the very rich store of Tyneside colliery songs … What I should like is to get on to some mine near the Tyne where working conditions are not too good, where the management are willing to co-operate with us in a programme which will boost British coal at the same time as it enlists sympathy for the miner.[28]

In the end Bridson settled for Brancepeth colliery in County Durham. Although it later transpired that the wage rates for the mine were slightly above average for the area, Brancepeth met the other requirements and also had its own brass band, which was important since Bridson wanted to ensure that the 'songs and brass band music to be included in this programme should be appropriate to the West Durham coalfield district rather than as arbitrary and non-commital as the music included in *Wool'*.[29] Bridson enlisted Joan Littlewood to work on *Coal* and she spent the month that it took to make the programme living with a miner's family and, dressed in special procured overalls, helped with hewing, loading and putting in the mine.[30] *Coal* was broadcast in November 1938 to critical and popular acclaim. Scannell and Cardiff have emphasised the undisclosed strategies that the programme employed, particularly Bridson's careful selection of the right kind of pit, reflected the 'hidden expediences' that furnished the claim to let 'the people' speak for themselves.[31] Whilst such measures may have manipulated listeners, these documentaries helped to secure acknowledged markers of north east cultural particularity, such as colliery songs, as pivotal in the *communicated* version of regional culture. This helped to shore up, from the inter-war years, regional signifiers that would remain enduring for most of the twentieth century.

Olive Shapley began her career with the BBC in 1934 working on *Children's Hour* and went on to become one of the North Region's leading documentarists. Her most innovative work made use of the new Mobile Recording Unit. Shapley's programmes were pioneering, touching on sensitive subjects, such as homelessness. She often used north east locations, as in *Homeless People*, broadcast on 6 September 1938 and featuring a training centre for young tramps in County Durham and the South Shields Seaman's Institute. The Prudhoe Street Mission on Westgate Road in Newcastle was also included, where dramatic contrasts were drawn between 'old men lying like sacks or heaps of rags on the hard floor' and 'the bustle and light of Saturday evening shopping in Newcastle: gleaming fruit and melting pastries; soft beds and rich carpets; warm, bright clothes and strong shapely shoes'.[32] Shapley's most distinctive work in the north east was *Miners' Wives*. Broadcast in 1939, this programme was the first to take a listener abroad at the BBC's expense. By the late 1930s mining was a familiar subject for social reportage, but Shapley's *Miner's Wives* broke new ground. The programme consisted of a factual account of daily life in Craghead by Shapley, with particular attention to the quality of housing, interspersed with comments from the miners' wives who had been carefully coached in 'the art of putting themselves across'.[33] There were further recordings of folk dancing, amateur dramatics, a WEA class and the town's cinema. Shapley's scripted comments provide an insight into her view of the mining village during the late 1930s:

> Saturday afternoon is a great day in Craghead … There is a cinema matinee and every child who can produce a penny goes to it. The hall is packed with children of every age, with cats and dogs as well; usually the film is a western, but before it begins the audience is encouraged to sing off some of its energy. This song, 'The Blaydon Races', is known everywhere in County Durham.[34]

Shapley's portrayal is a refreshing departure from what Alan Plater describes as the prevalent image of the north east as an 'angry essay by J. B. Priestley illustrated by Bill Brandt'.[35] *Miners' Wives* neither romanticises the exigencies of mining life nor exaggerates its awfulness. The programme also provides a rare insight into the lives of women in the region, often out of sight in much of the official investigation of such areas.

Olive Shapley arranged for Mrs Emmerson of Craghead to visit Marles-les-Mines, a mining village in Normandy. Accompanied by Shapley, Mrs Emmerson spent two weeks with a mining family in the French village. Her observations made up the second half of a programme which was well received and widely publicised.[36] In spite of Shapley's editorial control and the admission that she had coached the Craghead women in preparation for the microphone, Mrs Emmerson's reflections of life in Normandy and Durham provide a valuable insight into what she felt to be distinctive about her own village. Her opening statement described the French men coming in after work and switching on the wireless to hear the football results. Although she had felt nervous of her new environment, she was comforted by this familiar ritual, which had transported her 'right back to Durham on a Saturday with the men doing exactly the same thing'. Whilst it is likely that such reminiscences also relied upon the 'hidden expediencies' that characterised Bridon's *Coal*, the discrepancies between Olive Shapley's and Mrs Emmerson's accounts of colliery housing suggest that the commitment to actuality was upheld. In her 'factual' presentation of the town, Shapley described houses that had 'no pretensions to beauty', but Mrs Emmerson found the French miners' homes 'not near as pleasant to look at as most Durham houses'; without 'easy chairs' they seemed, to her, 'rather comfortless'. In many respects, Mrs Emmerson's impression of the French mining village was that its material culture was considerably less refined than in Craghead. She was surprised that young girls in the French village left school to become domestics or to take up dress-making in the home, 'just as was done in the colliery district in Durham 30 or 40 years ago'.[37] Thus she provided a rare account of a north-eastern village, where characteristics such as comfort, modernity and progress were emphasised alongside 'the dirt that we've got to contend with and the bad economic conditions'.[38]

The developments in radio led by Manchester programme makers have been characterised as pioneering a type of radio that would later be established as a central tenet of national popular radio. This style, with its characteristic intimacy between listener, speaker and subject, and its concern for 'dailiness', was appropriated by 'the nation' during the Second World War before becoming an accepted part of popular broadcasting. Programmes like *Miners' Wives* represented a departure from the earlier tradition of radio features in which the 'knowing collusion' between speaker and listener was organised by reference to social codes that excluded the subject, but, in the end, much of this work was concerned to represent the northern working class, rather than speaking in particular to north-eastern listeners.[39] This had a part to play in communicating northern culture in a way that probably was more sensitive to local peculiarities than earlier features had been, but it is difficult to gauge its influence on the self-identification of north-easterners, particularly given that levels of listening in County Durham, the setting for so much of this work, were amongst the lowest in England.

If anything, there was active hostility to Manchester broadcasts from listeners in the north east. Despite the commitment to regional broadcasting there was very little autonomy within the huge 'Northern Region'. As Briggs writes, 'Harding … was extremely successful in hitching Northern Broadcasting to the creative groups in Northern society and culture, but it was acknowledged without comment in 1937 that "Leeds acts in almost all things under instructions from Manchester"'.[40] The discussions surrounding the opening of a new north-eastern transmitter at Stagshaw near Corbridge confirm this reluctance to permit local freedoms within the North Region. In 1935, in his capacity as North Region director, Edward Liveing reflected on the challenges of greater independence for the north-eastern area:

> Northumbria and the surrounding counties have strongly independent cultural characteristics, which mark them out not only from the North of England, but, to some extent, from the whole of the rest of the country. In addition, Tyneside is, geographically, much more isolated from the Northern industrial cities than, say, Lancashire is from the West Riding, or vice versa.[41]

Liveing went on to argue against extensive independence on the grounds that 'the potential talent available for independent broadcasting is no more considerable than that, say of Merseyside or Leeds area'. This implied that Manchester would have to establish a new programme specialist staff in Newcastle, a proposition considered to be neither rational nor particularly efficient use of corporation resources. In the end Liveing recommended that existing output should continue, with extension to religious services, and talks on matters of local interest, as well as outside broadcasts and radio plays. Such material could be broadcast from the new north-eastern transmitter but would be supported by one new assistant and a small weekly allowance. Since Manchester programme experts would continue to be heavily used, Liveing felt justified in insisting 'that the general control would still have to be undertaken from Manchester'. The history of animosity between successive Newcastle station directors and Manchester staff may account for Liveing's self-protective tone. Interestingly the London Control Board was more permissive of local broadcasting freedoms than Manchester. In discussions of the new transmitter, the controller's meeting in London agreed that the 'Newcastle controller should have considerable local autonomy with regard to programmes', and that standard broadcasts be taken from London 'with *liberty* to dip into other Regional programmes if required'. Liveing, perhaps wishing to underscore the Manchester position, reiterated that all broadcasts from the Newcastle station must continue with 'full consultation and agreement from North Regional headquarters'. Further, he stressed that since the north regional programme was obliged to carry north-eastern contributions a certain amount of reciprocity should be expected of the Newcastle station.[42] The Newcastle station director, E. L. Guilford, whose very position was under consideration along with the plans for the new transmitter, made explicit the feelings surrounding the Manchester headquarters:

> As I told you there is a great dislike of Manchester up here among Newcastle people and there is no doubt that it would be much more popular if Newcastle could be separated entirely and, where any attachment was necessary, joined to London. Only the other day the opinion was expressed that they would rather hear the BBC Orchestra than a Halle Concert … The future position will require careful handling if the public here is to be satisfied with half the cake when they want the whole.[43]

The tensions between the Newcastle station, broadcasting in the north east and the Manchester headquarters were also reflected in the discussions over what the new transmitter's programmes should be called. The opening of the Stagshaw transmitter gave the north east two transmitters, one at Moorside Edge outside Newcastle and one at Stagshaw near Corbridge. Along with the suggestion that the transmitters adopt the names of the ancient kingdoms of Bernicia and Deira came the bold proposition that the programmes radiated from both transmitters be called the 'North Regional Programme'. This idea was strongly rejected by the BBC Control Board, which stipulated that 'Newcastle shall not be regarded as a Region in its own right, but as part of the North Region' and should emphatically not 'be given a title which gives it equal standing with the Northern Programme'. Transmissions from the Stagshaw transmitter would be known simply as the *Stagshaw Programme*. The corporation's view of the programme in its first operational year was that there would be little for export until the features side was developed and that most of the other material would be of limited interest beyond the local transmitter. After all, there were standards to uphold, especially in northern music: 'with the exception of duplications … every musical programme on Stagshaw must be suitable for the north programme'.[44]

Despite the financial and administrative obstacles to broadcasting in the north east under the regional scheme, the opening of the Stagshaw transmitter in 1937 brought new opportunities for radio in the region. The *Stagshaw Programme* schedule for March 1938 included a 'triple bill of north eastern dramatists' with plots described as 'Northumbrian'. Music included Tom Mearris (conductor of the Felling Male Voice Choir) leading a group of eleven 'Northumbrian singers', to be aired fortnightly. This programme found favour with the corporation and 'Northumbrian music' was considered worthy of its own special broadcasts.[45] The *Stagshaw Programme* also carried an independent features bill, including in 1938 *The Royal Northumberland Fusiliers*, *Tyne Bridges* and *The Northumberland Plate on Plate Day*.[46]

Initially responsibility for features on the *Stagshaw Programme* resided with Cecil McGivern, who went on to become the television programme director of the BBC in 1947. McGivern was a graduate of Durham University and had developed an early interest in acting and the theatre as a student. During the 1930s he became involved in radical theatre as a member of the People's Theatre in Newcastle, an episode which later provided material for his radio features.[47] Having joined the BBC in Newcastle in 1936 as a producer, by 1939 McGivern was promoted to the newly created post of Programmes Director for the North East.[48] This move was cut short by the outbreak of war and his subsequent move to London to work on the war programmes for which he became well known, including *Junction X*, *The Battle of Britain*, *Fighter Pilot* and *The Harbour called Mulberry*.[49] In the few months before his departure for London, McGivern presided over a marked increase in output of north-eastern radio material, such as a play called *Tenement*, written by Edwin Lewis and produced by McGivern, which was broadcast on the Northern Programme. The following excerpt of the script serves as an example of the character of north-eastern material making its way into the Northern Programme by the late 1930s.

> ANNOUNCER: This is the Northern Programme from Newcastle. We present 'Tenement', a play for the microphone, written by Edwin Lewis and produced by Cecil McGivern.
>
> The action of the play takes place in Tom Eldon's flat, Sam Wharton's flat and on the doorstep of the tenement, Paradise Buildings. Below the tenement flows the River Tyne, and the ends of scenes will be marked by sounds from the river.
>
> (*Fade up river sounds*)
>
> ANNOUNCER: Afternoon
>
> TOM ELDON: (*Tyneside dialect*) For God's sake, Alan, go and tell 'em to switch off that wireless
>
> ALAN: (*he had a secondary school education and his accent is far less pronounced than that of his father*) Why don't you try pricking the coupon with a pin, father?
>
> TOM: I've put Newcastle to win on both coupons.
>
> ALAN: Why not?
>
> TOM: With this system Manchester have to win.
>
> ALAN: Perhaps Manchester haven't heard of the system.
>
> TOM: There's no need to be sarcastic. Damn that noise. (*Gives a loud knock on the wall*) Oi! Oi! Andy Cracken. Will you stop that wireless? […]
>
> TOM: But according to the system Newcastle loses at home. It's against my conscience to mark 'em that way.
>
> ALAN: Think about that thousand pounds – what would you do with it?
>
> TOM: I'd move. I've gotten to dislike this place a bit. I suppose I've gotten big ideas after being on the dole five years. (*Laughs*)
>
> ALAN: How about Rothbury or Hexham-or perhaps a nice house on the coast?
>
> TOM: (*thoughtfully*) No, I don't think I'd leave the river.[50]

Compared to the stiff formality of much of the material broadcast from the north east under the Regional Scheme, this play, along with much of the output in the *Stagshaw Programme*, was humorous and irreverent. The writers and producers were evidently anxious to display their understanding of local audiences and their wider appreciation of vernacular popular culture. The rivalry between Newcastle and Manchester United, replicated in the politics of radio, spoke to the region's most important popular pastime and emphasised the connection between radio and established aspects of popular culture. *Tenement* was rooted in time and place and like Bridson's work sought to articulate a coherent sense of place. Whilst the nuances are lost in the written form, the text assumes that listeners knew where the largely middle-class enclaves of Rothbury and Hexham were and appreciated this appraisal of the region's geography of social class. That variations in dialect were deployed to reflect social difference suggests that writer and producer were confident that a play about 'someone in particular', was intended to be heard by 'someone in particular'.[51] Thirty years later, with an institutionalised acting profession concentrated in southern drama schools, Alan Plater found it difficult to recruit actors who could work in 'accents' other than the 'quaint form of English located halfway between Broadcasting House and Buckingham Palace'.[52]

In Sal Sturgeon, the comic writer Captain Walter Diericx of Spital Tongues in Newcastle found a professional actor with an established stage career who was able to read the part of 'Jenny Marley' in a series of humorous sketches broadcast from the north east during the late 1930s.[53] The following excerpt is taken from *Blaydon Races. A Tale of Geordie Marley* broadcast in the Northern Programme on 9 June 1937.

> ANNOUNCER: This is the Northern Programme. Here's a tale about the day the Marleys spent going to the place where Blaydon races were run. The famous races, that the song was written about, were held seventy-five years ago today, and Geordie Marley observed the anniversary … The story's by Walter Diericx and Sal Sturgeon will tell it.
>
> (*Open with record of the chorus of 'Blaydon Races'*)
>
> JENNY MARLEY: (*after humming concluding bars*) Hillo! (*Laugh*) ah'll back ye kna wat the tune is? Ay hinnies, 'Blaydon Races' Tyneside's National Anthem. Did ony o' ye owlder folk ivor *gan* te the Blaydon Races? Ah ownly went theor wance, an that was the day – the ninth o' June, an it wes some race an' aal, mind ye. Ah'll tell ye aboot it …
>
> Last neet wor Geordie cum in from the Club, full o' the joys of spring – ower full for ma fancy. 'Hinney', he says, 'D'ye kna wat day the ninth o' June is?' 'Ah!', ah says, lookin at the date on the *Evening Chronicle*, 'Next Wednesday'. 'Noa hinney', he says, 'Ah meen wat special day is it?' Wey the owny thin special ah cud think it wes, wes me Aunt Maggie's eighty-fourth borthday, an' ah said see. 'Hinney', says Geordie, as if he'd known aal aboot it since he was born, 'Think o' the words o' the forst vorse o' "Blaydon Races". "Ah went the Blaydon Races, twes on the ninth of June!" It's wan o' the ootsdandin dates in wor local history.' 'Wey' ah says, 'There's nowt to get worsel's in a swet aboot, is theor? Onyway, ah'll back ye hadn't jaloused that last neet.'[54]

The sketch recounts the adventures of Geordie, who along with 'aal the lads up et the Club' arranges a quoits match with 'aal the lads from Blaydon'. Jenny and the wives of other lads who suspect mischief and gambling follow the men to Blaydon hoping to avert the game. A bull from a neighbouring farm catches sight of one of the lads who had dressed up specially for the occasion: 'His weskit was broon, his coat was blue, an' he hed on wan o' them pull ower things the wes such a bright reed bobby dazzler'. The bull gives chase and the story ends with the men running for their lives round the streets of Blaydon.

The use of dialect, rather than 'accent', distinguishes this broadcast from earlier material emanating from the north east: the expressive idiom is deeply rooted in local popular culture and assumes that listeners will be able to tap into this humorous re-enactment of a nineteenth-century social ritual.[55] The *Stagshaw Programme*'s producers also hoped to ensure that both irreverent and 'factual' aspects of north-eastern culture were communicated so Diericx's material was broadcast alongside a feature on the Northumberland Plate, a horse race staged at Gosforth Park in Newcastle and the main attraction of Tyneside's unofficial holiday in the second week of June. A testament to enthusiasm amongst programme makers for material that played up to an acknowledged regional caricature, this type of radio also adds weight to Lancaster's suggestion that the changes brought to the geography of leisure by electronic and mechanical innovations sustained older cultural forms in the north east.[56] As Olive Shapley had noted, cinemas in Craghead regularly thronged to impromptu renditions of 'The Blaydon Races'. Whilst the actual races at Blaydon were eclipsed by the rise of the Newcastle Hoppins, the song remained anchored in popular culture, most memorably as an anthem for Newcastle United. Diericx clearly saw the potential in bringing such an immortal theme to the new media, and was able to capitalise on the overlap between an earlier participatory tradition and the growing pleasure of 'staying in' in the north east.

Although radio's new regional voice was eclipsed by the outbreak of war and the demands of the nation in 1939, many of the developments in radio usually associated with the 1940s were in embryo in the material broadcast from the Stagshaw transmitter after 1937. The format for *Wot Cheor, Geordie!* was nascent in Walter Diericx's early work, which deployed a self-consciously zany comedy usually located in radio developments during the 1940s.[57] More broadly, the programmes emanating from the north east during the late 1930s were characterised by a staged naturalness and an emphasis on the performance of social life, strategies that became established hallmarks of national popular radio after the Second World War.[58] Although the autonomy of north-eastern broadcasting, under the remit of the 'broadcasting north', remained ambiguous, the legacy of the 1930s flourish in north-eastern programmes meant that the region's programme makers were well placed to capitalise on the enthusiasm for regional broadcasting from within the BBC after 1945.

When John Polwarth took over as director of the Newcastle station after the Second World War, he was able to build on the broadcasts established under the *Stagshaw Programme.* In 1945 he requested a fee of £3.30 to be paid to 'Captain Walter Diericx' for a Tyneside sketch broadcast in *Wot Cheor, Geordie!*[59] The programme often took the form of an outside broadcast, introduced in the early years by Esther McCracken, an established local writer and radio performer, and featured humorous sketches and musical slots. During the late 1940s the appeal of this show apparently extended beyond listeners in the north east. In 1946 the assistant programme director in Manchester wrote to Polwarth expressing the hope that 'after the rigours of Durham on Saturday' he would still be able to tackle a 'Miners' Edition' of *Wot Cheor, Geordie!* which would round off a fine 'Miners' Week'.[60] Whilst nationalisation produced a renewed fascination with the region's mining communities, the programme time for *Wot Cheor, Geordie!* was cut in 1947, eliciting letters of protest from Nottinghamshire and East Yorkshire, as well as from within the north east.[61] In the same year the Newcastle radio station received over 4,000 postal applications to attend the next outside broadcast of the programme in Sunderland – surprising to the organisers, who had booked a hall in Seaburn with a capacity of 750.[62]

Wot Cheor, Geordie! began in 1945, possibly earlier, but gathered momentum following the arrival of Richard Kelly as assistant producer at the BBC in Newcastle in 1948. Kelly had worked for Cecil McGivern before the Second World War, when he was still a student in Newcastle, making programmes about jazz, his enduring passion. He joined the BBC again shortly after the departure of John Polwarth to become the BBC representative in Canada in 1947. This move brought a raft of new producers to the programme, including Ray Lakeland, Kenneth Poolman and Frank Wade, who was also instrumental in founding the Northern Sinfonia Orchestra.[63]

Kelly is often regarded as the architect of a Geordie 'golden age' of radio which spanned the 1950s, but as has been shown, both the content and style of the broadcasts he became known for had been established under McGivern during the 1930s. On the other hand, Kelly was clearly able to capitalise on the efforts to increase output from regional stations after the Second World War. During this time, the North Region was led by John Coatman, a passionate supporter of regional broadcasting.[64] As Briggs has written: 'between 1945 and 1955, so long as radio remained the dominant medium, the regions enjoyed a period of considerable autonomy'.[65] In 1968 Donald Edwards, the newly appointed general manager of local radio development, spoke of sound broadcasting's contribution to the 'amazing cultural revival in the provinces in recent years'.[66] Kelly confirmed that the 1950s gave local producers unprecedented creative freedom, recalling how 'there was an atmosphere of "there you are, there's the region, get on with it"'.[67] He exploited these opportunities, introducing comic writers and performers who would become integral to the 1960s 'cultural revival' in the north east. Building on earlier attempts to shore up the central position of radio in popular culture, one of Kelly's first programmes featured a visit by Newcastle United. Members of the team, including the manager George Martin, 'trained as a singer with a good tenor voice' and Colin Gibson, 'inside right and a very pleasing light vocalist', contributed to the programme's usual musical slot.[68] He also worked hard to establish the profile of *Geordie* beyond the region. In a list of northern programmes compiled for a BBC publicity document in 1948, *Wot Cheor, Geordie!* was included under a general heading of 'Northern Variety', whilst a separate category for north-eastern programmes included *Daily News Bulletins, Farmer Bewick's Barn Dances, Shipbuilding, Miners Gala* and *Down the Tyne*.[69] The following year, the head of variety in London wrote to Kelly requesting a recording of *Geordie*, which Kelly sent down with the following covering note attached: 'the dialect will be pretty broad … but could easily be toned down for a wider audience without losing its humour'.[70]

The belief in the universal quality and style of *Wot Cheor, Geordie!* is affirmed by one of the programme's most prolific contributors. In 1948 Leonard Barras, a clerk at Swan Hunter's shipyard, sent a sketch to Richard Kelly written for *Wot Cheor, Geordie!* Kelly quickly accepted the work and Barras's humorous sketches became an integral part of the programme until the early 1950s. The parts were read by well-known stage personas such as Sal Sturgeon, Edward Frame, Joyce Wright and Charles Brown, many having performed on radio before the war. He confirms that this was a time of relative creative freedom for writers and recalls that radio helped to generate a critical mass of artists working in the region.[71] This last point is reinforced by the playwright Alan Plater, who suggests that the autonomy of radio in this period provided an outlet for 'a lot of wonderfully renegade producers – which is a polite way of saying exceedingly left wing' that in its turn gave impetus to new and experimental writing in the north.[72] Whilst Barras acknowledged the importance of this development to writing in the north east, he was also sensitive to the ambiguous position of north east radio within BBC hierarchies, recalling how Kelly 'sweated a bit' under the pressure from Manchester. Kelly later described his time at the BBC in Newcastle as a campaign against the double imperialism of Manchester and London: 'We were little more than a colonial appendage of Manchester, which itself was little more than a colonial appendage of London'.[73]

Whilst Barras has come to be associated with the evolution of a specific north east comedy, in which he is distinguished by his characteristic 'Geordie surrealism', he was reticent about being cast as a 'regional writer'. His writing career began after the Second World War with a humorous column in the *Sunday Sun*, but he was also influenced by developments in national radio, particularly programmes such as *Round the Horn, The Goons* and *Take it from Here*. Having heard a couple of *Wot Cheor, Geordie!* broadcasts he recognised an opportunity to try his hand at radio comedy: 'I have always resisted the suggestion that I was a "Geordie writer". I have to be a writer who concentrates on writing funny material and if the circumstances require it, I'll write in Geordie ... the best comedy is universal anyway'.[74]

Although his scripts were spoken in local accents, he emphasised that the policy was to use accent rather than dialect: 'they wouldn't have been "taalking like that, ye knaa, aal the time" they certainly would not talk like that in a broadcast'. When Barras began collaborating with Kelly, a BBC audience survey revealed that a significant proportion of middle and upper-middle class listeners tuned in. Robert Silvey, head of BBC audience research, noted that this was typical of most Home Service variety broadcasts, with the caveat that *Wot Cheor, Geordie!* appeared to be attracting a disproportionate number of mature listeners.[75]

Barras's writing, which encompasses several published novels, plays – often premiered at Live Theatre – journalism, radio and television work, and a humorous column in *Northern Review*, is often described as 'Geordie surrealism', a term which he minded less than 'Geordie writer'. Whilst it is tempting here to search for past influences, Barras insisted that the surrealist tag, first used in a review of one of his plays in 1988, was a recent invention. He maintained that the descriptor would have made very little impression on radio listeners during the 1950s. But it is possible to acknowledge 'invented traditions' whilst believing in them at the same time: 'I didn't mind in the least, because I've come to recognise that quite a lot of my work can easily have that label attached to it and when that happens you to some extent capitalise on it and introduce those aspects all the more'. By his own admission Barras was heavily influenced by developments in national radio during the 1950s, and tried consciously to write in the style of programmes such as *Round the Horn* and *The Goons*. It could be argued that Barras's work was an interaction between new metropolitan-based comedy forms and regional particularity. Comedy was an integral part of his life from early childhood: 'I was brought up on comedy that wasn't particularly regional ... I've often told the story of my father falling off the fender reading *Three Men in a Boat* ... he read it over and laughed and laughed and that's the kind of atmosphere I grew up in, and there's nothing particularly regional about that'.[76] Commenting on Barras's surrealism, Alan Plater has nevertheless emphasised that his humorous column in a local Sunday paper during the 1950s was pioneering. Aided by the fact that the region was in possession of a local paper amenable to this genre, Barras became the north east's version of *Beachcomber*. Further, Plater suggests that whilst Barras may not have set out to reflect regional particularity, his work contains a nuanced range of references which may be more readily appreciated by audiences from the old industrial regions.[77]

Compared to Leonard Barras's pursuit of humour that transcended time and place, the arrival of Bobby Thompson to the BBC in Newcastle during the early 1950s introduced a comic to *Wot Cheor, Geordie!* who delighted in his role as

Geordie funny man. By the 1940s Thompson was an established stand-up comic, performing in workingmen's clubs and pubs throughout the region. Admired as the spokesman of the working class, a part which he relished, he frequently appeared in character as 'the Little Waster' and regaled audiences with tales of wife trouble, debt and the dole. During the early 1950s Richard Kelly orchestrated the rise of Bobby Thompson as a radio star – many felt Thompson excelled under the 'stern benevolence' of Kelly – introducing him first in *Wot Cheor, Geordie!* and later providing him with his own show, *Bob's your Uncle*. Evidently Kelly believed he had discovered an asset to north east radio:

> I think we have a find in Bobbie Thompson. His style has been compared to that of Al Read and there undoubtedly are certain similarities but it seems clear to me that he has developed his act quite independently of anyone else. I am devoting quite a lot of time to him and my practice is to record his act in the studio here and play it back to him, pointing out faults of tempo, passages of unintelligible dialect etc. He is, incidentally, almost illiterate … Wherever he is understood he brings the house down, which is why I am concentrating on ironing out dialect a little without spoiling the fun.[78]

The popular appeal of Thompson within the region was undeniable, but listener research undertaken during the early 1950s revealed that audiences elsewhere found the dialect difficult to understand. As one excise officer commented: 'the dialect was troublesome. The humour was of a kind that appeals only to a local'. In 1951, buoyed by the huge success of the programme within the region – by this time it was regularly enjoying audiences of more than a million in the north east – Kelly offered the programme to Scottish listeners.[79] To his surprise and disappointment, the director of Scottish programmes rejected the idea on the grounds that 'much of the content would be incomprehensible to Scottish listeners'.[80] It is possible that such setbacks contributed to Kelly's feeling in 1952 that the series had run its course: 'The programme seems to be doing very well just now but 28 weeks is, I think, long enough for the artists concerned, particularly on the comedy side'.[81]

In the event *Wot Cheor, Geordie!* was launched as a new series to popular acclaim in 1955, complete with 'the Little Waster', Willie Walker and his band, the Newcastle Ladies' Choir and the Northumbrian Serenaders.[82] The appeal of 'Northumbrian music' apparently extended to listeners beyond the north east. The 'Northumbrian Music' slot was established as a popular feature in the *Stagshaw Programme* during the 1930s and the Northumbrian Serenaders were the longest-standing musical performers featured on *Wot Cheor, Geordie!* Audience research based on the north regional section revealed that the most popular items of the whole broadcast were the songs sung by the Northumbrian Serenaders whilst Willie Walker and his band were also much liked.[83] Kelly, on the other hand, recognised music as a potential vehicle for the expression of cultural particularity. One of his early innovations was to turn the studio-based *Northumbrian Barn Dance* into a new live series 'with an authentic atmosphere from Dinnington Village Hall'. Musicians included Jack Armstrong and his Barnstormers playing for local dancers. For Kelly the 'staged naturalness' of a studio-based farm was offset by the advantages of showcasing the distinctive characteristics of Northumbrian music – 'no mere derivation of its Scottish equivalent'.[84]

The producer's attitude to broadcasting and regional culture was ambiguous. During the 1950s Kelly pioneered a form of radio documentary known as 'vox pop' which used local themes and settings. Whilst building on earlier initiatives in outside broadcasting, *Voice of the People* appears to have brought a novel dimension to radio for listeners in the north east. As one broadcaster recalled: 'it's impossible to convey the shock of hearing Geordie accents coming out of the Rediffusion wooden wireless set which had hitherto spoken only the voice of Whitehall and the occasional cockney comic. It was like seeing your granny suddenly reading the news on the telly'.[85] Whilst Kelly would probably have assented to the programme's success in harnessing the idioms of ordinary life, he was less comfortable with its function as a regional voice.[86] When the programme name was changed from *Voice of the People* to *Voice of the North*, Kelly complained: 'what was wrong with "people" and why it was changed to "North" I still don't know', pointing to the broadcast's wider importance with the claim that '*Today* started on the same day as *Vox Pop* … soon our idea of vox-pop was accepted by all other regions, and they started doing it. Not as well as we did mind you'.[87]

Kelly's cautious appreciation of north-eastern cultural particularity is explained in part by the tenuous position of the north east within the 'broadcasting north'. While the uneasy role of radio in the north east had been a continuity since the 1920s, tensions were heightened after the Second World War. This was a time of increased creative autonomy for regional broadcasting, yet the Newcastle station lagged behind many of its neighbours due to technical restrictions. The most pressing concern was poor reception. The north east had been equipped with a new transmitter in 1937, but the wavelength for Stagshaw continued to be shared with Northern Ireland, prompting one irate listener to complain to the *Evening Chronicle* in 1946 that 'The North East Region has been neglected ever since the commencement of public service broadcasting in this country'.[88] Coatman in Manchester was sensitive the fact that the 'failure (or inability) of the BBC to give Stagshaw … to "the people of Newcastle" seemed to suggest that the unity of the North was being taken for granted'.[89] Following his retirement he remained a staunch supporter of the fight for a north east wavelength.

This problem was compounded by the fact that the Newcastle station remained poorly equipped to develop a broadly based portfolio of radio programmes. BBC staff lists reveal that in 1956 the Newcastle station had thirty-five workers including two programme assistants, but no producers. By contrast the Leeds station had fifty staff, seven at producer level, including two specifically allocated to drama production. By 1962, Leeds had built on this strength with several staff in drama, talks and light entertainment across radio and television whereas the majority of workers at the Newcastle station were by now increasingly concentrated in news and documentary production.[90] By the early 1960s writers such as Leonard Barras were increasingly drawn to the production facilities offered by studios within the Leeds Manchester orbit. Barras's stories were broadcast from Manchester to national audiences by the producer Gillian Hush, who had started her career as an assistant to Kelly in Newcastle during the 1950s. During the 1970s Barras moved from writing for radio to television, still under the auspices of producers outside the north east such as the Leeds-based Alfred Bradley, who produced several of his stories for television and radio, with monologues and sketches often delivered by Alex Glasgow.[91]

The advent of radio in the north east presented a series of challenges and opportunities to cultural life in the region. On the one hand, radio appeared to furnish a platform for new cultural expression, echoing the manner in which music halls presaged the development of popular music during the nineteenth century. Arguably the oral qualities of north east popular culture, which underpinned the strength of music hall, offered similar opportunities to a medium that had sound as its anchoring concern and appears to have been highly complementary to a culture that 'lives on the tongue'.[92] To a degree these opportunities were realised in the north east, regional humour and music were immortalised to popular acclaim in the programmes featured in this discussion and both programme makers and writers confirmed that radio provided a forum for the intersection between writers, actors, comedians and musicians in the north east. This clearly built on existing cultural forms but in producing specifically for this new medium it could also be argued that it encouraged the development of new cultural practices. On the other hand, the imprint of the state and national culture was an overwhelming feature of radio policy and development in the period considered, and this imposed clear parameters on the development of regional culture through sound broadcasting. The obstacles to north east broadcasting were seen clearly in the tensions experienced under the Regional Scheme, which brought the radio north to listeners in the north east with limited local autonomy. The regionalisation of broadcasting prompted listeners in the north east to look favourably upon the National Programme and define themselves against the broadcasting north's headquarters in Manchester. At the same time, whilst there was little affiliation with radio's wider north, it could also be argued that the unsatisfactory radio provision was a catalyst to a growing regionalism within the north east: listeners and programme makers in the region only began using the term 'north east radio' as it became apparent that the region lacked adequate facilities for broadcasting.

In 1959 the Duke of Northumberland threw the switch that sent the studios of Tyne Tees Television live for the first time. The launch was accompanied by the strains of a specially collated 'Three Rivers Fantasy', a medley of north east songs including 'Bobby Shaftoe', 'Billy Boy', 'The Collier's Rant' and 'The Blaydon Races'. This selection was undoubtedly intended to reflect the new television company's erstwhile ambition to be the most regional of all the independent broadcasting companies.[93] It was also able to capitalise on the successful appropriation of popular song by radio and sought to extend this continuity to comedy. In that year, against the express wishes of Kelly, his *de facto* mentor, Bobby Thompson signed a contract for a show on the newly opened north-eastern commercial television station.[94] The show was a disaster. Thompson, a stand up, was profoundly uncomfortable performing sketches that had been written for him, an experience which proved equally unsettling for viewers. With poor ratings and an unenthusiastic cast the show barely lasted the year. The failure of the Bobby Thompson show was an unfortunate start for a television company that was inaugurated with the ambition to 'broadcast more programmes of north eastern interest than the BBC'.[95]

Notes

1 Scannell and Cardiff, *British broadcasting*, p. 6.

2 Scannell and Cardiff, *British broadcasting*, p. 10.

3 Scannell and Cardiff, *British broadcasting*, p. 13

4 *BBC Yearbook 1932* (London: BBC, 1932), p. 284.

5 Regional broadcasting was suspended during the Second World War.

6 Roger Burgess, *Babies and broadcasters: the story of 45 New Bridge Street* (Newcastle: Newcastle Building Society, 1994), pp. 11–20.

7 *BBC Yearbook 1934* (London: BBC, 1934), pp. 190–200 and 334–335.

8 Newcastle *Journal*, 8 January 1928.

9 BBC Written Archive Centre (hereafter BBC WAC), R16/201, Memo from Station Director Newcastle to Secretary, Central Council for School Broadcasting, 10 March 1933.

10 BBC WAC, R14/57, Memo from Newcastle Station Director to Mr Siepman, Head Office, 21 July 1930.

11 BBC WAC, R53/213/1, Report on the Proposed Regional Scheme by the Chief Engineer, 1929.

12 BBC WAC, R53/212, Chief Engineers Report on Relay Stations, 4 November 1929.

13 BBC WAC, Press Cuttings, 1926–1932.

14 Scannell and Cardiff, *British broadcasting*, p. 320.

15 BBC WAC, R34/734, Regional Directors' Meetings Correspondence, 19 September 1947.

16 BBC WAC, R28/141, Newcastle Local News.

17 *BBC Annual 1935* (London: BBC, 1935).

18 BBC WAC, R28/141, Memo from North Regional Director to Director of Programmes Head Office, 19 August 1931.

19 Scannell and Cardiff, *British broadcasting*, p. 335.

20 BBC WAC, Press Cuttings, 1926–1932.

21 A. Briggs, *The history of broadcasting in the United Kingdom volume II. The golden age of wireless* (Oxford: Oxford University Press,1965), p. 319.

22 *BBC Annual 1936* (London: BBC, 1936).

23 M. Pegg, *Broadcasting and society 1918–1939* (Kent: Croom Helm, 1983), pp. 48 and 59.

24 P. Scannell, 'The stuff of radio', in J. Corner (ed.), *Documentary and the mass media* (London: Edward Arnold, 1986), p. 14.

25 P. Stead, *Film and the working class: the feature film in British and American society* (London: Routledge, 1989), pp. 113–119.

26 Scannell and Cardiff, *British broadcasting*, p. 342.

27 Ibid.

28 BBC WAC, N2/16, D. G. Bridson, BBC Internal Memo – North Region, 3 September 1938.

29 BBC WAC, N2/16, D. G. Bridson, BBC Internal Memo – North Region, 5 October 1938, BBC WAC.

30 Scannell and Cardiff, *British broadcasting*, pp. 343–344.

31 Ibid.

32 Cited in Scannell and Cardiff, *British broadcasting*, p. 347.

33 BBC WAC, NR Scripts, 29 March 1939, p. 1.

34 BBC WAC, NR Scripts, 29 March 1939, p. 6.

35 A. Plater, 'The drama of the north east' in Colls and Lancaster, *Geordies*, p. 81.

36 Scannell and Cardiff, *British broadcasting*, p. 347.

37 BBC WAC, NR Scripts, 29 March 1939, p. 8.

38 BBC WAC, NR Scripts, 29 March 1939, p. 1.

39 Scannell, 'The stuff of radio', pp. 10 and 13.

40 Briggs, 'Local and regional in northern sound broadcasting', p. 180.

41 BBC WAC, R/361, E. Liveing, BBC Internal Memo, 3 September 1935.

42 BBC WAC, R/361, E. Liveing, BBC Internal Memo, 22 February 1937.

43 BBC WAC, R/361, E. Guilford, BBC Internal Memo, 13 April 1937.

44 BBC WAC, R45/87, Northern Programme, provisional programme arrangements for Northern and Stagshaw transmitters, January–March 1938.

45 Ibid. The world-renowned Felling Male Voice Choir, with roots in Methodism, was formed in 1920 and has toured nationally and internationally since the mid twentieth century.

46 Ibid.

47 I am indebted to Alan Myers for this insight.

48 *The Times* (6 February 1963), p. 15.

49 A. Briggs, *The history of broadcasting in the United Kingdom volume IV. Sound and vision* (Oxford: Oxford University Press, 1979), p. 223. See also Briggs, *The golden age of wireless*, pp. 167–169, and A. Briggs, *The history of broadcasting in the United Kingdom broadcasting volume III. The war of words* (Oxford: Oxford University Press, 1970), pp. 393 and 710.

50 BBC WAC, NR Scripts, 23 March 1939.

51 P. Scannell, *Radio, television and modern life* (Oxford: Blackwell, 1996), p. 37.

52 Plater, 'The drama of the north east', p. 74. The BBC were also aware of this problem, having complained in 1951 that there was a shortage of actors who could perform in regional dialects, *BBC Yearbook 1951* (London: BBC, 1951), pp. 60–61.

53 Sal Sturgeon was active in the Newcastle Players' Repertory Co. during these years and with Esther McCracken provides an example of the crossover between dialect drama and comedy on radio and amateur theatre, as exemplified by the People's Theatre in Newcastle. I am grateful to Jimmy Donald for this insight.

54 BBC WAC, Northern Region Scripts, Walter Diericx, *Blaydon Races. A tale of Geordie Marley.*

55 The acclaimed writer Tom Haddaway, who often used dialect, has defined it as a language within a language which is accessible only to the cognoscenti; this distinguishes it from accent, which can be appreciated by a larger audience. T. Haddaway, 'Comic dialect' in Colls and Lancaster, *Geordies*, p. 85.

56 Lancaster, 'Sociability in the city', p. 333.

57 P. Goddard, ' "Hancock's Half Hour": a watershed in British television comedy', in J. Goddard (ed.), *Popular television in Britain* (London: British Film Institute Publishing, 1991), pp. 86–87.

58 Goddard, ' "Hancock's Half Hour" ', p. 57.

59 BBC WAC, N9/534, Internal Memo from John Polwarth, 30 July 1945.

60 BBC WAC, N9/534, Memo to Mr John Polwarth, June 1946. There is some uncertainty as to the date for the first *Wot Cheor, Geordie!* broadcast. Leonard Barras suggested that broadcasts began before the war, and, based upon Polwarth's memo, this may well have been the case.

61 BBC WAC, N9/53, Memo from Edward Wilkinson, Assistant Director, Manchester, to John Polwarth, 6 August 1946.

62 BBC WAC, N9/53, Memo from John Polwarth to North Region Headquarters in Manchester, 4 April 1947.

63 Burgess, *Babies and broadcasters*, p. 30.

64 Briggs, 'Local and regional in northern sound broadcasting', p. 181.

65 A. Briggs, *The history of broadcasting in the United Kingdom volume V. Competition 1955–1974* (Oxford: Oxford University Press, 1995), p. 624.

66 Ibid.

67 Richard Kelly, cited in Burgess, *Babies and broadcasters*, pp. 30–31.

68 BBC WAC N9/53, Memo from Richard Kelly to Manchester Headquarters, 23 November 1948.

69 R. Jordan, (ed.), *This is the North of England Home Service* (London: BBC, 1948), p. 24.

70 BBC WAC, N9/53, Richard Kelly Memo to Standing, 29 September 1949.

71 Recorded interview with Leonard Barras, 8 March 2004.

72 Recorded interview with Alan Plater, 6 June 2004.

73 Kelly, cited in Burgess, *Babies and broadcasters*, pp. 30–31.

74 Recorded interview with Leonard Barras, 8 March 2004.

75 BBC WAC, N9/53, Robert Silvey Memo to Richard Kelly, 15 February 1951.

76 Recorded interview with Leonard Barras, 8 March 2004.

77 Recorded interview with Alan Plater, 6 June 2004.

78 BBC WAC, N9/53, Memo from Richard Kelly, 21 November 1951.

79 P. Sagar, 'The development of regional identity in North East England 1800–1900' (Newcastle, University of Northumbria MPhil thesis, 2006).

80 BBC WAC, N9/53, Memo from Director of Scottish Programmes, 6 July 1951.

81 BBC WAC, N9/53, Memo from Richard Kelly to Manchester HNRP, 29 February 1952.

82 Newcastle Library Local Studies Collection, *Wot Cheor, Geordie!* Script for Sunday, 2 October 1955.

83 BBC WAC, N9/53, LR/50/621, BBC Listener Research Report, 4 April 1950. These findings nevertheless need to be treated with caution given that the sample used was extremely small.

84 Newcastle *Journal*, (15 November 1950), p. 3; Judith Murphy, 'Selling coals to Newcastle: the media and publishing in relation to North Eastern folk music, 1945–1975', *Papers in North East History*, 17 (2008), pp. 3–55.

85 J. Walker, 'How to rise invisibly to the top', in J. Finch, M. Cox and M. Giles (eds), *Granada Television: the first generation* (Manchester: Manchester University Press, 2003), p. 50.

86 Scannell, *Radio, television and modern life*, p. 74.

87 *Evening Chronicle* (1 January 1970), p. 9.

88 The shared frequency between the north east and Ulster is a theme that was explored by Gordon Burn in his *The North of England Home Service* (London: Faber, 2004).

89 Briggs, 'Local and regional in northern sound broadcasting', p. 185.

90 BBC WAC, BBC Staff List 1952; BBC Staff List 1962.

91 Recorded interview with Leonard Barras, 8 March 2004.

92 Lancaster, 'Sociability in the city', pp. 319–341.

93 B. Sendall, *Independent television in Britain, volume 2. Expansion and change, 1958–1968* (London: Macmillan, 1983), p. 7.

94 J. Ging, *A Geordie scrapbook* (London: Constable, 1990), p. 66.

95 *The Viewer*, 1 (1959), p. 3.

3

Television and regional broadcasting culture: 1953–77

The television broadcast of the coronation in 1953 has come to be seen as a landmark moment in British post-war history. With television the full spectacle of national pageantry was for the first time brought to the intimate and informal domain of individual homes. This intersection between public and private spheres is widely regarded as signalling the beginning of the end of 'old society'. The 'decline of deference' that accompanied this shift was underlined by the consolidation of a youth culture characterised by the distinctive developments in popular music by the 1960s. The extent and geography of these changes can undoubtedly be contested, but the position of television, as the major vehicle for popular culture, was established during this period. With legislative developments, such as the introduction of commercial television in 1955, and with the expansion of BBC channels during the 1960s, the nature of British broadcasting was very different to the state-defined national service, operating in the public interest, that had been launched in the 1920s.

With the widening of broadcasting horizons, it is no surprise that television would 'bring fundamental tensions and contradictions within the established cultural system into high visibility'.[1] The attempts to secure television services in time to broadcast the coronation in the north east demonstrated television's potential to articulate dissent from establishment culture. As one BBC executive commented: 'the chief concern [in the north east] … is not whether the transmitter will be radiating in time for the Coronation, but whether it will be working in time for them to see the Cup Final!'[2] This reflects regional attitudes towards national institutions. The opportunity to investigate regional culture is further enhanced by the 'opening up' of television with the development of commercial television. 'People's television', to use Sir Robert Fraser's words, was developed as a regional networked service and introduced non-metropolitan competition to British broadcasting for the first time.[3] The rationale for the development of commercial television's regional focus was also clarified by the 1954 Television Act, which stipulated that commercial television should be distinct from and not compete with the BBC's national remit.

The exploration of television in the north east represents a continuation of themes addressed in relation to radio. Whilst the 'oralcy' of north east popular culture arguably lent itself well to radio and its concern with 'the voice' – a feature which allowed north east programme makers to capitalise on the rich resources of dialect humour and song – television demanded a distinct form of representation. Scannell has written that with the advent of commercial television and the growth of consumer choice, the successful broadcaster had to negotiate the tension between the foreground and background, speaking to 'our society' whilst also providing a particularised version of ourselves.[4] This insight on the communicative character of broadcasting is meaningful to the question of regional television. During the 1970s, the findings of a parliamentary committee investigating the future of broadcasting in Britain suggested that audiences wanted to know 'what was happening in their region and the impact which national events are going to make on their region' and that they were well disposed to 'programmes picturing events in the region which have national importance'.[5] The response of north east broadcasters and audiences to the challenges of a new medium will concern us here.[6]

Institutional developments such as the resumption of regional radio networks after the interruption of the Second World War and the development of a regional television service with the advent of commercial television in 1955 produced a flourish of programmes with a regional focus. In television this was not initially an autonomous response to regional culture amongst broadcasters but reflected the stipulation of the 1954 Television Act that commercial television should develop a regional focus to distinguish it from the BBC. The north, or more precisely the north west, quickly assumed a dominant position. In 1968, Donald Edwards, the first general manager of local radio development, spoke of an astonishing provincial cultural revival: 'The North, in particular, was asserting its identity through Liverpool even more than Manchester'.[7] These developments reiterate the importance of understanding north east culture in terms of its status as a region within a region. By the 1960s the fascination with northern industrial culture which had preoccupied social reportage during the 1930s found new expression in television, and the north's 1960s cultural moment was crystallised with the advent of programmes such as *Coronation Street*, *Z Cars*, *The Likely Lads* and *The Liver Birds*.[8]

Whilst commercial television played an important part in bolstering the representation of non-metropolitan culture this did not derive from developments in northern or other British regions alone. Indeed critics of commercial television in Britain saw its initiatives as evidence of an American-led global threat to national language and culture, a view shared by critics in France. In Britain the tenor of anxiety was reflected in the placing of the independent television companies within the orbit of the ITA in 1954.[9] It will be important to consider the significance of this perceived threat for regional culture: did the advent of 'Americanisation' through commercial television, held responsible by its critics for eroding British tradition and the British way of life, pose a similar threat to regional culture? For some historians this period signifies the end of regional distinctiveness as expressed through class differences, reflected in the breakup of working-class communities that greater affluence had helped to engineer.[10] Whilst developments in commercial television were symptomatic of this process, as the major agency of popular culture, television served as an important vehicle for the representation of working-class life in the north of England in the post-war period.

The advent of television was eagerly awaited in the north east and during the 1950s there was a sustained political campaign to secure a transmitter for the last part of England to be without access to TV. Following successful lobbying by two delegations of Tory politicians, the second led by Lord Ravensworth, a temporary station was established at Pontop Pike, a bleak moorland hilltop near the steel town of Consett in County Durham. The challenges of realising broadcasting ambitions in a small, peripheral area were evident already at this stage.[11] In the event, the rise to dominance of the north in television during the 1960s was to become synonymous with the development of Granada, the company that was awarded the licence to broadcast in the large, populous north west region in 1956. Quickly acknowledged as the most socially conscious of the commercial companies and renowned for making distinctive drama based on the everyday lives of northerners, Granada was undoubtedly related to the 1960s visual cult of the north. Three years after Granada had begun transmission the north east's commercial television station was launched with the claim that it would be the most 'regional' of all the commercial television stations.

As distinct from BBC television, which was anchored in an existing national framework, independent television originated in the regions and following its inauguration in 1955, coverage was established in London, the Midlands and the north west.[12] Viewers in the north east, 'well accustomed to finding themselves near the end of any national queue', were to wait until 1959 before sampling this new form of regional representation.[13] The site for the new transmitter, Burnhope, another moorland hilltop in County Durham, had been chosen already in 1957, and whilst the contract for the north east station was awarded in the same year, it took two years of legal wrangling over financial control before independent television went on air in the region. Applicants shortlisted for the contract included a *Guardian* group headed by Laurence Scott, a consortium led by Viscount Tenby and a team directed by Sir Richard Pease, local industrialist and JP in association with the Darlington-based solicitor Claude Darling. The latter had backing from the *Daily News* company in Peter Cadbury as well as from the brothers George and Alfred Black, members of a long-established family of north east theatrical impresarios. This group impressed the judges, not through the presence of members of the region's elite, or the Black brothers' show business credentials, but because they proposed an impressive array of locally produced programmes, with a strong emphasis on educational features and issues of topical regional interest, a fact that was reinforced by the appointment of Professor Eaglesham of Durham University to assume responsibility for the station's educational output. After some deliberation the new station was named 'Tyne Tees Television'.[14]

The problems of financial control were common to all independent television stations, but were arguably more pressing for Tyne Tees because the station was amongst the last to be inaugurated. The 1954 Television Act stipulated that all commercial television companies be independent of each other, a requirement which resulted in the resignation from the board of directors by Peter Cadbury because of his *Daily News* connections. This left the company short of capital. Eager to redeem loan stock quickly, the company persuaded the ITA that the financial structure could change with the sale of non-voting shares, providing that 40% of the total equity would always consist of voting shares.[15] The share interest of the board of directors, illustrated in Table 1, provides an insight into the structure of the new media in the region; in 1964 the board of directors comprised members of the original Richard Pease Group including the Black brothers, Anthony Jelly and Sydney Box but also Viscount Ridley. In 1968, alongside Pease, Ridley and other regional aristocratic magnates such as R. H. Carr-Ellison, newly appointed directors included Lionel Jacobsen, the managing director of Burtons, and T. Dan Smith.

Table 1 Share interests of Tyne Tees television directors 1967 and 1968

	1967		1968	
	Voting	Non-voting	Voting	Non-voting
George Black	416,000	138,000	106,500	46,000
R. H. Carr Ellison	14,000	–	14,000	2,500
G. H. J. Daysh	8,300	1,080	8,300	1,080
R. H. Dickinson	–	5000	–	5,000
E. J. R. Eaglesham	20,000	850	20,000	850
E. G. Fairburn	80,000	102,400	80,000	102,400
J. P. Graham	500	–	500	–
Lionel Jacobson	250,000	50,000	250,000	50,000
J. A. Jelly	10,900	150	10,900	150
D. G. Packham	4,000	–	4,000	–
R. A. Pease	20,000	–	100	–
Viscount Ridley	44,500	7,595	48,000	–
T. Dan Smith	75,000	–	75,000	–
Totals	943,200	305,075	617,300	207,980

Source: *Tyne Tees Television Limited, Report of the Directors 1968*

The presence on the board of the industrial and landed elite, such as Pease, Ridley and Carr Ellison, invites comparison with the arguments that underpinned the Benwell Community Development Project's investigation of the dispersal of elite capital from local industrial concerns during the twentieth century. On closer inspection, however, the significant holders of both voting and non-voting shares in Tyne Tees Television were drawn from the middle class, represented by entrepreneurs in the retail and entertainment sectors of the north east economy.[16] As sons of the 'Moss Empires', the Blacks, former pupils of Durham School, had promoted repertory and their investment in Tyne Tees owed much to their earlier financial success with the Adelphi Theatre in London.[17] Whilst the Blacks' fortunes had been made outside the region Lionel Jacobson's investment reflected the strength of the retail economy in the north east. His Newcastle-based company, Jackson the Tailor, spearheaded mass-produced clothing during the 1950s with such success that the Leeds-based Burtons clothing company had negotiated a reverse takeover by 1953. By the early 1960s, Jacobson was chairman of Burtons.[18] As a politician, T. Dan Smith would appear to be at variance with the profile of Tyne Tees directors, but, as is well known, Smith had amassed considerable commercial interests by this stage and was as comfortable in the presence of the regional business elite as he was in his role as Labour councillor.

The first meeting of the directors of the new independent television company took place in Newcastle in January 1958 and by the following October Tyne Tees Television had established its studios in the City Road, Newcastle. Richard Pease was appointed the company's first chairman whilst other members of the board included Claude Darling, the film producer Sidney Box and George and Alfred Black.[19] In June 1958 Anthony Jelly, sales director of Scottish television and former sales manager with ATV, was appointed managing director of the company.[20] Joint directors were George and Alfred Black, with Bill Lyon Shaw, former head of BBC Light Entertainment, as controller of programmes. Whilst their local contacts and entertainment backgrounds did little to impress ITA bosses, it was the Black brothers 'with their close north east connections … and their flair for show business' who made the headlines in the north east.[21] They quickly became the face of the new station, inaugurating its weekly magazine, *The Viewer*, with a manifesto to their regional commitment:

> In our happy task of planning Tyne Tees Programmes, we start with a considerable advantage. We were born and educated in the area. We know it and understand it. That is a good deal more important here than it might have been elsewhere, for the region stretching from beyond the Tees in the south to well beyond the Tyne in the north is a region with a culture, a tradition and a way of life entirely its own. Yet none of this has so far been reflected by either steam radio or TV. Those days are now over. Right from the start we shall originate at least fifteen percent of our programming. We shall in fact, be broadcasting every week more programmes of north eastern interest than the BBC has done in years.[22]

The new station's remit included establishing studios and an outside broadcast unit in Newcastle. The first scheduled broadcast of the new station correspondingly included locally produced news featuring an interview with Prime Minister Harold Macmillan, formerly MP for Stockton on Tees. This coup was nevertheless followed by an episode of *Highway Patrol* (a formulaic American police series) and an evening of entertainment programmes including *I Love Lucy* and *Double Your Money*.[23] Whilst the first schedule culminated with a special epilogue from the bishop of Durham and massed local choirs, the initial promise of educational and documentary emphasis was difficult to discern in the early days of Tyne Tees. Synonymous with the Black brothers' brand of variety by the early 1960s, this bias towards light entertainment quickly elicited criticism from viewers including the barbed complaint that, in preference to talks from Sir Kenneth Clark (showing in other regions), Tyne Tees viewers were subjected to endless repeats of *Highway Patrol*.[24]

Alongside imported American serials the style of much of the locally produced output was typically light hearted and oriented to variety style comedy and music. The *One O'clock Show*, on air daily from 1959, was characteristic of this era of programming policy. Launched as 'a light-hearted programme with a bit of everything: comedy, personalities, music – even audience participation' its target audience was female. *North East Roundabout* was launched in the same year and went out every Friday evening; although ostensibly a news programme designed to reflect local news and 'views of the week', the programme was principally about regional sport.[25] The *One O'clock Show* built on Bill Lyon Shaw's earlier success with *Lunchbox* at ATV in Birmingham, but it was specifically intended to capture female viewers on Tyneside and took into account the fact that a British region with a historically low level of women's employment would have a large female audience.[26] From 1961 the *One O'clock Show* was exported twice weekly to Border Television. On balance much of Tyne Tees's local output did deviate from the initial group's emphasis on education, but this dimension of programme policy could equally be seen as a measure of the station's success. Tyne Tees Television was an undeniable agent of popular culture, no small achievement considering the social profile of the board of directors. Equally, responding to the appetites of their viewers was salient in such a small broadcasting region where failing to sustain viewing figures would have been disastrous; experimenting with the socially conscious educational material attractive to the ITA was ultimately a gamble that Tyne Tees proved unwilling to take.

Alongside the clear dominance of light entertainment there were also efforts to widen the cultural palette of north east viewers with the programme offer. According to Lyon Shaw the station helped to establish Northern Sinfonia and brought classical music, opera and ballet to the region; as he puts it, 'we were educating the viewers without it being obvious'.[27] Some programmes were even explicitly didactic. For example, *Spotlight* was launched in 1959 and was designed to air topics of regional interest, including: 'What is the case for and against comprehensive schools? What has gone wrong, if anything, with the British coal industry? What can be done about river pollution? Can anything be done to improve the town of Blyth?'[28] At the same time the repeated criticisms of its local output raise the question: in a region with a strong popular culture, what should the function of a regional television station be? As Malcolm Morris, programme controller during the late 1960s reflected: 'It wasn't easy to give the area a definable image … the Scots could spray a few kilts and pipers around the studio' and guarantee the programme an instant dose of authenticity, 'But what's the quick recipe for creating a comparable entity out of a region … especially at a time when everybody is trying to forget about the cloth cap anyway'.[29]

The station also had its own reasons for wishing to consign the cloth cap to memory. One of Tyne Tees's first attempts to 'bring the north east to north east viewers' resulted in *The Bobby Thompson Show*, also on air in 1959. Introducing Thompson to television was an idea inspired initially by Richard Kelly, who had reaped the rewards of Thompson's comic persona on radio, and also reflected the Black brothers' familiarity with the north east comedy circuit. But whilst Thompson's brand of humour worked well on radio, he was uncomfortable with the comedy sketches written for television. His performances were consequently stilted and wooden. Viewers switched off en masse and the show was shelved quickly and quietly. Whilst the station may have been able to capitalise on certain aspects of popular culture, the failure of the show suggests that televised comedy was difficult to realise. Thompson was acclaimed as a stand-up, but he was no actor, and by the early 1960s successful television comedy was characterised by self-conscious moves away from the variety format, reflected in the use of episode-length narratives and the replacement of the 'funny man' with gags, by character actors who were more suited to the growing enthusiasm and popular appetite for situation comedies.[30] Embracing these changes would have required close collaboration with a body of writers able to tap into the latest developments in radio and television comedy. Whilst there was clearly a pool of north east writers working in the early 1960s, the station had limited success in harnessing this talent. Michael Beale, the entertainment reporter for the *Evening Chronicle*, felt that the region's dramatic resources were underused by the station: 'with all the local talent in the Playhouse and People's Theatre it could have been quite possible to cast original plays at no great cost'.[31] Compared to its rivals, Tyne Tees produced no regional drama of note at a time when northern drama and serials were at the forefront of redefining popular attitudes to working-class culture. As with radio during the inter-war years, many of the most memorable northern programmes of this era were penned by north east writers. Dick Clements and Ian La Frenais are acknowledged for their television work during the

1960s, especially for *The Likely Lads* (1964), which went out on the BBC to instant acclaim. Alan Plater's scripts for the BBC's *Z Cars* during the 1960s secured him a national reputation for northern television drama.

Born in Jarrow, Plater spent much of his writing career away from the region and describes himself, in contrast to Leonard Barras, Tom Haddaway and Sid Chaplin, as absent but eternally haunted by Tyneside.[32] Having left the north east for Hull as a child, he returned during the 1950s to study architecture at Newcastle University. Here he nourished his secret ambition 'to be a writer, cartoonist and celebrated wit … a wacky sort of notion for a kid born in Jarrow and brought up in Hull'. He describes the 1950s as presenting many challenges for the apprentice writer from Tyneside ('[m]ost novels and plays seemed to be set in the Home Counties, lubricated by gin and tonic and speckled with witless epigrams') and he turned instead to Celtic writers, such as Gwyn Thomas, whose representation of the Welsh working class inspired Plater in his writing about Tyneside.[33] Whilst the literary canon may have yielded little for a north east writer before the arrival of the 'angry young men', it was nevertheless a period which Plater identifies as seminal to the flourishing of northern culture during the 1960s. He describes Newcastle student life at this point as a time of 'ferment', the '1960s getting pregnant':

> I mean Ian Carr was there, David Mercer was there and all the gang in the art school, my special mate was Jim Collier [who later became Professor of Architecture at Dundee despite, like Plater, having failed the fourth year] … our special mates were Jack and George, abstract painters working in the art school and yes it was very exciting and I have this theory that the four of us, had we not been separated … with other add on people who were around at that time, like Jack Shepherd the actor, we could have become 'Beyond the Fringe' … I know after I left they did an alternative review at the People's Theatre which Jack Shepherd was involved in, which was probably as way out, if not further out than what those Oxbridge boys were doing.[34]

Whilst much creative activity outside this 'legitimate' cultural axis could be subjected to similar claims, there was clearly a pool of creative north east talent growing in embryo in Newcastle during the 1950s, often made up of the core of first-generation working-class grammar school boys, which, as in many other cities, would be central to the popular cultural developments of the subsequent decade. Given these assets, the failure of Tyne Tees to capitalise on indigenous talent is all the more remarkable. As Plater confirms:

> They had a golden opportunity and they blew it, they had a talent base to die for and what real drama has emerged from Tyne Tees Television? They made one film which I think was about West Auckland winning the world cup, but that was because Dennis Waterman came across the story and effectively produced it himself, came up here and said 'you've got to do this' forced it through … I think

it's been a major problem … I mean what did George and Alfred Black care about the region? Absolutely nothing. I think the tempo of the times was that there was this thing called ITV and everyone should buy a slice of it.[35]

The commercial incentive did not preclude the emergence of regional drama elsewhere; rather, Plater pinpoints Tyne Tees' unwillingness to look beyond material considerations and to harness indigenous creativity as their most significant shortcoming. He further maintains that this has been a serious impediment to cultural representation in the north east, particularly in view of Granada's contribution to the emergence of the televised north as 'the people's theatre' during the 1960s. Just as sound broadcasting played a pivotal part in articulating the relationship between the north east, the north and 'the nation', programmes such as *Z Cars* and *Coronation Street* helped to shape the image of the north in the popular imagination during the 1960s.

In addition to BBC initiatives, the input of Granada, the largest northern commercial television company, has been readily acknowledged. For Plater Granada's importance lay in the commitment to making television drama in the north, which he argues created an unprecedented outlet that allowed the region's latent writing talent to move into television.[36] This view acknowledges the contribution of the north region's cultural resources to the success of the company, or, as Colin Clark, producer and director of documentaries and drama on GTV amongst others, writes, the secret of Granada's extraordinary success 'was Manchester. It was the north'.[37]

If Manchester made Granada, why did the north east fail to generate a similar dynamic for Tyne Tees Television? In part the explanation lies in the strength of the relationship between writers and the media in the Manchester region, consolidated by the city's role as headquarters of the BBC north region under the regional scheme from 1929. Manchester's Deansgate area also housed the printing plants and northern editorial offices of the major national dailies as well as the locally based *Manchester Guardian*. This greatly enhanced the city's writing and journalistic pool of talent. By the early 1960s, the strength of this inheritance was reflected in the fact that a move from BBC radio in Newcastle to BBC radio and subsequently television in Manchester was an established pattern for north east writers, directors and producers. Leonard Barras's work was being produced by Alfred Bradley for BBC radio in Leeds in the early 1960s and later in Manchester. Regarded as the north's most assiduous talent spotter, Plater also worked with Bradley during the early 1960s.[38] By the mid 1960s the Leeds radio studios had established a reputation as a 'northern writers' club' and it was during this time that Plater collaborated with Bradley as the editor of a radio programme called *Northern Drift*. The programme was intended to provide air space for new writers in the north and the response to this creative initiative was overwhelming. Plater was forced to hire a secretary to manage the hundreds of scripts sent by writers including Ray Hindes, Alan Garner, Carla Lane and Trevor Griffiths. Plater subsequently secured a position with the BBC in Manchester, working with Vivian Daniels, who was producing eight television plays per year for the network from the Manchester studios in 1963.[39] It was at that time that he came to the notice of Granada staff and was 'poached' in 1964 to write his first work for the company, a play called *Fred*.[40]

Whilst Granada was clearly able to capitalise on a burgeoning media culture which the BBC in Manchester had helped to nurture, the company's ability to enlist the corporation's key writers equally reflects the attraction of the new station led by Sidney Bernstein. Jim Walker, who started as a radio presenter of *Voice of the People* with Richard Kelly in Newcastle and subsequently went on to work with Bill Grundy for the BBC in Manchester, was similarly 'poached' by Granada. For Walker, the attraction of Granada was that it captured the *esprit de corps* of the 1960s in a fashion unrivalled by the BBC: 'As the 1950s differed from the 1960s, so Granada differed from the BBC. I was lured to Quay Street … it was bruited darkly that to get into Granada you had to be Jewish, a Communist or queer'.[41] Indeed, despite the identification of 'Granadaland' with northern culture during the 1960s, the location of the company in the region was something of a historical accident. On starting his post at GTV Walker was told that he had been considered attractive because of his Lancashire accent. When he confessed that he was from Newcastle, two hundred miles away, his boss replied casually, 'Well you know, northern'.[42] As Colin Clark writes, Granada's success in the north was bound up with the 'Granada family': 'a group of relatively young men and women who were united by a single aim, which was to produce, from Manchester, the best television programmes they possibly could … we were pioneers, and although we were almost all from the South, we began to feel immense pride for the North'.[43] 'Granadaland' was in fact entirely Sidney Bernstein's invention and could easily have been located in the south as the initial team had applied for one of the lucrative London franchises. But Bernstein 'accepted the north with good grace' and the region proved to be fertile for the kind of television he set out to make.[44]

As migrants who had arrived in Britain during the 1880s, the Bernsteins, like the Blacks, had begun by developing business interests in cinema and music hall. Sidney Bernstein and his brother Cecil developed the Granada cinema chain during the 1920s and 1930s. Sidney's commercial initiatives also reflected his political affiliations: he had joined the Labour Party at the age of seventeen and was a founder member of the London Film Club in 1925. During the 1940s he nurtured a relationship with Alfred Hitchcock in Hollywood and with this background in film and politics he established his television company with a commitment to make programmes that reflected the lives of its northern audiences as well as his own political convictions. As Julia Halam writes: 'he wanted to ensure that Granada productions had a staunch social message; to this end, writers with regional roots and voices such as John Finch, Alan Plater and Jack Rosenthal were encouraged'.[45] Such writers were happy to rise to this challenge, even if it often meant that the social message took precedence over the setting – often a fictionalised north recognisable to viewers in the region and beyond because its characteristics were non-metropolitan, working class and 'gritty'.

In Rob Shields's assessment, the 'Kitchen Sink' cycle of British films produced during the 1950s and 1960s similarly projected an undifferentiated 'north' in which external authority was thinly veiled in the apparently 'natural shots' of smoky industrial horizons.[46] Plater confirms that the enthusiasm for 'northern' writers in both the BBC and Granada did not require a great deal of topographical accuracy, rather 'an ill-defined, generalised lump of good old earth called "the north"'.[47] On the other hand, the dramatist acknowledges that this was an important point of departure for the later development of plays that were much more specific and allowed him to explore the nuances of the 'northern' setting in greater depth. *Z Cars* was his metropolitan gesture, the programme that allowed him to go on and write about the north east.[48] Equally this moment of metropolitan fascination with the northern working-class subject provided a platform for the subsequent emergence to popular and critical acclaim of more complex representations of 'the north' in the work of writers such as Alan Bleasdale and Willy Russell.

Granada's most notable contribution to the visual quest for northern authenticity came with *Coronation Street*, Britain's longest-running soap opera to date and a programme that provided an image of the north that was instantly recognisable, an intimate vision of 'our north' the north of 'community'.[49] Paradoxically, whilst Granada clearly played a pivotal role in bringing 'northern' culture into sharper national focus, the station was also associated with the generalised fear that commercial television, with its Hollywood movies and cheap American programme imports, would erode British national culture. This paradox points to the contested nature of 'Americanisation'.[50] Bernstein's commitment to making authentic northern drama reflected his interest in drama with a social message, which was in turn influenced by his partnership with Alfred Hitchcock. On the other hand, Granada was also a vehicle for the kind of 'America' that critics feared to be eroding the traditional way of life which *Coronation Street* represented. The critical appreciation of *Coronation Street* has undoubtedly increased in subsequent decades, but the programme arguably represents the first major British adaption of the American invention the 'TV soap opera'. Whilst Granada was able to interweave American media influences with the recognisable knowable appeal to 'someone in particular', stations like Tyne Tees were apparently unable to resist the allure of filling air time with American imports that *appeared* to have little connection to north east culture. This had become a recognised problem for the company soon after its launch, as one critic in the *Northern Echo* observed in 1960: 'The company policy has been ... *to give the public what it wants*. This is the natural result of its commercial nature. The bulk of its time has been consequently devoted to American serials, give away shows, variety and drama'.[51] Whilst its commercial 'nature' clearly influenced programme policy, the admission that Tyne Tees was satisfying its public could surely also be seen as a measure of its success as a regional television station. Many seemed to continue to apply the, possibly unfair, yardstick of BBC public service broadcasting to commercial television, failing to appreciate its role as being distinct from the BBC.

Furthermore, the American influence on Tyne Tees and other commercial television stations helped to bring to screen some of the most memorable northern programmes of this era. When Hugh Greene was appointed director general of the BBC in 1959, his strategy to recover audiences from ITV was geared towards producing programmes that would distinguish the corporation from the kind of popular low-quality entertainment that brought the maligned *Highway Patrol* to long-suffering Tyne Tees viewers. *Z Cars* was first broadcast on the BBC in 1962 and reflected the ambition to engage with popular culture but also to rival the mundane imports offered on the independent television stations. According to Laing, *Z Cars*, a police drama set in an industrial northern town and featuring 'real life' crime, presented viewers with an alienated, dangerous but instantly recognisable version of northernness.[52] Two years later, the advent of BBC 2 provided the corporation with new opportunities to exploit the televisual appeal of northern realism. The first episode of *The Likely Lads* was broadcast on 16 December 1964 on BBC 2 and broke new ground with its combination of situation comedy and northern realism. It was quickly repeated on BBC 1 on the prime-time slot of 8 p.m. as part of a comedy scheduling plan designed explicitly to pull audiences across from ITV. By 1965 ten million viewers were regularly watching *The Likely Lads*. The programme was written in partnership by Dick Clement and Ian La Frenais. Whilst the former was from Essex, La Frenais grew up in Whitley Bay and *The Likely Lads* was set in the north east. Like many writers of this time, La Frenais had left the region during the early 1960s in search of work in London. He met Clement through the two men he shared a flat with in Notting Hill Gate – Maurice Hardaker and Brian Flint, who were both writing for Tyne Tees – and the first sketch for the show was written in a pub on Old Brompton Road. 'Double Date', which switched between two men and two women talking about their shared night out, was first performed on the London stage by the Ariel Players as part of their 1961 Christmas revue. It was, as Clement recalls, 'of its time when a more realistic, northern drama and humour was emerging. With shows like *Coronation Street* and *Hancock's Half Hour* we were moving away from the surreal to a northern working-class style'.[53] Clement was subsequently accepted on a BBC director's course where he impressed the corporation hierarchy with a short film set in Liverpool. This move secured his employment in the BBC as a producer as well as the commission of three episodes of a situation comedy based on 'Double Date'.

The Likely Lads followed the lives of two men: Bob Ferris played by the Yorkshire actor Rodney Bewes and Terry Collier played by James Bolam, who was born in Sunderland. The decision to feature the lives of the two men reflects La Frenais and Clement's ambition to tap the nerve of northern realism with this situation comedy. As Clement has said, 'we had been influenced by all these British black and white films of the period: *Saturday Night and Sunday Morning, Billy Liar* and *The Loneliness of the Long Distance Runner*'. The choice of title similarly signals the desire to explore the theme of working-class masculine identity and in particular the generational shifts experienced during the 1960s. Bob and Terry, two young workers in an engineering factory, enjoying newfound sexual and financial freedom whilst still anchored in a culture of working-class respectability, could have been referred to by older men in the north east factory as 'likely', 'there's a likely un', an ambivalent quality which conveyed rueful admiration for the flamboyance of youth.[54]

Whilst La Frenais' north east upbringing provided inspiration for the show, the lives of Bob and Terry bore little resemblance to his own; as the son of a corporate accountant in Whitley Bay, La Frenais never worked in a factory. But as a youth he frequented the seaside arcades of Whitley Bay 'and tried getting to know the guys there, who wore drape jackets. They were all apprentices working in the factories and this is what we decided to make Terry and Bob'.[55] Both Clement and La Frenais were convinced that the north east was the ideal conceptual location for the comedy because of its ready affiliation with the aspects of northern realism they wished to convey: it was suitably industrial and had a strong male working-class culture. But like many of the northern television programmes made during the 1960s, 'the north' they presented eschewed precise identification. In part this anonymity of setting reflected the constraints of the industry; Clement, echoing Alan Plater, confirmed that there was a distinct shortage of character actors capable of working in dialect. Further, economic consideration meant that location filming was a rarity and much of the first series was filmed in London, close to Television Centre. A street in Willesden Junction provided many shows with the ideal northern location: 'two rows of proper back to back houses with little brick loos at the end of the garden'.[56] Audiences in the north east must have found it difficult to recognise their region in this setting given that 'back to backs' with gardens were unusual in north east industrial housing stock. In the event the region first sampled the comedy when it was repeated on BBC 1 since BBC 2 was not available to north east viewers until November 1966.[57]

The success of *The Likely Lads* depended not on the integrity of its regional representation but rather on its successful combination of situation comedy with northern realism, a feat which Clement claims as pioneering for the show. Like

Hancock's Half Hour the programme used character actors and similarly represented a conscious break with variety-inspired comic performances of most radio
routines during the 1940s and early 1950s. Despite the clear appeal of this genre,
the comic format adopted by Tyne Tees Television during the 1960s continued
with variety style skits and sketches, which, given the dramatic failure of *The
Bobby Thompson Show*, is suggestive of the overwhelming influence of George
Black, who assumed the dual role of senior programme executive and founder
of the board, prompting Bill Lyon Shaw, programme controller, to resign in
1963.[58] Whilst early criticism of the station's programme orientation was
tempered to a degree by the growing reputation of its local news broadcasts,
the changing financial climate of the later 1960s brought uncertainty to the
fledgling company. In 1968, Chairman Professor Daysh reported tersely that
'profit after tax and minority interests was £258,149 and must be regarded as
disappointing'.[59] The following year the change in frequencies resulting from
the introduction of BBC 2 altered transmitter coverage so drastically that it jeopardised the future of both Yorkshire and Tyne Tees as independent companies.
The formation of Trident Television Ltd., to assume responsibility for the two
companies with the agreement of the ITA, provided the initial solution.[60]

The creation of Trident provides an opportunity to compare the programme
profile of Tyne Tees to that of its other northern rival Yorkshire. In 1978 Yorkshire
Television's strength in drama was singled out as noteworthy by the chairman,
Ward Thomas. At that time the station could boast a portfolio of acclaimed
writers including David Mercer, Alan Plater, Harold Pinter and Jack Rosenthal.
Tyne Tees on the other hand was praised for *What Fettle*, a programme designed
by Heather Ging in her capacity as producer during the early 1970s. Described
as 'exploring music, ballads, humour and folk culture and the history of the
north east to the huge appreciation of a discriminating audience' in the Trident
annual report, the programme helped launch Ging's career as a producer and
she recalls it with affection.[61]

> It was my opportunity as a new producer, to put my interests in local music and
> history onto the screen … the people who were involved, say coal miners, with
> their songs and stories, made it very cohesive and emotional, and something with
> which television audiences could identify.[62]

Given the popularity of this programme with north east audiences, it is remarkable that the station did not seek to capitalise further on the mining theme. By
the late 1960s the fascination with north east mining culture had reached its
zenith, encouraged by regional and national cultural agencies, such as the Arts
Council, regional art galleries and museums. Norman Cornish, the region's most
celebrated 'pitman painter', was beginning to find the 'pitman' sobriquet weari-
some. By 1970 he had exhibited extensively, been the subject of a BBC *Monitor*
series and generally acquired the status of 'northern legend'. Although Laing

suggests that the moment of metropolitan fascination with the northern working-class subject had passed by the time the second series of *Z Cars* was screened in 1965, interest in the mining theme, an enduring feature of broadcasting since the 1930s, was revived during the 1960s.

In part this reflected the developments in the history of mining since nationalisation in 1947. The Second World War temporarily revived coal mining and with the pits belonging to 'the people', the industry came to symbolise the ambition for a modern Britain. The commitment to building better futures was given a boost in the north east in 1963 following the appointment of Lord Hailsham as minister with special responsibility for the area. These initiatives were further enhanced by the return to office of a national Labour government in 1964 similarly intent on realising the rationalisation of the coal industry. The mining industry during the 1960s experienced both rapid change and tragedy which touched upon deep local and national emotions and was the subject of intense media attention. This period witnessed the closure of many old pits strategically offset by the opening of larger, more modern coastal sites, combined with housing and planning initiatives designed to improve the standard of living for miners in the widest sense.

The relationship between mining and modernity had hardly been cemented, however, when the Aberfan colliery disaster struck in 1966 and once again served as a reminder of the drudgery and suffering that British mining communities continued to endure. Television played an important part in articulating the tensions that underpinned the attempts to modernise the coal industry. The BBC were applauded for their coverage of the Aberfan disaster; their rejection of the advice of Lord Robens, chairman of the Coal Board, that there be no live coverage of disaster, produced unedited footage which was unanimously praised for its sensitivity and responsibility.[63] During these years both the BBC and Granada produced television dramas that reflected the national tensions plaguing the attempts to modernise coalmining. Many of these productions were set in the north east and arguably they helped to shore up the mining theme as a central feature in representations of north east culture on television.

In 1969, 'one of the first network plays written and played in full blooded north-east accents' was screened on BBC 1 in the evening slot allocated to the 'Wednesday Play'.[64] Initially written for the stage, *Close the Coalhouse Door* was the brainchild of Sid Chaplin, a former miner, well-known regional novelist and full-time journalist employed by the NCB, who in his turn had been inspired to write a play about the history of a mining village by Bill Hay's production of Brendan Behan's *The Hostage* at the Newcastle Playhouse during the 1960s.[65] Written collaboratively by Sid Chaplin, Bill Hayes and Alan Plater, with music by Alex Glasgow, *Close the Coalhouse Door* captures the essence of Tyneside history and culture on stage. As Plater reflects: 'As far as my Tyneside is concerned, history began with the industrial revolution and everything I have written about the area springs from that perception … What I tried to do in *Close the Coalhouse Door* was to embrace the music-hall tradition – the jokes, the stand-up routines, the funny hats and above all, the subversive energy'.[66]

Music hall was Plater's vehicle for engaging an audience rarely found in the stalls of the local rep; part of his enduring commitment to writing plays for 'people who do not go to the theatre'. The play was received rapturously in Newcastle when it opened and its enduring appeal in the north east was confirmed by a successful revival by Live Theatre on the Newcastle Quayside in 1994. The play was also favourably reviewed in London; despite the loss of intimacy with the local audience the successful communication of the universal theme of the 'love hatred of the pitman towards his … employment' was well received.[67] A screening on national television the following year was preceded by a special edition of *Panorama* with Lord Robens discussing the politics of coalmining in the presence of some 'well scrubbed colliers'. By contrast the screening of *Coalhouse Door* was described as a more honest attempt to deal with the grimmer realities of the industry. The play's use of music was less favourably received, with one television reviewer finding the combination of 'music hall ditty' and historical reconstruction contrived: 'there were periods when the whole thing became an unpersuasive charade'. But the metropolitan appetite for the 'pitman's struggle' was undiminished and praise was heaped on the authentic representation of the miner's 'dignity and despair'.[68]

The response to the comic format of *Coalhouse* illustrates the difficulties of realising humorous peculiarities on television. In the wider sense the play reinforced the enduring interest in the mining theme, heightened during the 1970s in the context of the 1973/4 miners' strikes. In 1974 Labour was back in power and mining was never far from the national consciousness. Granada's thirteen-part adaptation of A. J. Cronin's *The Stars Look Down* went on air the following year. The story of a north east mining community between 1910 and 1932 was adapted by Alan Plater and directed by Howard Baker, Alan Grint and Roland Joffe.[69] It was filmed in Langley Park, County Durham, a location with arguably more integrity than the Lake District, which had been used for the pre-war film version. Nevertheless local reaction to the authenticity of the television production was mixed. Many inhabitants felt that it was a slight on Langley Park to be chosen to depict life in the Depression, and whilst inhabitants enjoyed the bustle of the film crew the consensus was that the series exaggerated the extent of material deprivation in the area for visual effect.[70] For metropolitan critics, however, such strategies represented good aesthetics and the programme prompted one *Times* reviewer to enthuse that the photographic composition could be likened to Lowry. At the same time there was a growing feeling that the mining subject was being overworked: 'Perhaps television has spoilt us too much and too recently with similar parts'.[71] On the other hand the serial brought welcome opportunities for regional actors to work on projects based in the north east. As the Sunderland actor Rod Cuthberston, chosen to play the part of football-crazy miner Hughie Fenwick, commented, 'I'd love to live in Sunderland if it were possible. I hate London – but I've just got to live there because of work'. Cuthberston was nevertheless nurturing the wider ambition that this project would help to secure his position within the 'Granada family' and open the door to a part in *Coronation Street*.[72]

In 1976 the BBC produced a rival serial for the national network depicting north east mining life during the Depression with *When the Boat Comes In*. The programme focused on the life of a Tyneside mining family during the Depression, following the progress through the union ranks of a young miner, Jack Ford, played by James Bolam. The thirteen-part series was produced by Leonard Lewis. Sid Chaplin, Tom Haddaway and Alex Glasgow, who also wrote the theme tune, all contributed episodes for the first series, whilst the second series was written by the London-based James Mitchell.[73] The programme was well received in the north east:

> first indications are that it is much superior to *The Stars Look Down* and if it is slightly nearer the soap opera edge than *Days of Hope* the stories are rounded and transfixing. North country language is spoken lucidly and without any comic Scott Dobson overtones … Certainly if you are looking for Geordie creations whom the rest of the country may believe in then this characterisation is the first I have seen on telly. It bears no relationship to the music hall of Mike Neville: it has dignity and depth.[74]

This reference to the stereotypical 'pub man Geordie' emphasises the difficulty of connecting the Geordie music hall comic tradition to a national audience.[75] During the twentieth century these features of north east culture have travelled less easily beyond the region than the image of the long-suffering pitman, and, despite the ubiquitous comic appeal of Andy Capp, the humorous representation of north east culture often evoked unease within the region. In contrast, the tenacity of the mining theme was sustained by voices from within the region, as much as by outside onlookers. Applause for the rejection of Geordie caricature in *When the Boat Comes In* was echoed by Catherine Cookson, writing in the *Radio Times* in 1976:

> I had gathered that James Mitchell and his fellow writers had decided not to lard their scripts with thick Geordie dialect, and they were wise, for our esoteric speech can be transmitted adequately by the use of idiom and inflexion and still remain comprehensible … for me the test of a play is when I become involved to such an extent that I am actually transported into the time and place being presented. The second series was so authentic that I was living the life at the kitchen – which was accurate right down to shape of the sugar basin and the beaded cover for the milk jug … What struck me most forcibly was the authenticity of the backgrounds. I had thought that the old north east had been mostly pulled down, but the camera crew found that there were still back to backs and cobbled streets in existence.[76]

This appreciation of the programme's authenticity by Tyneside's 'favourite daughter' provides an interesting insight into the relationship between television drama and the representation of regional culture in the north east. As Colls has written, Cookson's account of life 'in a back street' expressed in her novels but equally in the much nurtured legend of her own upbringing, was strenuously concentrated on the production of memories of hard times: 'Cookson's Tyne Dock and Jarrow were not only ugly, they were wretched; their people not only poor but scabrously so … This is "hard" "gritty" "northern" "industrial" "life" – make no mistake'.[77]

Catherine Cookson's appreciation of *When the Boat Comes In* needs to be set in the context of her contribution to the legend of north east hardship, and her enthusiasm for the programme read as a reflection of perceived support for her own account of Tyneside authenticity. This underlines the role of television as an agent in the consolidation of regional particularity. Clearly a region with as significant an industrial inheritance as the north east produced writers that were drawn to the exploration of this theme, but the broader fascination was rooted in a national preoccupation with class and the politics of mining. This provides an interesting reversal of Joyce's suggestion that regional identity during the nineteenth century was equipped to override social differences.[78] With the advent of television, regional nuances were often subordinated to the overriding ambition to communicate class differences which the 'gritty north', often the north east, was well placed to intimate. As Charlotte Brunsdon has observed, television requires viewers to be 'competent within the ideological and moral frameworks, the rules' of its subject to make sense of it.[79] Whilst left-leaning television makers claimed to be challenging the social order with their radical representation of the working class, these programmes similarly had to connect with national codes. In the depiction of north east culture, a preoccupation with class allowed the mining theme to dominate television drama, also helping to ensure that regional homogeneity was portrayed at the expense of diversity. The appetite for this theme was clearly reflected in the critical acclaim which *When the Boat Comes In* enjoyed: in 1977 the series won a prestigious award from the Radio Industries Club.

Meanwhile there were sustained complaints that Tyne Tees was failing to satisfy its brief as a regional television station. In 1969 the *Evening Chronicle* asked its readers: 'is the station fulfilling its role as a medium reflecting the region?', a view that was more forcibly expressed by the ITA in 1971 with the warning that the company stood to lose its licence unless it increased both the volume and quality of local output.[80] But perhaps the most damning criticism of the company came with the publication of the Annan Report in 1977. Chaired by Lord Annan, the committee was established to investigate the future of British broadcasting in 1970.[81] The investigation itself was a response to the criticism sustained throughout the 1960s that broadcasting in Britain was elite, closed and generally insensitive to the needs of a rapidly changing society. Repeated calls for broadcasting to be 'opened up' finally led to the formation of the Annan Committee.

Regional broadcasting, by the BBC and independent stations, was heavily criticised in the final report. Investigation into the eight British regional television stations of the BBC, which included Newcastle, had found that 'staff felt isolated and disregarded … morale was low … their budget and facilities were totally inadequate to compete with the ITV companies on equal terms'. The peripheral status of the regional stations was further reinforced by the unwillingness to produce programmes in the regions: 'London crews would come out to film for London produced programmes', and, in general, the regions were expected by the London departments to be 'bizarre and rustic'. It concluded that despite the alleged provincial flourish noted by Donald Edwards in 1968, many staff in regional stations felt that a metropolitan bias had increased since the 1960s.[82] The investigation concluded that there was little future for corporation regional broadcasting with stations that were inadequately equipped to compete with commercial broadcasting; further plans for more local programmes should be shelved in order to 'concentrate on producing contributions from the regions for the network services'.[83]

These recommendations aroused indignation in many BBC regional stations. Jim Graham, regional television manager of BBC north east during the 1970s, writing in the *Evening Chronicle*, defended Britain's 'island sites', claiming that the BBC would be 'cut off from its roots in England' if Lord Annan's suggestions were carried through. In the north east, whilst the regional station would retain *Look North*, 'the feature programmes that reflect the broader life of the region would go … if you're young "Lindisfarne" would never have been heard'.[84] Whilst the Annan report found the BBC regional services wanting, praise was directed towards many of the independent stations including Granada, Thames and Yorkshire for their distinguished contributions to the network. Lord Bernstein and Sir Dennis Forman at Granada were named for their extraordinary contribution to the development of independent television in Britain.[85] By contrast, the north's smaller commercial stations, including Tyne Tees and Border, were strongly criticised, and especially Tyne Tees for failing to open up the scandal surrounding corruption in local government during the late 1960s. The feeling was that the station suffered from a 'too cosy' relationship with leading local citizens and that the level of investigative journalism was poor: 'We asked Tyne Tees why they didn't think they had a duty to do more than just report it in news bulletins … they replied that they could not afford the costs of a team of investigative journalists … Tyne Tees thought they were right to leave this story to Granada, who certainly did not tackle the story early in the day'.[86] Neither the station nor the report openly raised the T. Dan Smith question: a leading figure in the unfolding scandal, Smith had also been both a shareholder and director of the company until 1970.[87]

The criticism directed at Tyne Tees helps to crystallise the problems that beset the station in the two decades after its official opening in 1959. The company did indeed have an intimate relationship with the region's leading citizens, with key members of the local financial and political elite dominating the board of directors throughout the 1960s. Their broadcasting interests were reflected in the document that secured the initial contract for the company in 1959 and were characterised by a didactic programme profile with a distinctly paternalistic edge which the ITA had found attractive. Much of the initial proposals were never realised in Tyne Tees Television programme policy, and the station favoured popular variety style light entertainment that leant heavily on American imports. The character of Tyne Tees's programme policy also reveals that the north east, along with the other British regions, encountered difficulties in sustaining comprehensive broadcasting facilities because media culture was overwhelmingly centralised. The peripheral status of the north east was also compounded by its diminutive size, and the difficulties of realising effective broadcasting in the region often came into sharpest focus in the ongoing tensions with the larger 'broadcasting north'. The disparity between the size of the region and its demands for cultural representation go to the heart of the 'conflicting rationalities' at the centre of broadcasting.[88]

In 1977 the Annan Report summarised viewers' expectations for regional broadcasting: 'they want the nation to know about themselves … they like programmes picturing events in the region which have national importance; they want to infiltrate London with homegrown talent; they want to feel that broadcasters are members of their own region and belong to no-one else'.[89] The challenges of broadcasting in relation to regional concerns are clear. As the intelligibility of any television programme is dependent on its ability to reflect viewers' personal narratives as well as generalised understandings of 'our society', the ambitions for the televisual representation of a region such as the north east were likely to be greater than the resources available for this task.[90] The difficulties of realising the dualism between reflecting life in a region whilst also representing the region's national significance contributed to the problems experienced at Tyne Tees.

This issue was complicated by structural factors which impinged on the region's cultural representation throughout this period. The question of resources had a distinct regional dimension in the north east, where the low number of viewers, in comparison to most other regions, limited the advertising revenue available for the development of commercial television from the outset. A similar situation pertained at the BBC, where the distribution of resources to regional stations was apportioned according to the volume of local licences. The programme profile adopted at Tyne Tees was as much a product of low advertising revenue as it was a conscious rejection of the educational and topical repertoire promised from the start. Indeed, the recent incorporation of Tyne Tees into 'Granadaland' echoes the strategy of the BBC's 1930s Regional Scheme in which economic and technical considerations dictated the boundaries of the sound broad-casting regions. At the same time, the question of the region's size needs to be set in the context of a palpable and historic absence of cultural patronage.[91] Given such impediments, it is no surprise that commercial television in the north east experienced difficulties in realising its initial ambition to originate more programmes locally than the BBC.

Perhaps as a response to the Annan Report Tyne Tees did try to address their deficit in local drama. During the 1980s the station produced several acclaimed series based upon the novels of Catherine Cookson. In 1990 their production of C. P. Taylor's *And a Nightingale Sang* won the prestigious Prix Europa. But unfortunately the days when commercial television was 'a licence to print money' were over and this late dramatic flourish was brought to an abrupt end by the closure of the station's drama facilities and an increase of low-budget imported soap operas such as *Prisoner Cell Block H*. One commentator has argued that the decline of regional production facilities at both Tyne Tees and the BBC further undermined the potential for a critical mass of regional creative talent to thrive and remain in the north east. Lancaster has gone so far as to argue that Liverpool's burgeoning television industry in the last decades of the twentieth century was a major factor in the city's successful campaign to be European Capital of Culture in 2008. This has been contrasted to the demise in production faculties in Newcastle during the same period.[92]

The challenges of regional broadcasting were not restricted to commercial television. In 1970, the BBC launched a programme called the *Great North Road Show* produced by John Mapplebeck, whose ambition was to capture the essence of north east culture in a fashion that was unprecedented on television: 'the entertainment traditions of the north east have never been effectively cap-tured on TV … *Wot Cheor, Geordie!* was a great success on radio but nothing like it has been attempted on TV. North East humour is so distinctive that it is impossible for it to go down with the rest of the country, so this will be a purely regional programme … we shall draw on traditions of Tyneside and graft on some of the newer aspects'.[93] When the first *North Road Show* was screened by the BBC in 1970 there were complaints from dissatisfied viewers who would have preferred to watch *Monty Python's Flying Circus*, which was being broad-cast in other regions.[94] Alongside structural constraints the ambition to develop a regional television service clearly had to contend with the cultural shifts of the 1960s. Mapplebeck was building on the radio initiatives of Richard Kelly, with whom he had worked during the 1960s, but the essence of north east radio comedy did not always make the transition to television. In part this was a reflection of the accelerating pace of cultural change. The problem of representing verna-cular culture on television was also symptomatic of the growing chasm between developments in wider, youth-oriented popular culture and local traditions, which had lent themselves well to radio development. An enduring theme in the history of broadcasting media, as reinforced by the 1977 Annan Report, is the ever present tension between the wish to present the local vernacular against the desire for many people and viewers in the region to participate in the wider national radio and television culture. Occasionally some local programmes were popular and did find an audience, in part thanks to the tenacity of local producers in harnessing the strong history of dialect humour for broadcasting purposes. However in the long run it is difficult not to conclude that viewers' appreciation of the popular vernacular was fluctuating, particularly if these programmes happened to clash with an episode of *Highway Patrol*.

Notes

1 J. Corner (ed.), *Popular television in Britain* (London: BFI, 1991).

2 BBC WAC, T 16/221/ TV Policy, From Robert Steal HNRP to C.P.

3 Briggs, *Competition*, p. 623; C. Johnson and R. Turnock, 'From start-up to consolidation: institutions, regions and regulation over the history of ITV', in C. Johnson and R. Turnock (eds), *ITV cultures: independent television over fifty years* (Maidenhead: Open University Press, 2005), pp. 15–36.

4 Scannell, *Radio, television and modern life*, p. 21.

5 Annan, Lord, *Report of the Committee on the Future of Broadcasting, Cmnd 6753* (London: HMSO, 1977), p. 153.

6 Goddard, '"Hancock's Half Hour"', p. 16.

7 Briggs, *Competition*, p. 625.

8 R. Shields, *Places on the margin: alternative geographies of modernity* (London: Routledge, 1991), p. 219.

9 A. Briggs and P. Burke, *A social history of the media, from Gutenberg to the Internet* (Cambridge: Polity Press, 2002).

10 J. Halam, 'Introduction: the development of commercial TV in Britain', in J. Finch in association with M. Cox and M. Giles (eds), *Granada Television: the first generation* (Manchester: Manchester University Press, 2002), pp. 2–23.

11 BBC WAC, T16/221/1, Memo from Stephenson.

12 Briggs, *Competition*, p. 623.

13 A. Brown, *Tyne Tees Television: the first twenty years* (Newcastle: Tyne Tees Television, 1978).

14 Other suggestions included 'North East Television', which was rejected because it was too imprecise, along with the convoluted 'Tyne Tees and Wear Television'. B. Sendall, *Independent television in Britain Volume 2: Expansion and change 1958–1968* (London: Macmillan, 1983), pp. 3–5.

15 Sendall, *Expansion and change*, p. 7.

16 Benwell Community Development Project, *The making of the ruling class: two centuries of capital development on Tyneside* (Newcastle: Benwell Community Development Project, 1979).

17 Newcastle Local Studies Collection, Durham School Register, 3rd edn to 1939, p. 597; *Evening Chronicle* (17 November 1970), p. 1.

18 N. Vall, 'The emergence of the post-industrial economy in Newcastle 1918–2000', in Colls and Lancaster, *Newcastle*, p. 57.

19 N. Vall, 'Regionalism and cultural history: the case of North East England 1918–1970', in Green and Pollard, *Regional identities in North East England*, p. 191.

20 Sendall, *Expansion and change*, p. 7.

21 Vall, 'Regionalism and cultural history', p. 192.

22 *The Viewer*, 1 (1959), p. 3.

23 Sendall, *Expansion and change*, p. 8.

24 Ibid.

25 *The Viewer*, 1 (1959), p. 6.

26 G. Philips, *Memories of Tyne Tees Television* (Durham: G. P. Electronic Service, County Durham, 1998), p. 92.

27 Philips, *Memories of Tyne Tees Television*, p. 20.

28 *The Viewer*, 1 (1959), p. 7.

29 *Evening Chronicle* (31 October 1969), p. 4.

30 Goddard, '"Hancock's Half Hour"', pp. 86–87.

31 *Evening Chronicle* (22 January 1971), p. 10.

32 Plater, 'The drama of the north east', p. 76.

33 A. Plater, 'My favourite books', *Socialist Review*, 174 (1994) http://pubs.socialistreviewindex.org.uk. Accessed 31 August 2009.

34 Recorded interview with Alan Plater, 10 June 2004.

35 Ibid.

36 Ibid.

37 C. Clark, 'What was the secret?', in Finch, Cox and Giles, *Granada Television*, p. 37.

38 *The Times* (30 January 1964), p. 7.

39 Recorded interview with Alan Plater, 10 June 2004.

40 A. Plater, 'Behind the cycle sheds', in Finch, Cox and Giles, *Granada Television*, p. 116.

41 J. Walker, 'How to rise invisibly to the top', in Finch, Cox and Giles, *Granada Television*, pp. 51–52.

42 Ibid. Walker joined GTV in 1968 working initially with *Octopus the Campaign* then on local nightly news and subsequently producing programmes including *World in Action* and *New North* before finally leaving the company in 1989.

43 Clark, 'What was the secret?', p. 37.

44 Halam, 'Introduction', pp. 2–23.

45 Halam, 'Introduction', p. 17.

46 N. Vall, 'Bohemians and pitmen painters', *Visual Culture in Britain* 5: 1 (2004), p. 3.

47 Plater, 'The drama of the north east', p. 73.

48 Recorded interview with Alan Plater, 10 June 2004.

49 S. Laing, 'Bang in some reality: the original *Z Cars*' in Corner, *Popular television*, p. 127.

50 V. Camporesi, 'The BBC and American broadcasting, 1922–55', *Media, Culture and Society*, 16 (1994), p. 626.

51 *Northern Echo* (14 January 1961), cited in Sendall, *Expansion and change*, p. 8. Emphasis added.

52 Laing, 'Bang in some reality', p. 127.

53 R. Webber with D. Clements and I. La Frenais, *Whatever Happened to the Likely Lads?* (London: Orion Media, 1999), p. 12.

54 Webber, Clements and La Frenais, *The Likely Lads*, p. 21.

55 Webber, Clements and La Frenais, *The Likely Lads*, p. 25.

56 Webber, Clements and La Frenais, *The Likely Lads*, p. 24.

57 BBC WAC, T16/641, TV Policy.

58 Sendall, *Expansion and change*, p. 10.

59 Tyne Tees Television Ltd., Annual Report (1968/9), p. 4.

60 Trident Television Ltd., Annual Report (1978), p. 3.

61 Trident Television Ltd., Annual Report (1978), p. 2.

62 Philips, *Memories of Tyne Tees Television*, p. 70.

63 Briggs, *Competition*, p. 536.

64 Plater, 'The drama of the north east', p. 76.

65 Sid Chaplin's early development as a writer can be traced back to the inter-war years, when, like Norman Cornish, he was a participant at the Spennymoor Settlement in County Durham, where the warden, William Farrell, helped him to secure a place at Fircroft College to study economics. N. Vall, '"Polishing the pitmen": cultural improvers in north east England 1920–1960', *Northern History*, 41: 1 (2004), pp. 163–180; A. Plater, 'Song for my father: the C. P. Taylor Memorial Lecture', *Northern Review*, 3 (1996), p. 12.

66 Plater, 'Song for my father', pp. 14–15.

67 *The Times* (23 October 1968), p. 6.

68 *The Times* (23 October 1969), p. 13.

69 A. Plater, 'Behind the cycle sheds', p. 117.

70 *Evening Chronicle*, (19 September 1974), p. 18.

71 *The Times* (5 September 1975), p. 7.

72 Newcastle *Journal* (24 September 1974), p. 2.

73 Newcastle *Journal* (27 March 1977), p. 11.

74 Newcastle *Journal* (15 January 1976), p. 8.

75 J. Murphy, 'Heritage and harmony' (MA Dissertation, Sunderland University, 2003).

76 *Radio Times* (14 February 1976), p. 62.

77 R. Colls, 'Angel of the north: an appreciation of Catherine Cookson', *Northern Review*, 7 (1998), pp. 59–61.

78 P. Joyce, *Visions of the people: industrial England and the question of class 1848–1914* (Cambridge: Cambridge University Press, 1991), pp. 289–292.

79 C. Brunsdon, 'Crossroads: notes on soap opera', *Screen* 22: 4 (1981), pp. 32–37.

80 *Evening Chronicle* (31 October 1969), p. 4; Newcastle *Journal* (25 May 1971), p. 1.

81 Briggs, *Competition*, pp. 995–997.

82 Annan Report, 1977, p. 100.

83 *Evening Chronicle*, (4 April 1977), p. 8.

84 Ibid.
85 Annan Report, 1977, p. 148.
86 Newcastle *Journal* (25 March 1977), p. 5.
87 Smith sold the majority of his shares in 1969, Newcastle *Journal* (9 October 1969), p. 10; Border Television was similarly criticised for allowing vested interests to inhibit the coverage of the planned redevelopment of Carlisle city centre. Annan Report, 1977, p. 154.
88 Scannell, *Expansion and change.*
89 Annan Report, 1977, p. 153.
90 Scannell, *Expansion and change.*
91 For instance, Newcastle Corporation resisted instituting a public library well into the nineteenth century. O. Ashton and J. Hugman, 'Letters from America: George Julian Harney, Boston, U.S.A., and Newcastle upon Tyne, England, 1863–1888', *Transactions of the Massachusetts Historical Society,* 107 (1995), pp. 165–185; B. Griffiths, *Northern Sinfonia: a magic of its own* (Newcastle: Northumbria University Press, 2004).
92 B. Lancaster, 'As seen on TV or why Newcastle/Gateshead didn't win', *Northern Review,* 13 (2003/4), pp. 5–11.
93 *Northern Echo* (1 August 1970), p. 9.
94 Ibid.

4

Artists and impresarios: 1959–79

Bill Griffiths, poet and dialect scholar, praised the tenacity of this 'modern art form', with its humour and echoes of music hall irreverence. Appetite for the local idiom has nevertheless waxed and waned. Between 1959 and 1979 the appreciation of vernacular culture widened demonstrably. This shift can mainly be attributed to the contributions of a group of impresarios, from a variety of backgrounds, who promoted vernacular art. The discussion so far has centred upon the broadcasting institutions and the approach taken here is distinguished by its focus upon the agency of individuals. We begin by examining the, sometimes nostalgic, revival of regional culture that characterised the 1960s, focusing upon a range of events, including the Blaydon Races centenary celebrations, the creation of Beamish open-air museum, the Morden Tower poetry scene and dialect revival in the context of Frank Graham's publishing initiatives.

Much of the material at the core of the north east revival was nineteenth- and early twentieth-century songs celebrating male work culture.[2] Likewise dialect revival promoted a distinctly muscular industrial inheritance and we explore how far this and other examples of revival can be read as a crisis of masculinity. The near absence of women from the core of the 1960s impresarios is noteworthy, particularly given that the few women who entered this world tended to support the masculine narrative with the same fervour as their male colleagues. Was the wide appeal of vernacular revival therefore rooted in longstanding traditions of popular celebration that were impervious to developments in mainstream culture? Or was the influence and authority of the impresarios indeed so great as to warrant the claim that the 'Geordie cult' of the north east was mere artifice, part of the 'well nurtured myth' of Tyneside culture?[3]

Equally the 1960s and the 1970s provided new opportunities for women to shape the cultural region and the discussion of both the Morden Tower poetry movement and Live Theatre reveals that beat poetry and radical theatre reflected the contribution of female artists and organisers committed to the representation of both vernacular and working-class cultures. But the 1970s were also to be an apotheosis for the cultural left and the ensuing discussion details the difficulties of reconciling the political radicalism of the early initiatives with the growing institutionalisation and bureaucratisation of such endeavours by the end of the decade.[4]

T. Dan Smith is often regarded as a politician who more than any other shaped the region's sense of self-awareness both culturally and politically. His youthful Trotskyism was supplanted by a successful business career in the immediate post-war years. He joined the Newcastle Labour Party and his political acumen and charismatic personality facilitated his rapid rise to dominance in the party, both in the city and at a regional level. Smith had his finger on the popular pulse and was well versed in the nuances of working-class culture. He was also a politician of his period. Like many in the Labour Party nationally he was in favour of corporatist-style politics and a continental-style planning process both nationally

Fig. 1 T. Dan Smith

and regionally. He was an enthusiastic adherent to George Brown's corporatist agenda. This background allowed him to take up the dominant position in regional politics and in particular his rise to the chair of the regional economic development council seemed appropriate to the political climate of the mid-1960s. He was unquestionably the most famous and important regional politician in England and his subsequent downfall on charges of political corruption severely damaged the reputation of local government.[5]

Smith had an undeniable appetite and talent for harnessing vernacular culture for political ends. During the early 1960s his influence over the Blaydon Races centenary celebrations provides an opportunity to consider the issue of how political actors contributed to regional cultural revival after the Second World War. As Lancaster has written in his historical dissection of Newcastle's urban sociability, 'in June 1962 something extraordinary took place. People took to the streets in their hundreds of thousands and many travelled continents; for what? To celebrate the centenary of a fictitious proletarian bus ride to a shady unregulated "flapping track"'.[6] This public spectacle was no spontaneous occurrence but had in fact been carefully staged by a special committee established in 1959 to oversee the planning of the event which would 'embrace all aspects of local and regional culture in the field of sport, recreation, drama, and music'.[7] In 1960, Smith had made enquiries into the history of the event in response to the feeling *in Newcastle* that measures should be put in place to mark the centenary of the race 'in respect of which George Ridley had composed the words of the famous Tyneside song'.[8] The song's wider popularity was well known and there are numerous examples of its pivotal role as a marker of established as well as new cultural practices. As Olive Shapley noted during the 1930s cinema goers in County Durham often punctuated the occasion with an impromptu rendition of the song and after one of their more spectacular national victories during the early 1950s, members of the Felling Male Voice Choir treated their bandmaster to a spontaneous performance of 'The Blaydon Races' as they assembled on the steps of the Royal Albert Hall. During the late 1930s the song also featured as part of Walter Diericx's radio plays in the nascent broadcasts of *Wot Cheor, Geordie!*

The Blaydon Races centenary committee was quick to capitalise on this inheritance, enlisting Esther McCracken, also an early pioneer of radio drama in the north east, to provide plays for the celebration with appropriate local or regional character.[9] Richard Kelly was a prominent supporter of the centenary, suggesting that a 1962 counterpart of 'Geordie Ridley's' show at the Mechanics Hall in Blaydon in 1862 could be televised during the celebrations. Whilst a new venue would have to be found Kelly stressed the importance of staging a 'Tyneside Variety show traditional to the area'.[10] Further evidence that the proposed celebrations drew upon and helped to coalesce existing ferments of revival can be gleaned from examples such as Cecil Geeson's letter to the centenary

Fig. 2 Centenary of Blaydon Races, 1962

celebrations soliciting assistance with the publication of his book *Northern Dialect Words* in time for the celebrations.[11] Whilst the event was clearly rooted in a political agenda, the case for reading this celebration of Tyneside culture as an instance of heavily stage-managed political invention needs to consider the clear confidence in the city-region's cultural activists to supply suitable entertainment for the event. There is little evidence that aspects of regional culture were exaggerated, and the overall impression is one of enthusiasm for Smith's ambition to harness local culture to his vision of the modern region.

The celebration's main route proceeded along the Scotswood Road and this was used to great effect by Smith to focus attention on the remodelling of the area that encompassed the construction of brand new 'system built' flats. The political effort to bring the celebration of north-eastern cultural heritage to an exercise in urban replanning was largely unprecedented. The use of cultural material for political and territorial agendas was attributable to the particular brand of regionalism witnessed during the period of Smith's Labour ascendancy; the range of his vision was reflected in the fact that he wanted to call these celebrations 'the first Northumbrian festival'.[12] Whilst Smith, as a local man and regionalist politician, saw no difficulty in meshing his interests in the region's cultural inheritance with the plans for its physical and economic renewal – the new flats' communal entrances were to be adorned with mosaic commemorations of the Blaydon Races – for others these processes were harder to reconcile. Delegates from the Newcastle City Council visiting the Civic Trust in London as part of an attempt to raise the profile of the centenary and to discuss external support for the festival alongside a housing exhibition planned for the same year were told in no uncertain terms that whilst the housing exhibition might be supported by the trust, the organisation was 'not interested in the Blaydon Races as a festival' concept.[13] Undeterred, the centenary committee continued planning extravagant promotional visits to the Northumbrian and Durham countryside to show 'the visitor the special historical significance and the present day potential of the north east as a compact region' to act as springboard for the launch of a 'positive policy in regard to the appreciation and preservation of ... buildings of special merit architecturally both old and new'.[14] The celebrations were also seen as vital to the Labour council's promotion of the area's dynamism. Councillors hoped that the event would help to consolidate the national perception of Tyneside as a cohesive unit.[15] This geo-political undercurrent quickly roused suspicion amongst Conservative opposition, expressed in criticism of the centenary's historical anachronisms: 'there has been a take over bid. This programme appals me ... the day when the brass band was the pride of almost every mining village in Northumberland and Durham has gone down and down. At the Durham Miners' Gala the greatest attraction was a band from the American Airforce'.[16]

The festival was nevertheless a successful realisation of Smith's ambition with half a million people attending street parties, fireworks and 'significantly during this period of restrictive licensing hours, all-day drinking'.[17] Whilst drawing on existing strands of revival, the occasion also provided impetus for the preservation of practices and traditions that might otherwise have been declining in significance after the Second World War. For instance, this politically driven event facilitated the rehabilitation of 'Balmbras' music hall that had once hosted local artists including Corvan, Wilson and Ridley, the region's major nineteenth-century song writers.[18] A member of the centenary committee spent many months during 1960 working with the proprietors of the 'Carlton Hotel', as it was then known, on the conversion of a billiard room to its original state as a music hall. It was decorated with pictures relating to the Blaydon Races and was renamed 'Balmbra's' in time for the celebration. The hall became Smith's venue of choice for entertaining civic dignitaries and subsequently other public bodies often chose Balmbra's as the venue for fundraising events.[19] This process of public rehabilitation also appeared to provide a boost to the ongoing popular music hall revival. Balmbra's soon became host to music hall enthusiasts, such as Joe Ging, later curator of the Joicey Museum for popular culture, and a man who, alongside his wife Heather and friend Mike Neville, ensured that music hall, although marginalised on local radio by the mid-1960s, found its way into television where the region's stations remained committed to locally based variety programmes into the 1970s.

The rehabilitation of Balmbra's provides an example of how popular demand was boosted by official endorsement and backing. 'Northumbrian music' also benefited from similar support and was enthusiastically featured in the centenary celebrations. Joe Bennett, director of the 'Northumbrian Traditional Group', saw the week of celebrations as a turning point in his efforts to pre-serve 'traditional' music in the region. In an interview in 1972, great emphasis was placed on Bennett's credentials as an aficionado of traditional music: 'he is steeped in the traditions of the Keelmen who plied their trade along the "coaly" Tyne. He has an intense love of their songs and dances, handed down from father to son over the generations'.[20] Like many contemporaries his ambition to be a musician and composer was cut short by the outbreak of the Second World War, but on his return to Newcastle Bennett used his spare time to play the accordion in pubs and clubs as a member of the 'Barn Dance Band' led by Jack Armstrong, the Duke of Northumberland's personal piper. As Bennett recalls, 'in these post war years, there was a real danger that country dance teams, choirs, music hall artistes, clog dancers and Northumbrian pipers might disappear' and whilst Murphy has identified this as an enduring sentiment in the north east, the political impulse to preserve what Bennett collectively called 'Northumbrian music' was unprecedented. Hitherto the efforts to encourage and preserve musical practice had come through voluntary channels such as the folk revival movement and the musical tournaments of the inter-war years. Acts including the Royal Earsdon Sword Dancers, which had been a regular feature of the North of England Musical Tournament, an annual event in Newcastle between 1919 and 1961, were profiled once more by the centenary celebrations. Bennett joined the Earsdon dancers as accordionist after 1962, subsequently bringing the Shiremoor Marras, the Seaton Valley Dancers, the champion clog dancer Hylton Pomeroy, alongside Northumbrian piper Colin Ross into the fold of what was to become the 'Northumbrian Traditional Group'.[21]

The centenary committee's enthusiasm for traditional music also reflects the growing and mutually beneficial relationship between broadcasting and vernacular culture. As we have seen, Richard Kelly was involved in staging a 'Tyneside Variety Show' for the event and more broadly the organisers were able to benefit from what Murphy describes as a 'comfortable interplay between commerce/media and folk/vernacular' that characterised the cultural region by the early 1960s.[22] By contrast Northern Arts were less obviously involved in the festival and 1962 was primarily recorded by the arts association as a year in which the first sub-stantial grant in support of Northern Sinfonia was made, as well as the appoint-ment of the association's first Gulbenkian-funded arts officer to carry out a survey of 'cultural talent' in the area.[23] Perhaps it is unsurprising therefore that ten years later when Northern Arts held an 'evening's entertainment at Balmbra's Music Hall (a deliberate choice) ... attended by managers and trade union leaders ... to create a feeling of good will towards Northern Arts', this was an initiative of the then Director, Dave Dougan, who like his friend Scott Dobson had a background in regional sound and television broadcasting and journalism.[24]

In 1958, one year before Newcastle Council began its preparations for the Blaydon Races centenary, the plan to create a museum which would make a significant contribution to the image of the cultural region had begun to take shape in County Durham.[25] In 1958 the county council's sub-committee for museums considered the recommendation that collections of 'folk life' and industrial material should be built up and that an open air museum for County Durham ought to be created.[26] Beamish Museum, England's first open-air museum, was established in 1971. Frank Atkinson, the architect and first director of the museum, brought up in a pit village near Barnsley, was a graduate of Sheffield University and had nurtured an interest in museology from an early age. He was appointed director of the Wakefield City Art Gallery and Museum in 1949 at the age of twenty-nine and subsequently directed Halifax Museum, where he discovered the possibilities of using broadcasting media as a means of publicising museum activities, forging good relationships with producers and presenters in Manchester and Newcastle.[27] In 1958 he became director of the Bowes Museum in County Durham, home to some of the region's most prestigious examples of French and Spanish fine and decorative art, including works by Goya. Shortly after his appointment he suggested to Durham County Council that an area with such a strong industrial heritage needed another museum to reflect everyday life and the more recent past.[28] In 1960 Anne Ward was appointed 'folk life assistant' at Bowes to assist Atkinson with a process that engaged people throughout the region in the collecting objects and artefacts of 'folk life' in preparation for the open-air museum.[29]

Writing to publicise the initiative in 1964, Atkinson claimed to have taken inspiration for Beamish from 'its highly successful and popular Scandinavian forerunners'. A visit to the Lillehammer Folk Museum in Norway in 1952 had persuaded him that there was a need for such a museum in England. However, apart from a booklet issued in 1949 by the British Ethnographic Committee, entitled *A Scheme for the Development of English Life and Tradition*, there had been no similar attempts to establish a national museum based on the Scandinavian model in England.[30] Whilst acknowledging a debt to his Nordic predecessors, Atkinson emphasised that in County Durham the museum would through its contents more clearly demonstrate the region's uniqueness and particularity.[31] 'Skansen', Sweden's largest open-air museum, was established in Stockholm at the beginning of the twentieth century, and designed to ensure that regional particularity was strongly linked to the idea of national unity.[32] Unlike the Scandinavian museum, Atkinson's ambition was for a museum that projected and celebrated regional associational life. Beamish quickly established itself as part of the ferment of growing regional identity and was the venue for discussions by the nascent campaign for regional devolution. But it was not officially connected to the regionalist political movement. Nor was the motivation to reflect the cultural heritage of the northern coalfield a response to the decline of the regional economy, which was enjoying a relatively buoyant period in the context of nationalisation. Rather the modernisation of the industry and the corresponding rise of new towns such as Peterlee prompted the concern to preserve the material culture of the Durham pit village and invested the project with a sense of popular urgency.

Like the Blaydon Races centenary, this exercise in public history, achieved largely as a result of the singularity and determination of Atkinson, appears to have functioned as a positive affirmation of regional culture. The curators had confidence in 'the people' to assume responsibility for their own self-representation. Contributions to the museum's collection by the public were invited with no apparent attempts to screen or vet these artefacts for their suitability as exhibits. As Atkinson has written: 'I formulated the "you offer: we'll collect it" principle'. Whilst a coherent strategy was precluded by limited resources and time – Atkinson was particularly alive to the need to salvage material from the process of slum clearance underway in many parts of the County – the ad hoc character of the early curatorial policy does bring a novel angle to post-modern *and* critical perspectives of 'heritage', which have celebrated and berated the industry's reliance on historical pastiche in equal measure.[33] On the other hand, Atkinson was clearly the impresario of this particular initiative, playing the part of cultural go-between and emerging as crucial in the active manifestation of regional projection by the 1960s. The role of broadcasting in facilitating this process is also noteworthy. When Newcastle University held a conference in 1968, to launch the 'Friends of the North of England Open Air Museum' with Professor Daysh as its first president, BBC 2 seized upon Atkinson's idea that it should be made into a television documentary entitled, *The Man Who Was Given a Gas Works*.[34]

Compared to the Blaydon Races centenary, political will appears to have played a less central part in the development of Beamish. The idea for a regional open-air museum first came about following withdrawal of financial support by County Durham in 1965. In response to the boundary changes proposed by the 1966–9 Redcliffe Maude commission on local government, which led to the creation of metropolitan councils in 1974, the county stood to lose significant population on south Tyneside, which, combined with a strong sentiment that 'the old black industrial image' should be obliterated, resulted in the withdrawal of support for the project. Atkinson, by this stage deeply committed to the museum concept, sought to tap the ongoing ascendancy of political regionalism in the north east in order to elicit a broader base of support for the project. In this he was largely successful, and, boosted by a national Labour victory in 1966, a regional working party was established which included representatives from Northumberland, Durham, the North Riding of Yorkshire, Cumberland and Westmoreland councils, and the county boroughs of Newcastle, Gateshead, North Shields, South Shields, Sunderland, Hartlepool, Darlington and Middlesbrough.[35] But Durham County Council resisted, and the project that would provide an enduring public celebration of Durham industrial culture progressed without their endorsement.

Atkinson clearly relished his role as impresario, describing himself as the 'puppet master' of the initiative. It must have been disconcerting for him to learn that political support for the project was to be ephemeral. Following the local elections in 1967, the Conservatives replaced Labour in several of the region's councils, including Newcastle. Under the leadership of Arthur Grey, the newly elected council took the decision to withdraw financial support for the Beamish project. Gateshead and Tynemouth quickly followed, as did Sunderland. Faced once again with the prospect of losing the project, Atkinson turned to the media, with whom he had already established cordial relations. There ensued a flourish of articles in the regional press urging north east politicians to support the project. Television also played a significant part in profiling the museum and Atkinson identified the contribution of Ray Sutcliffe, producer of the BBC chronicle film *The Man Who Was Given a Gas Works*, as pivotal to the project's public relations success during the critical period of 1967–8.[36] Following growing publicity Arthur Grey in Newcastle relented, and the museum was open to the public from 1971.

The role of Beamish in stimulating an appetite for the region's industrial material cultural was reflected in its popular success. During the August bank holiday in 1971 Beamish sustained two-hour queues and 50,000 visitors, a national record prior to the British Museum's Tutenkamen exhibition. The following summer bank holiday Beamish received 90,000 visitors and it has continued to sustain this level of attraction since it opened.[37] Whilst enthusiasm for the history of material culture was clearly awakened by the initiative, it is important to underline that popular demand was not the driving force for the creation of the museum itself. Although Atkinson acknowledged that strong regional awareness had underpinned the museum's success, he was single-handedly responsible for initiating the project and able to exploit the idea of a cohesive regional culture in securing support for the creation of a new institution. That the project endured despite the absence of coherent political support reinforces the strong part played by the media in the process of promoting the vernacular cultural region.

Alongside the Blaydon Races centenary and the creation of Beamish Museum, a broader ferment in regional culture was gathering momentum by the early 1960s. There were also connections between regional revival and the blossoming urban avant-garde community. By the early 1960s, Newcastle, as the centre of regional student life, sustained a thriving *demimonde* of jazz and cafés that was allowing a bohemian world to flourish away from London. Boosted by the inmigration of a young population from the regional hinterland and beyond who were free of the cultural and economic constraints imposed on their predecessors by Depression and war, this development contributed to a clear shift in the urban cultural landscape.[38]

As elsewhere, new influences such as American beat culture played a significant part. Developments in popular music saw the emergence from the local scene of bands such as the Animals that also drew heavily upon American sources; Eric Burdon was described at one stage as Britain's finest white blues vocalist.[39] Clubs like the Marimba and A GoGo provided a forum for the fusion of the different strands of Newcastle's avant-garde community, but particularly jazz, poetry and art. Mike Carr from South Shields formed the EmCee Five during this time. He gathered around him a talented group of musicians, including his brother Ian, a student at Newcastle University, and began performing regularly at venues around the city by the early 1960s.

Ian Carr reflects that the 'artistic flowering' evident in Newcastle was consolidated by the arrival of the Animals, but has also identified as important the wider developments in regional culture such as the return to the north east of the writer Sid Chaplin and his wife Rene during the late 1950s. Carr singles out the publication of *The Day of the Sardine* in 1961 as reflecting the growing cross-over between avant-garde and vernacular culture: 'Sid was a long time jazz fan who had spent some time in New Orleans savouring the music and had an ear for vital sounds. He was also a kind of social and artistic catalyst … he seemed to know every nook and historical wrinkle of Newcastle'.[40] Chaplin the regional enthusiast also appears to have provided a link between bohemian and official cultural revival: 'I remember going to a meeting with Sid and two city councillors, T. Dan Smith and Ted Fletcher, to discuss how to promote Newcastle and its riches, artistic, historical and otherwise. Dan pulled a scroll of paper from his pocket and proceeded to read a poem he had written in octosyllabic couplets about pulling down of the old Scotswood Road'.[41]

Poetry of a rather different kind nonetheless played a central part in the revival of vernacular culture during the 1960s. In 1964 Basil Bunting wrote to the local newspaper requesting support for Connie Watson and Tom Pickard, who had recently established a poetry centre in the Morden Tower. Two years earlier Connie Watson (later Pickard), a teacher at Kenton Comprehensive School, and Tom Pickard, a young poet who with Watson was part of the wider People's Theatre group, hitchhiked to the Edinburgh Festival where they encountered Jim Haynes at his 'Paper Back Bookshop'.[42] They were immediately struck by the informality of the shop. Connie Pickard recalled: 'they gave you a cup of coffee when you walked in and I'd never seen that before in a bookshop … people were sitting around talking, having informal discussions about everything that was new in literature'.[43] The lack of stuffiness that characterised Haynes's operation, the accessibility of the books (they were inexpensive paperbacks and there was no obligation to buy) added to the shop's democratic ambience.

On their return to Newcastle Connie Pickard recalled that 'we wanted to be Jim Haynes ... and we started plotting our literary takeover of Tyneside'. Their quest for premises for the Tyneside 'Paper Back Bookshop' led them to the town hall, where a clerk in the property department offered them a tower on the northern remains of the medieval town wall. Pickard rejected this offer without viewing, determined to obtain a cellar space in St. Mary's Place, close to the university and the wider student bedsit community. But the clerk was persistent and eventually she agreed to take a look. Carrying a very large key she found the tower on her old school route to Fenham. It had been peripheral to her younger self's visual horizon, and as she looked up to behold the tower for the first time she was struck by this mysterious room within the ancient wall. Perched on the tower's top was an angel: 'and I saw this little Angel on the roof and thought we somehow have got to do it'. The clerk arranged a rent of 'ten bob a week' for the purposes of running a reading and book room. With Turkish carpets and drapes, 'long haired' people sitting on the floors, the air of mystery was unmistakeable. Connie compares herself to Harry Potter as she opened the doors for the first time to the room that the couple had stumbled across in their quest for a Jim Haynes style bookshop on Tyneside.[44]

In 1963 the Pickards were still trying to acquire stock for their venture. Following conversations with Haynes they also discussed the acquisition of suitable stock with Richard Hamilton at King's College (later Newcastle University). As a student of arts and architecture at the college Connie Pickard had been deeply influenced by the art teaching of Richard Hamilton. Hamilton himself was closely connected to the US avant-garde, particularly those who were part of the Black Mountain College movement.[45] Prompted by Hamilton, the Pickards wrote to Jonathan Williams, a member of the Black Mountain group and the publisher of Charles Olson and Robert Creeley, requesting stock. Generous in his reply, Williams concluded by asking them to pass on his regards to Richard Hamilton and Basil Bunting. The Pickards looked at each other and said: 'Who is Basil Bunting?'

Bunting is acknowledged as one of the twentieth century's most important poets. Recognised during the 1930s as a pivotal modernist poet by Ezra Pound and Louis Zukofsky, he would achieve wider acclaim following the publication of *Briggflatts* in 1966. Described by Cyril Connolly as 'the finest long poem to have been published in England since T. S. Eliot's *Four Quartets*', the poem is also an evocation of his native Northumbria. Bunting also represents a direct connection with the radical tradition in American poetry that is often distinguished from the British 'poetry movement'.[46] Having served in the RAF during the Second World War and subsequently working for the British Diplomatic Service in the Middle East, Bunting returned to his native north east with his young Iranian wife and gained employment as a financial journalist with the local press. His output diminished during the 1950s, when he was busy bringing up a young family.

Nevertheless, the contribution of the by now middle-aged Bunting in establishing the Modern Tower and promoting Tom Pickard's early development as a poet should not be underestimated. The Pickards and their associates developed an early affinity with the American poets, particularly the Objectivists, the Black Mountain group and the Beats. Curious about Bunting, Tom Pickard visited him at his home in Wylam, persuading him to attend the first reading by Peter Brown in June 1964. Bunting was thrilled by the atmosphere and enjoyed the company of bright young men and women who were frequenting the tower, many of them students of Richard Hamilton. And the young warmed to him: 'of course they loved him because he was so unusual and amazing and kind of mysterious'. The Pickards asked him to read after his first visit to the tower, expecting him to decline, but he accepted readily.[47]

Basil Bunting first read at the Morden Tower in July 1964, followed by Dennis Goacher in September and Alexander Trocchi in October, an event which immediately produced a flurry of letters to the local press demanding that somebody do something about 'these long haired people, these poets, coming to Newcastle'. But they didn't stop coming. Trocchi's reading was followed by Robert Creeley's visit later the same month, and by Gael Turnbull and Michael Shayer in December. The tower inaugurated the spring of 1965 with readings from Edwin Morgan, Hugh MacDiarmid, Pete Brown, Gael Turnbull, Adrian Mitchell and Basil Bunting.[48]

In 1965 Tom Pickard wrote to Allen Ginsberg inviting him to read at Modern Tower. He received a reply on a postcard of Blake's *God Judging Adam* which read: 'Dear Sir Tom I do deeply desire to visit Newcastle and touch the feet of Mr Bunting whom I've read since 1952 … could you find me a place to sleep for the night and introduce me to gangs of long haired Rockers?'[49] Allen Ginsberg, Lawrence Ferlinghetti and Gregory Corso all visited and read at the tower in 1965. Ginsberg affectionately recalled that 'Basil Bunting … had found companions among the young in Newcastle … more charmingly, the young had sought out and found the older Bard in his obscurity near the city, and drawn him out to word-joust and night-intoxication properly renewed by their own attentive enthusiasm and good cheer'.[50]

In many respects the early 1960s cultural world centred around the People's Theatre, nearby bohemian Jesmond with its large student population, Richard Hamilton and the art school and poetry at the tower can be compared to Liverpool Eight, Merseyside's contemporary cultural engine room. It comes as no surprise that the 'Liverpool Beats' were frequent visitors to the tower. The Liverpool and Newcastle poets shared a common affection for local urban vernacular imagery and a high regard for contemporary, radical American poetics. In 1965 Pickard's

Fig. 3 Gregory Corso at the Morden Tower. Basil Bunting is far right, sitting on the floor.

Fig. 4 Allen Ginsberg and Tom Pickard

use of dialect became more pronounced and following his visit to Newcastle in 1965, Lawrence Ferlinghetti was to describe Pickard in *Esquire* as the next Dylan Thomas: 'he came to Oxford with us and read a poem in this Newcastle dialect – he really woke things up – he could be another kind of Dylan Thomas in a different kind of way. I mean a different original voice'.[51] Pickard's dialect poems were also enthusiastically promoted in the local press, where they were contrasted to earlier obscure and 'aloof' works. By contrast those in 'the traditional regional vernacular' were likened to 'the cutting edge of protest songs'. By 1967 Pickard was part of a band called Living Mythologies that accompanied his poetry sessions with improvisations of 'cosmic folk'. The poet himself acknowledged a debt to the nineteenth century's regional musical inheritance, citing songs such as 'Waters of Tyne' and 'Gan to Kye' as inspiration.[52]

The cross-over between avant-garde poets and the celebration of vernacular music and dialect is worth probing still further. For the arrival of the 1960s and its 'anxiety of cool' has often been associated with the divorce of the avant-garde from the working classes which brought to an end the convergence of mutual interests that had been sustained during the 1930s.[53] The example of Tom Pickard and the Morden Tower poetry scene points to a different reading of this era. The poet was connected to the 'new' culture of the international avant-garde through the beat poetry scene, but did not remove himself from the longer-established tradition of popular dialect writing and music. Ferlinghetti's responsiveness to Pickard's poetry perhaps also reflected the democratic nature of American beat poetry, open to the new, as opposed to the often cited elitism of the British poetry 'movement'. Another poet increasingly drawn to the tower was Bill Griffiths, whose early work used the idiomatic language of west London hell's angels and 'prisonspeak'. Now regarded as one of Britain's great contemporary poetic voices, Griffiths eventually settled in the region, not only utilising local language in his poetry but also producing a magisterial series of scholarly dialect dictionaries and writings on the language of the north east.[54] The mutual admiration of Griffiths and Pickard is captured in their co-authored *TYNE TXTS*, published in 2002 to commemorate refurbishment of the tower.[55]

It remains important to recall that the existence of the tower and its role in the renaissance of poetry during the second half of the 1960s was also attributable to the, often tireless and largely voluntary, work of organisers and promoters who were not necessarily artists in their own right, but most definitely part of 'the scene'. The contribution of Connie Pickard deserves particular attention. From a working-class Catholic mining family in Leadgate, County Durham, which included several aunts who had enjoyed some theatrical success, Connie Pickard had been taken to the theatre by her aunts as a child. This nurtured an interest in the performing arts and she was gradually drawn to the world of the People's Theatre as a schoolgirl and university student. Living in nearby Jesmond she became part of the young company that distinguished the People's in the early 1960s. She was well aware of the role of the Trevelyan family in the life of the theatre and recalls 'seeing Sir Charles in the audience with his white hair' as a schoolgirl. The Trevelyans invited the youngsters from the People's to Wallington Hall for a short holiday each year and she further recalls the 'erecting of a Maypole in the Great Hall and the company performing traditional dancing against the backcloth of Bell Scott's Pre Raphaelite murals'. As a student she was a friend and contemporary of young Philip Trevelyan, who later made a short film of the Pickards.

Connie Pickard was rooted in the 'old order' of private arts patronage and voluntarism: 'we didn't expect to get paid for anything we were there to enjoy it'. Tom Pickard was also a part of the People's scene and when they embarked upon their tower venture they carried this informal background with them. The success of the tower brought with it pressures that tested the resources of the couple, now with a young family. They were forced to seek financial support from the state and the informal world of the young poetry scene was to struggle with the demands of public sector bureaucracy. It is worth keeping in mind that the Tyneside poetry scene, arguably the jewel in the crown of 1960s regional culture, was 'made' by the determination of Connie and Tom Pickard to recreate the Edinburgh literary world of Jim Haynes on Tyneside. During its early years the tower survived on Connie Pickard's willingness to subsidise the venue from her schoolteacher's salary.[56]

The connections between avant-garde and vernacular revival are further encapsulated by the varied and colourful career of 'Scott' Dobson, the 'professional Geordie' often seen as the architect of Geordie revival during the 1960s. Dobson's dialect writing was not in circulation until the end of the decade and equally important to the wider question of north east cultural revival was his support and advocacy for the 'pitman painter' Norman Cornish for much of the decade in question. Born in the mining and shipbuilding town of Blyth in 1918, Dobson was firmly established in Newcastle's bohemia by the 1960s, having studied at King's College, at Freckleton in Lancashire and at Leeds College of Art before becoming a teacher at Manchester Grammar School. He returned to Newcastle and became one of a group of 'hard up' artists experimenting with abstract expressionism. He combined this with a career as a teacher, gallery owner and journalist – first of art, and later of jazz and Newcastle nightlife – *and* worked as a psychedelic light show operator.[57] Employed as an art critic for the *Evening Chronicle* during the early 1960s he was also part of a community of artists working in the abstract mode, including the 'fireman' artist Ross Hickling, as well as the 'amateur' artists Harry and Alan Lord. This was nevertheless the era of Victor Pasmore and Richard Hamilton's ascendancy at King's College. Whilst the flourishing amateur scene supplied enthusiastic recruits to the college's extra-mural art classes, the dominant influences for college students were metropolitan.[58] Similarly, whilst both Victor Pasmore and Lawrence Gowing,

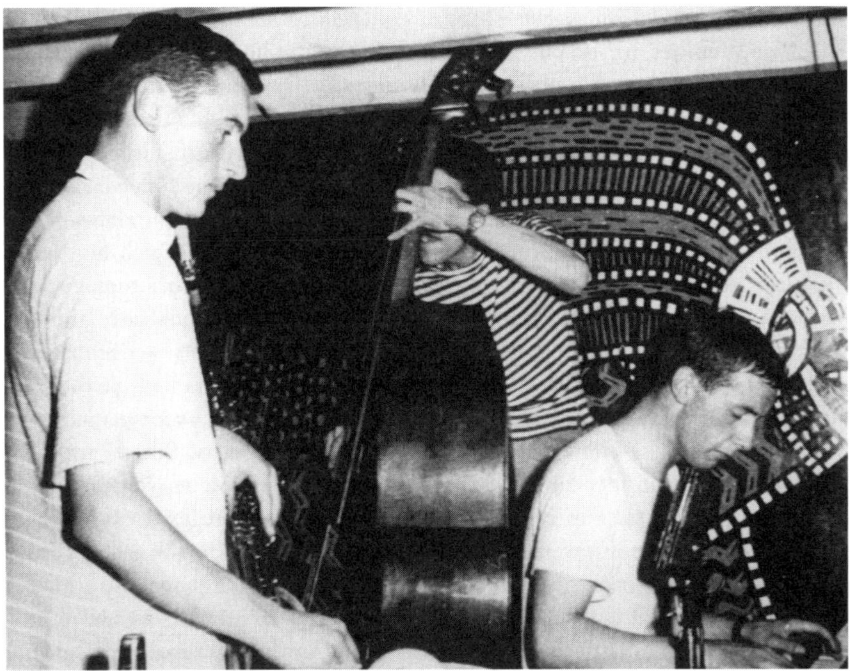

Fig. 5 The EmCee Five playing at the Marimba. Note the Scott Dobson
mural in the background.

head of the fine art department between 1948 and 1958, subscribed to the socially
relevant art of the Euston Road School during the 1930s, Pasmore's abstract
mode increasingly came to dominate King's College.[59] As an artist, Scott Dobson
expressed contempt for the amateur local art scene. He had rejected realism
initially and as a journalist he was often an uncompromising critic of the paro-
chialism of north-eastern audiences and their tenuous grasp of abstraction. He
also championed Richard Hamilton's Pop art and reserved much enthusiasm for
the kind of development that allegedly alienated most working-class artists, who,
having believed that 'all art began with an altruistic purpose', have often been
characterised as 'unsettled' by the version of ordinary life offered by Pop art.[60]

For a short time Dobson appeared able to negotiate the tension between his
avant-garde 'art' and Geordie personas. However his subsequent transition from
abstract to figurative and the celebration of vernacular pastiche has parallels in
the realism and local immediacy of Sid Chaplin's early 1960s novels and perhaps
even the rootedness of Bunting and Pickard's poetry in regional themes. In some
respects the paintings of Cornish and writings of Chaplin can be seen in a spectrum that incorporates the new northern realism and connects to a wider national
movement, meshing with the novels of Silitoe and the New Wave cycle of British

films. As a regional journalist, Dobson contributed to the growing appeal of the region's miner artists, but particularly Cornish, who frequently dominated his column inches in the Newcastle *Evening Chronicle* during the 1960s. His commitment to the authenticity of the pitmen painters remained unflagging. Commenting on a Newcastle exhibition in 1959, Dobson distinguished Cornish from other artists: 'products of an orthodox art school training', they lacked the 'authority of Cornish'. Although closer to his own particular taste they were, for him, 'less satisfying': 'Cornish's roots lie deep in tradition which he uses to augment his burning conviction – a tendency disturbing to more sophisticated painters who are often the unfortunate possessors of too much taste and too little feeling'.[61]

Dobson, a grammar school boy and art college tutor, could combine the celebration of vernacular authenticity with participation in an avant-garde world whilst artists such as Cornish rarely entered bohemian society. But we are more interested here to understand why impresarios like Dobson actively cultivated and indeed developed a career based on the promotion of regional authenticity and working-class culture at a time usually associated with the avant-garde's separation from the parochial. Cornish, as well as being championed by Dobson, found that he was in demand from other quarters. Northern Arts sought to promote the artist as evidence that the region could produce international cultural phenomena to match its economic aspirations. Political interest in the artist was also growing, as reflected by Durham County Council's commission in 1963 to create a giant canvas of the Miners' Gala for the new modernist county hall. The National Coal Board considered the undertaking to be of sufficient importance to grant the artist leave from his mining job. The canvas also fetched a higher sum than the council's other commissioned work, a neo-classical representation of monks building Durham cathedral, by the Newcastle artist Thomas Pattison.[62] The visual representation of regional politics found slightly different expression in Newcastle, where Pasmore murals and Jacob Epstein sculptures adorned the city council's new civic centre. But here the connection between official and popular vernacular also resonated in a building which would have been a comprehensive homage to architectural modernism, but for its centre piece, a campanile which loudly radiates 'Blaydon Races' from the city's political heart.

Throughout the 1960s Dobson continued to applaud the 'old brigade' of worker artists, whose 'masculine and gutsy' industrial images were 'unbothered and uncluttered by what the boys in London are doing now or whatever is the current line among provincial art school politicians'.[63] And by the end of the decade Dobson had returned to depicting local scenes in his own work. At a solo show held at the Westgate Gallery in 1969 he exhibited a series of paintings of 'Northern people' and 'the corners of Newcastle that reflect Scott's interest in the older, character filled features of the city'. His tenacious insistence on the vernacular integrity of visual imagery, alongside his own rejection of art school avant-garde, reflected a cultural environment in which individuals had to jostle for influence with a growing and increasingly confident arts and cultural bureaucracy.[64] It was during this time that Dobson began to cultivate his interest in dialect, a move that turned out to be a popular and commercial success thanks to the work of Frank Graham Publishers as well as the demand for this genre of writing from the regional television stations.

Dobson's apparently seamless transition from art critic to dialect writer may have been less easy to realise outside the north east, however, as Dobson himself conceded: 'The' wud a hoyed as oot o' Manchester Grammar School when ah tort theor if aad sed to me art pupils: "Gan on, clag your paint on lads"'[65]. Undoubtedly this would also have been the experience had Dobson been teaching in one of Newcastle's grammar schools, but, as has been stressed, avant-garde and vernacular cultures often converged in the north east during the 1960s. One commentator has even suggested that Ferlinghetti's review of Pickard in 1965 acted as a catalyst to the wider use of dialect in popular culture, particularly in music hall revival on stage and on television.[66] This is nonetheless difficult to verify and needs to be countered by the evidence that popular enthusiasm for dialect had been awakened by Richard Kelly's initiatives from the 1950s, themselves indebted to broadcasts in dialect from the 1930s. Moreover the extent to which Dobson cultivated dialect revival as part of a conscious rejection of establishment cultural politics should be tempered by the evidence that his motivation was more likely opportunistic. Heather Ging, writer and producer for Tyne Tees Television during the 1970s, describes the period as one in which there were 'a number of like people around feeding from each other ... it was to do with that pot boiling in the region ... we were part of this, but not aware of it, not conscious of it'. Impresarios like Dobson clearly played a decisive role by heightening the consciousness of 'that pot boiling'. But, as Ging confirms, Dobson gave publicity to these issues, not because he was intrinsically committed to reviving regional culture, but because, 'he was one of these minds that had his eye on the main chance ... he saw a chance to do the Scott Dobson books and just recognised there was a market for it'.[67]

Dobson was only able to capitalise on this ferment by tapping into a growing infrastructure for the representation of regional culture. Frank Graham Publishers, which pioneered works on north-eastern culture including the seminal *Larn Yesel f Geordie*, made a significant contribution to this new environment of responsiveness to vernacular culture. The press was established during the late 1950s by the Sunderland-born schoolteacher Frank Graham, a veteran of the Spanish Civil War and Communist Party member. His initial venture into publishing began when he was employed as a WEA tutor on Holy Island and published his own historical guide to the island as a teaching aid. When the initial print run of 3000 sold out in the first year he became convinced that there was a wider and untapped regional market for putting 'the past in print'. By the early

1960s he was assembling and publishing a wide variety of authors on north east history. His output was not confined to the region's industrial heritage and Graham sought to defend himself against criticism of his populist approach to history with the claim that the most important book he published was on Hadrian's Wall during the Roman period.[68] Whilst acknowledging the success of the Geordie Beuks, when interviewed, this 'quiet, bespectacled teetotaller' rarely referred to the Dobson initiative despite having sold more than a quarter of a million of Dobson's works by 1971, preferring instead to draw attention to his more serious publications on the north east and Northumbria.[69] His numerous publications included many scholarly works and for many years Graham acted as a *de facto* regional academic press.

Whilst Graham may have been less inclined to court the media interest achieved by self-promoters such as T. Dan Smith, Frank Atkinson and Scott Dobson, his press played an important part in shaping the parameters of the cultural region from the 1960s. These boundaries arguably corresponded to the geography of the northern coalfield which, as has been well documented, stretched far into the regional hinterland and ensured the convergence of urban and rural cultures. But from the 1960s cultural practices, including Graham's publishing initiatives, arguably strengthened this characteristic. Externally the presence of Geordie Beuks may have helped to reinforce the broadcast media driven assumption that the north east sustained a cohesive regional culture shared by conurbations and rural areas.[70] By contrast the creation of 'Scouse Press' in Liverpool by Fritz Spiegle in 1966 was popular on Merseyside but had little wider regional purchase. Spiegle's first publication was his own edited *Lern Yersel Scouse*, in print from 1966, a 'scouseology' which, like Dobson's works, drew on earlier initiatives in radio comedy by local broadcasters such as Billy Butler and Brian Jacques. Belchem writes that *Lern Yerself Scouse* was the first of a series of heritage publications that sought to:

> look back beyond the early 1960s when the Beatles – four lads who shook the world – brought Liverpool to global attention. As hero-worshipped drug abusers, they stand condemned along with other exponents of the Mersey sound, and the accompanying (but soon southern-based) 'professional scousers', the novelists, poets and playwrights of the 1960s Mersey boom.[71]

Whilst Graham may have been equally circumspect about similar aspects of youth culture, his contribution to the north east revival was never posited upon the rejection of a 'metropolitan Geordie' and there was no Beatles equivalent in the north east. Moreover, his publication of Dobson's Geordie Beuks is credited with helping in the revival of the dialect and culture of Tyneside and Durham, the region's 'industrial zone'. In contrast to Spiegle's rejection of modern Liverpool, Griffiths has suggested that Dobson's work should also be seen as more comfortably present minded: '[a] definite link back to a music hall ambience? But the scale is more intimate, the humour closer to the society it works in … this typically modern art form – suitable for fireside pub or public transport'.[72]

> Where's Stotty Cake Raa? Whey, ye must knaa, ye canna miss it.
> Ye knaa Clartybank Coll'ry? Well then, ye get off the bus at the Mechanic's Haal, torn left b'the Club, ower the railway line, three pigeon duckets doon the allotments, through the hole i' the pityard fence, bear reet pas the screens [i.e. pit washery], doon b' the back o' the Store butcher's midden, past the bettin shop, torn left opposite the thord netty past the rain barrel, and anybody'll tell ye.[73]

But Geordie dialect revival was appreciated beyond the informal world of pubs and buses, having entered north east television culture by the early 1970s. As the sales of *Larn Yersel* accrued, its popular appeal was reflected in its adoption by the BBC as the programme idea for *Geordierama*. Scripted by Dobson, the show in 1974 included comic performances by Mike Neville, George House and Dick Irwin accompanied by Joe Bennett's Northumbrian Traditional Group. At the same time Dobson had extended the horizons of his 'Geordie inventions' to include LPs, shows at Newcastle City Hall, Geordie car stickers, passports and driving licences.[74] The Scott Dobson television initiative was largely an expression of the regional pastiche, of which this professional Geordie had become the master by the 1970s. *Geordierama* nevertheless drew on a more varied and complex array of influences than the programme title suggested, many of which had sustained the revival of north east culture since 1945.

Actors such as Dick Irwin also helped to carry music-hall comedy influences through to television during the 1970s. Irwin had discovered his talent for joke telling whilst serving on the western front during the Second World War – a gift which Richard Kelly was quick to recognise – and subsequently appeared amongst the cast of *Wot Cheor, Geordie!* During this time he complemented his comedy with his musical interests, developed during the 1930s as part of a country and western 'concert party' performing in workingmen's clubs throughout the region. Following the rehabilitation of Balmbra's as a music hall during the 1960s he performed the part of 'Barker' on stage there for almost a decade. By the 1970s Irwin had established a role as a Geordie comedian – he was publishing with Dobson by this time – alongside a fledgling career as a 'serious' actor. In 1974 he appeared in the cast of the network production *When the Boat Comes In*.[75] Such programmes clearly offered further opportunities for the convergence of comic and serious performance that echoed the wider interconnection between the vernacular cultural revival and the flourishing of northern realism during the 1960s. But, as Alan Plater has noted, actors like Irwin were able to move between the worlds of 'serious drama' to vernacular stage comedy in part due to the scarcity of north east actors capable of working in dialect. Demand for actors who could work in dialect expanded with the consolidation of the 'television north' after the 1960s, which opened up new opportunities to work both within and outside the region.[76]

George House, also instrumental in the development of *Geordierama* during the 1970s, had been the first television news presenter for the BBC's initial transmissions in the north east. His national reputation was secured in 1958 when his interview with Cissie Charlton, the mother of the footballing brothers, was broadcast nationally on *World at One*. Unsurprising therefore that he should wish to underline the national significance of his television work, claiming in 1978 that 'the two Ronnies are doing now what Mike [Neville] and I were doing years ago'.[77] But, as the success of Heather Ging's *What Fettle* showed, by the early 1970s these programmes anchored in regional culture were driven by popular demand. This surprised senior executives who remained sceptical of local programmes, especially when *What Fettle* produced the highest audience ratings ever experienced at Tyne Tees.[78]

In contrast to the often nostalgic promotion of regional culture that characterised dialect revival during the 1960s, the 1970s witnessed the use of vernacular with more political and radical overtones. The legacy of the anti-Vietnam War campaign, the 'moment of 1968', the rise of feminism, the election of a Conservative government and the miners' strikes of 1972 and 1974 all served to energise many young cultural practitioners and move them towards an overtly political agenda. In Britain and across Europe the 'hippy movement' gave way to the rise of a more politicised 'cultural left'. In the north east this shift

Fig. 6 Live Theatre Newcastle

was reflected in the emergence of a new generation of cultural workers that can also be said to reflect the tradition of the individual acting as cultural impresario. Most notably the region's modern 'alternative' theatrical tradition can be traced back to the establishment of Live Theatre in 1973, which set in train a new theatrical movement. Helping to sustain playwrights including C. P. Taylor, Live also gave rise to new writers committed to working in the vernacular, including Tom Haddaway. In addition these writers were connected to the nascent north east documentary film movement centred round the Amber Collective.

Geoff Gillham and Val McLane started Live Theatre in Newcastle in 1973. Currently acknowledged as one of the UK's leading centres for nurturing and developing new writing talent, Live Theatre has also become a central institution in the story of Newcastle's revitalised East Quayside area. With a £1 million capital award from the National Lottery in 1996, the 'building based' Live Theatre is referred to by the Arts Council as an 'ideas factory' for the development of new writing.[79] This is a long way from its beginnings as a socialist 'partnership' over thirty years ago. As co-founder of Live with the late Gillham, Val McLane's background in theatre is relevant to a broader understanding of the cultural left during the 1970s. Like Scott Dobson, McLane first trained to be a teacher following a degree in English at Leeds University during the early 1960s. But her 'real love' was the theatre and whilst at university she had joined the flourishing student drama society. Through the society McLane travelled abroad for the first time, performing Pinter in Turkey and the former Yugoslavia, which opened up a new world in which she also became politically active. However, subverting her love for the theatre, she initially pursued a career in education: 'I always really wanted to be in the theatre. But I knew that, for a working-class girl that was ridiculous'.[80]

Nevertheless the late 1960s were an era of opportunities for gender and social mobility and following some years teaching McLane was recruited by the head of BBC radio in the north, whom she had met 'by chance in a pub in Leeds', to present the newly established BBC Radio Newcastle in 1970. As a radio journalist she exploited her links with regional theatre, interviewing the artistic director at the Newcastle Playhouse and encountering the playwright Cecil Taylor, who had recently come to work at the same theatre. In this milieu of radio and the arts McLane was approached by Gillham with the proposal to form an alternative theatre company: 'and he said it's going to be completely non-bureaucratic it's against the bourgeoisie, it's for working-class people, I want working-class actors and we are going to perform to the working classes'.[81]

Gillham, originally from Essex, was similarly a former teacher and had a vision for the theatre as a 'social concept with a social purpose'. Drawn to the idea, McLane was persuaded to provide fifty per cent of the funding for the venture, encouraged by her husband who acknowledged that her artistic ambitions had been sidelined by both marriage and her mother's dream that she enter the teaching profession. This also coincided with the loss of her position at Radio Newcastle, where the station manager, revealing the limits of gender equality in regional broadcasting, 'said that because I was a married woman I shouldn't be earning so much money'.[82]

From 1973 McLane, together with Gillham, Madeline Newton, Loraine Lingard and 'a boy called Ned Smith', comprised the 'founding group' of Live Theatre and began devising sketches, which they performed initially in pubs. But the ambition to be sustained by the proceeds of these efforts was swiftly dashed: 'of course we got next to nothing … and it was a wonderful idea to work for a working-class audience but of course they had no interest particularly in theatre and we were just sort of going in there and forcing it on them in the pubs and … we struggled so a lot of the savings disappeared quite rapidly'.[83] Undeterred by their misfortune, and the loss of Ned after the first show, the three women and Gillham turned their attention to education and started by writing scripts influenced by R. D. Laing for a series of successful school shows. This allowed them to hire actors in order to stage a pantomime.

Whilst arguably removing Live from the original idea of the theatre as 'social concept', the pantomine brought much-needed funds and also drew wider attention. Director and producer Leonard Lewis, 'up from London', saw their production of *Dick Whittington* and offered roles to both Madeline Newton and Val McLane in the forthcoming *When the Boat Comes In*. Although McLane, as a new mother, was unable to take the part, she identifies this period as one in which the development of Live was increasingly coming to the attention outside the region. Such acclaim also roused the interest of the Arts Council and in 1975 Northern Arts' drama advisor encouraged the founders to apply for Arts Council funds. Despite their ongoing financial difficulties the group was resolute in their rejection of official arts sponsorship: 'we said no we don't want to do that, that would be far too bourgeois, we don't want to have anything to do with the so called legitimate theatre, we're alternative'.[84]

But funding continued to be a major concern and sometimes the quest for resources prompted the group to find ingenious ways of circumventing their socialist convictions. In 1974, joined by a young Tim Healey, the group put together a community show in Kenton in west Newcastle. Funding was secured from the Arts Council in a manner palatable to the group because the 'people of Kenton' applied for a grant and then hired Live Theatre. Working in this way Live devised a play called *Kenton Do*. Tim Healey took the part of 'Buster Kenton' and parodying 'Buster Keaton' they used slapstick freely but also incorporated circus skills and with the help of Dave Whittaker developed a successful piece of audience participation: 'and we had a great celebration actually: the story behind it was their celebration of having moved from Scotswood and living in the West End and having gone up to Kenton'. Kenton was the brave new world of T. Dan Smith's modernism, incorporating the city's first comprehensive school, whose teaching staff included Connie Watson, and Swedish architect-designed housing.

Despite this and similar successful school shows the tension between the need to raise funds and the group's social focus was becoming increasingly pronounced. The crisis came in 1975. In the middle of preparations for a school show Gillham announced dramatically that he had 'joined the Workers' Revolutionary Party and that the rest of the group should abandon the theatre and join the revolution'. All bookings were to be cancelled and all funds to be gathered to support the impending revolution and 'to do shows outside the factory gates [the shipyards]'.[85] This proved to be a defining moment for the group. The majority, including McLane, although sympathetic towards the cause, were not prepared to support Gillham's call. This episode precipitated a split amongst 'the founders' and heralded Gillham's exit from Live Theatre. The remaining group subsequently continued into the second half of the 1970s, still committed to the representation of working-class lives and audiences, but now noticeably distanced from their radical beginnings.

By 1977 Live Theatre had attracted a wave of new actors and directors including Michael Mould, later of the community theatre group 'Bruvvers', and Murray Martin, of the Amber Film Collective, who directed the theatre for a year in 1977. Formed in London by a group of students from Regents Street Polytechnic, from 1969 Amber was based in Newcastle and worked with a specific commitment to film making and photography representing working-class communities in the north east. Documentaries such as *High Row* and their first feature film for Channel 4, Haddaway's *Seacoal* (1985), which was named as best European Film of the Year, were to achieve critical acclaim.[86] Martin met Tom Haddaway through Live Theatre and this lead to a fruitful and long-lasting creative relationship that saw Haddaway 'working alongside' Amber in the production of features such as *In Fading Light*. Based on Haddaway's life in the North Shields fishing industry, the script was written in close collaboration with Amber. As Martin would later remember: 'we sent the actors out on their boats and they came back with their stories … and they told Tom what had happened and he would write it down'.[87] Haddaway shared Amber's political commitment and, perhaps in an effort to distinguish his writing from the Scott Dobson genre of regional pastiche, would later comment that 'having our dialect tolerated as merely amusing is one way of rendering us powerless'.[88] But despite Amber's explicit political content and commitment to representing working-class communities, the group, in contrast to Live, appear to have sustained a fruitful relationship with Northern Arts.

In 1971 Northern Arts established its first fellowship in creative photography with support from the Northern Gas Board. The second fellowship was won by Sirkka-Liisa Kontinnen in 1972. Konttinnen had come to the north east from

Finland in 1968 and would achieve wide recognition for her photographic documentary of Byker from 1970. Described as an 'outstanding' talent by Northern Arts in 1972, Konttinnen's montage of the process of urban renewal would culminate in *Byker* in 1983, an Amber production supported by Northern Arts. Martin would later defend the criticism that this was an overly nostalgic portrayal of working-class communities, arguing that the integrity of the portrayal lay in the affection for its subject.[89] It is noteworthy that the vernacular industrial north represented by Amber, which drew upon and nurtured a cross-over of writers between the theatre and film collective, was readily sponsored by Northern Arts; further, the Arts Council were often cited as the group's only committed benefactor, whereas Live consistently refused, before the 1980s, to seek sponsorship from these patrons of 'legitimate' culture.

The flourishing cross-over between the documentary film movement and Live Theatre also reflected the influence of Cecil Taylor. Born in Glasgow in 1929 of Jewish parents, he left school at fourteen and had various jobs, ending up as a travelling salesman. He came to Newcastle, where his mother had grown up, in 1955 and staged his first play *Aa Went t' Blaydon Races* in 1962. His Jewish background and socialist beliefs impelled him to work with the disadvantaged, particularly within local working-class communities, which were reflected in the themes of much of his work. He became the key figure in the emerging Tyneside playwriting scene and inspired newcomers such as Tom Haddaway. Alan Plater described Taylor as 'founding father and inspiration' to a generation of actors and playwrights, and his no-frills style of narrative, with songs and direct address to the audience, has informed much of the Live Theatre tradition.[90] McLane developed a creative rapport with Taylor and had worked with him at Northgate Hospital in Morpeth, Northumberland, where a project with disabled children resulted in the writing of a play called *Operation Elvis*.[91]

In 1978 the importance of a growing critical mass of writers drawn to Live was quickly acknowledged by the group's new director, Teddy Kendal. McLane was initially surprised to learn of the appointment of the 'flamboyant' American and veteran of the Vietnam War: 'I thought this is interesting, what's he doing here in Live Theatre which is supposed to be a local company ... for Geordies, for local people, working-class Geordies'. In part this reflected the expanded Live Theatre 'group', who had recruited the new director from outside the region. Kendal was connected to the growing national movement of community arts and had been involved with experimental theatre in Coventry, but as director of Live he quickly sensed the artistic importance and local significance of the relationships between Cecil Taylor, Tom Haddaway and Murray Martin, which he actively reinforced. With rehearsal rooms above the Amber Collective's Side Gallery and a performance space in a warehouse on the Newcastle Quayside, McLane recalls this as an exciting time: 'we did some amazing shows we worked in tenant's community huts and we tried the Social Clubs under Murray

Martin. And that was hard. But it was incredibly exciting. Because again this was a non-theatre audience who responded actively to what was going on'.[92]

The challenge of audience participation was revealed during a performance of Taylor's *Give Me Sunshine* to an audience in Kenton. One of the actors, playing a fifteen-year-old girl in a jazz band, was in the middle of a scene in which she swore at her mother whilst revealing that she was pregnant. This elicited a memorable response from an elderly woman in the front row, who brought the whole performance to a standstill when she jumped up exclaiming: 'you, how dare you use language like that to your mother!'[93]

Whilst Live's performances in the north east often pointed to the mistaken assumption that working-class audiences would be responsive to, and appreciative of, socialist or radical scripts, by the late 1970s the theatre was achieving acclaim beyond the region. In the early 1980s Live toured the country and many of its members would go on to enjoy careers in national television drama: McLane secured roles in West End theatres as well as in the second series of *Auf Widersehen Pet*. During this time she also performed at the Sheffield Crucible in the musical *Gregory's Girl*, derived from the first play written by a young Lee Hall.

In September 2007 Lee Hall's *Pitmen Painters* 'opened the expanded Live Theatre on Newcastle Quayside after a £5.5 million refit'.[94] Hall, from a working-class family in Walkergate, had been influenced by Live during the 1970s as a pupil at Benfield School, where the theatre staged its early school shows. However, Live's transition from a collective run by individual activists during the 1970s to a 'writers' factory' and example of successful culture-led regeneration thirty years on has not been straightforward. In many respects the transition from a peripatetic company with a strong political agenda to a building-based company is a story that is often neglected in official and broadcast narratives. By the 1980s Live had retreated from outright opposition to 'legitimate culture' and had accepted Arts Council sponsorship. Shortly afterwards the shifting political climate was felt in terms of money that was available for such explicit representatives of the cultural left. Following a series of cuts a number of independent theatre groups, including McLane's independent feminist theatre, Major Diversion, Wearabout in Sunderland and Michael Mould's Bruvvers in Newcastle, experienced funding cuts or the threat of closure. Live Theatre survived but in 1984 was forced to relinquish its status as a partnership, a move that resulted in McLane's partial removal from the theatre and a time that she recalls as increasingly difficult for regional representatives of the cultural left: 'we were working under Thatcher and there were cuts being made left right and centre, partnerships were being forced to give up and become charities or close down, and so it was a huge attack on the cultural left'.[95]

As we have seen, McLane notes that the rise of her fortunes as an actor based upon her rich experience with Live brought success which drew her to other companies and venues. Her partial departure and the divisions within the original group based upon the political turmoil of the 1970s and 1980s helps to explain the transition from an itinerant to a permanent company symbolised by the transformation of its early performance premises just off the quayside into a permanent theatre. Similarly, the demands of Amber's ambitions necessitated permanent premises and an administrative capability to bid for the high level of funding necessary for film production. Amber have been criticised by some members of the 'community arts' movement. Keith Armstrong has described the Amber oeuvre as voyeuristic, a view echoed by John Mapplebeck, former head of the Newcastle BBC station, who has described their work as 'incredibly soft centred'. Armstrong described Martin's shift to television work with substantial funding as a betrayal of Amber's earlier small-scale independent film-making background.[96] However, it could equally be argued that Martin was responsive to a quickly shifting landscape for arts funding and recognised that Amber would need to engage with a growing and increasingly complex funding bureaucracy in order to survive. Martin's funding strategies appear to have carried the support of the collective, most notably the radical and politically astute artist Tom Haddaway. Amber produced Haddaway's first film, *The Filleting Machine*, in 1981, a workerist account of deskilling in the regional fishing industry. The film was written originally in the early 1970s and adapted for the stage, with Martin producing and directing it for Live Theatre as part of their social club circuit of plays. A raw account of life on the North Shields Ridges Estate (later renamed Meadowell), this was the basis for the film that was produced with sponsorship from Northern Arts in 1981. Two years later Channel 4 purchased the film and commissioned Amber to produce a contextualising piece which incorporated interviews with residents of the estate to discuss the integrity of the representation, an initiative that was praised by the British Film Institute.[97]

Despite the nobility of their early ambition it is difficult not to conclude that in order to achieve their initial aims many of the endeavours of the impresario activists were dependent upon institutions. As Amber has demonstrated, survival was often predicated upon engagement with, and sponsorship from, the representatives of 'legitimate culture'. Moreover by the 1980s, the world in which it was possible for an individual artist to move between the bohemian avant-garde, journalism, publishing and television, as encapsulated by Scott Dobson's embodiment of both 'Geordie' and avant-garde personas, had significantly changed. Live abandoned its early, itinerant format and as a building-based company had to fall in line with the bureaucratic regime that is perhaps an inescapable aspect of public patronage. Similar pressures resulted in Connie Pickard leaving Morden Tower in 1975. This shift was in no small part due to the growing and formal administration of the arts. The informal world of the 1960s, when clerks in the town hall could hand out keys to ancient monuments for 'ten bob a week', when small theatre companies had little difficulty finding space, when the 'professional Geordie' had easy access to print and broadcasting, was shrinking. The 'can do' milieu of the vernacular vanguard was disappearing fast.

But their achievement also needs to be set against the world which they had helped to change. Jack Common, arguably the most gifted writer from the region during the twentieth century, published his masterpiece *Kiddar's Luck* in 1951. Common used dialect speech in the book and although it received good reviews it failed to sell well even in the region, a problem made worse when his London publisher went bankrupt. The book was written in the evening in Newcastle after working during the day as a council garden labourer. He had drifted back to his native city from London, when the literary world of which he had been a fringe member disintegrated at the end of the war. It is not too fanciful to speculate that if Common had been writing in the early 1960s rather than the early 1950s his fortunes would have been very different. The region would certainly have embraced his enormous talent and perceived him as part of a larger cultural project rather than a lone voice.[98]

Many in the region hoped that the publishing tradition established by Graham would find a home in Bloodaxe Books, a company established by two Newcastle-based journalists in 1978. In its early years it appeared to be fulfilling these hopes with the publication of Jimmy Forsyth's *Scotswood Road* in 1987 and their reprint of Jack Common's *Kiddar's Luck*, previously published by Graham. The company does produce works by some local poets and picked up Basil Bunting's work in 2000. But increasingly since the early 1990s, Bloodaxe, a non profit-making company and thus ideally placed to take advantage of Arts Council funding for producing work by new artists, has established itself as a leading international poetry publisher and the only serious rival to Faber and Faber in the realm of poetry publishing.[99] The company left its offices on Newcastle's Quayside in 1997 and is now located jointly in North Northumberland and Bala, in North Wales.

Undoubtedly the most prominent of the artist impresarios were men. It could be argued that this was a reflection of the dominant male discourse of north east society. But the role of role of women cultural innovators was often central to the cultural achievements of the 1960s and 1970s. The persona of the professional Geordie established by Scott Dobson was supported as much by the work of Heather Ging, as Tyne Tees producer and writer, as it was through the efforts of Frank Graham. Similarly, Frank Atkinson's vision of Beamish as the 'people's museum' was realised in no short measure by the role of his first employee, Rosemary Allan, the long-serving curator. Without Connie Pickard it is difficult to envisage the success and reputation of the Tyneside poetry scene. Equally Val McLane's role in Live Theatre was pivotal and would often challenge the dominant gender stereotype of the masculine north east, with theatre content that was influenced by both socialist and feminist principles. However both of these women had their careers interrupted by the demands of motherhood in an age when there were few resources for working women who lacked private benefactors or family means. In the long run both their careers demonstrated that the 'glass ceiling' was as present in the bohemian world of the cultural left as elsewhere.[100]

The election of Mrs Thatcher in 1979 posed a threat to both the regional economy and the multi-faceted cultural world that the 'left leaning' vernacular impresarios had created. Paradoxically the effects of Conservative economic policies did not herald a new era of individualism; rather the sharp economic decline of the early 1980s forced many artists and organisations to become more dependent on the public purse. Northern Arts, as the 1980s progressed, struggled to assuage this demand and at the same time respond to central government cuts and insistence upon greater accountability. The subsequent management overhaul of the organisation during the 1980s was to pose major challenges to small organisations and individual artists. 1962 seemed a distant memory and the future looked bleak.

Notes

1 'Superstitions of Olden Days', anon., cited in B. Griffiths, *North east dialect: the texts*, rev. edn (Newcastle: Centre for Northern Studies, 2002), p. 139.

2 Murphy, 'Selling coals to Newcastle', pp. 3–61.

3 D. Rowe, 'The north east', in F. M. L. Thompson (ed.), *Cambridge social history of Britain vol. 1* (Cambridge: Cambridge University Press, 1990); N. McCord and R. Thompson (eds), *The northern counties, from AD 1000* (London: Longman, 1998), p. 400.

4 For our purposes the 'cultural left' refers to cultural workers with a left-leaning political agenda, many of whom were drawn from a voluntaristic tradition in the north east, but particularly radical or experimental theatre groups.

5 T. D. Smith, *Dan Smith: an autobiography* (Newcastle: Oriel Press, 1960).

6 Lancaster, 'Sociability in the city', p. 336.

7 TWAS, MD/NC/94/22, Joint Committee as to the Centenary of the Blaydon Races, 23 March 1960; 3 December 1959, p. 196.

8 Ibid.

9 TWAS, Newcastle City Council proceedings, Report of the Joint Committee as to the Centenary of the Blaydon Races 20 April 1960, pp. 1110–1111.

10 TWAS, MD/NC/94/22, Joint Committee as to the Centenary of the Blaydon Races, 23 March 1960, p. 213.

11 TWAS, MD/NC/94/22, Joint Committee as to the Centenary of the Blaydon Races, 23 March 1960, p. 212.

12 TWAS, MD/NC/94/22, Joint Committee as to the Centenary of the Blaydon Races, 23 March 1960, p. 196.

13 TWAS, MD/NC/94/22, Joint Committee as to the Centenary of the Blaydon Races, 6 April 1960.

14 TWAS, Proceedings of the Newcastle Council, Report of the Joint Committee as to the Centenary of the Blaydon Races, 20 April 1960, p. 1111.

15 TWAS, Proceedings of the Newcastle Council, Report of the Joint Committee as to the Centenary of the Blaydon Races, 5 July 1961, p. 195.

16 TWAS, Proceedings of the Newcastle Council, Report of the Joint Committee as to the Centenary of the Blaydon Races, 5 July 1961, p. 190.

17 Lancaster, 'Sociability in the city', p. 320.

18 D. Harker, *Fakesong, the manufacture of British 'folksong' 1700 to the present day* (Milton Keynes: Open University Press, 1985), pp. 51–52. In Robert Colls's account Tyneside song is distinguished by the self-mockery of the pitmen/keelmen characters, a feature which endured the transition from radicalism to patriotism and jingoism. The pitman, Colls suggests, was self-aware and 'revelled in his caricature'. R. Colls, *The collier's rant: song and culture in the industrial village* (London: Croom Helm, 1977), p. 56.

19 TWAS, MD/NC/94/22, Centenary of the Blaydon Races, Publicity Sub-Committee, 27 April 1960, p. 240.

20 *North Magazine* (9 March 1972), p. 12.

21 Ibid.

22 Murphy, 'Selling coals to Newcastle', p. 24.

23 Northern Arts Annual Report, 1970/71 'The story of the first ten years' (Newcastle, 1971), p. 1.

24 Northern Arts Annual Report, 1970/71, pp. 4–5.

25 Beamish Museum remains a subject of interest to historians and museologists. See especially J. Walton and G. Cross (eds), *The playful crowd: pleasure places in the twentieth century* (New York: Columbia University Press, 2005), ch. 6 and for critical perspectives see J. Iles, '"Gone with the wind": versions of history at Beamish', *Northern Review*, 5 (1997), pp. 47–52.

26 TWAS, LA/PA/806, Beamish, First Report of the Joint Committee of the North of England Open Air Museum, 1978, p. 15.

27 F. Atkinson, *The man who made Beamish: an autobiography* (Gateshead: Northern Books, 1999), pp. 13–50.

28 Atkinson, *The man who made Beamish*, p. 73.

29 TWAS, LA/PA/806, Beamish, First Report of the Joint Committee of the North of England Open Air Museum, 1978, pp. 15 and 16.

30 F. Atkinson, *The man who made Beamish*, p. 85.

31 F. Atkinson, 'An open air museum for the north east', *Journal of Industrial Archaeology*, 1 (1964–5), p. 1.

32 Aronsson, 'The old cultural regionalism', pp. 251–271.

33 D. McCrone, 'Imagining Scotland: a heritage industry examined', *Networking Europe: essays on regionalism and social democracy* (Liverpool: Liverpool University Press, 2000), pp. 321–363.

34 Beamish, First Report of the Joint Committee of the North of England Open Air Museum (1978), pp. 15 and 16.

35 Following the decision to locate the museum in County Durham, the group lost the support of Cumberland and Westmoreland and the North Riding of

Yorkshire, leaving for the museum a region that stretched from Northumberland to Cleveland, and which Atkinson recognised as 'a more valid cultural entity and just about the right size'. Atkinson, *The man who made Beamish*, p. 98.

36 Atkinson, *The man who made Beamish*, p. 183.

37 Beamish, First Report of the North of England Open Air Museum, Joint Committee, Spring 1978.

38 Between 1940 and 1960 Newcastle gained over 14,000 inhabitants. Whilst the city centre areas benefited from a growing student population which would remain an enduring feature of post-war demography, this development was offset by the considerable decline in population from the industrial riverside wards, such as Scotswood, site of the historic celebrations and Smith's physical regeneration. N. Vall, *Cities in decline? A comparative history of Malmo and Newcastle after 1945* (Malmo: Malmo University Press, 2007), p. 82.

39 B. Lancaster, review of G. Pearson, *Sex Brown Ale and Rhythm and Blues*, in *Northern Review*, 9 (2001), pp. 133–135.

40 I. Carr, 'Novocastrian jazz 1950s and early 1960s', *Northern Review*, 4 (1996), p. 14.

41 Ibid.

42 J. Haynes, *C'est ma vie folks and thanks for coming! An autobiography* (London: Faber, 1982). Haynes, originally from Louisiana, also co-founded the London Arts Laboratory, which was to influence the young Peter Stark, director of Northern Arts from 1984, in his early career as a cultural manager. See A. Rickman and J. Haynes, 'A fortress and a haven for adult games', *Arc* (winter 1969), pp. 22–28, for details of the first Arts Laboratory.

43 Recorded interview with Connie Pickard, 27 August 2009.

44 Ibid.

45 V. Katz, *Black Mountain College: experiment in art* (Cambridge, MA: MIT Press, 2003).

46 www.bloodaxebooks.com. For a discussion of this movement, incorporating Bunting and Pickard, also see Andrew McAllister (ed.), *The Objectivists: an anthology* (Tarset: Bloodaxe Books, 1996).

47 Recorded interview with Connie Pickard, 27 August 2009.

48 Ibid.

49 T. Pickard, 'Work in progress 1', *Northern Review*, 8 (1999), pp. 40–45.

50 A. Ginsberg, in Pickard, 'Work in progress 1', p. 44.

51 L. Ferlinghetti cited in T. Pickard, *High on the walls* (London: Fulcrum Press, 1967).

52 *The Journal, Weekend Review* (20 May 1967).

53 S. Sillers, 'Carbo verbun factus est: British art in the 1960s', in B. Moore Gilbert and J. Seed (eds), *Cultural revolution? The challenge of the arts in the 1960s* (New York: Routledge, 1992), p. 273.

54 The best overview of Griffiths's life and work can be found in the W. Rowe (ed.), *Salt companion to Bill Griffiths* (Cambridge: Salt Books, 2007). Griffiths's *Dictionary of north east English*, 2004; *Stotties 'n' spicecake*, 2006; *Pitmatic: the talk of the north east coalfield*, 2007; *Fishing and folk: life and dialect of the north sea coast*, 2008 were all published by Northumbria University Press, Newcastle upon Tyne.

55 T. Pickard and B. Griffiths, *TYNE TXTS* (Newcastle: Amra Imprint and Morden Poets, 2002).

56 Recorded interview with Connie Pickard, 27 August 2009.

57 M. Hall, *The artists of Northumbria: an illustrated dictionary of Northumberland, Newcastle upon Tyne, Durham and north east Yorkshire painters, illustrators, caricaturists and cartoonists born between 1625 and 1950*, rev. edn (Bristol: Art Dictionaries Ltd., 2005), p. 109.

58 M. Scott, 'Post-war developments in art in Newcastle: was it a golden age?', *Northern Review*, 4 (1996), pp. 38–40.

59 Vall, 'Bohemians and pitmen painters', p. 14.

60 Sillers, 'Carbo verbun factus est', p. 273.

61 *Evening Chronicle* (23 April 1959).

62 Vall, 'Bohemians and pitmen painters', p. 14.

63 Ibid.

64 Ibid.

65 *Evening Chronicle* (13 May 1970), p. 6.

66 I am grateful to Connie Pickard for this insight.

67 Recorded interview with Heather Ging, 6 September 2004.

68 *Northern Echo* (14 January 1992), p. 7.

69 Newcastle City Library Local Studies Collection, Local Biography, vol. 56b, p. 47. N. Vall, 'Northumbria in north east England during the twentieth century', in R. Colls (ed.), *Northumbria: history and identity 547–2000* (Chichester: Philimore & Co. Ltd., 2007), p. 288.

70 Ibid.

71 Belchem, *Merseypride*, p. 53.

72 Griffiths, *North east dialect texts*, pp. 21 and 138.

73 Ibid.

74 *Journal* (18 December 1974), p. 5.

75 *Geordie Life* (May 1976), p. 14. It is a measure of this movement that it actually spawned the publication of 'waiting room magazines', and that this prompted little reaction provides evidence of the extent to which the projection of vernacular in popular publishing had become integral to the region's cultural landscape by the 1970s.

76 Plater, 'The drama of the north east', pp. 92–113.

77 *Northern Life* (September 1978).

78 Recorded interview with Heather Ging, 6 September 2004.

79 www.artscouncil.org.uk/regions/project_detail.php?rid=4&sid=18&id=223 (accessed 15.8.09).

80 Recorded interview with Val McLane, 18 June 2009.

81 Ibid.

82 Ibid.

83 Ibid.

84 Ibid.

85 Ibid.

86 N. Young, 'Forever Amber: an interview with Ellin Hare and Murray Martin of the Amber Film Collective', *Critical Quarterly*, 43: 4 (2001), p. 61.

87 Young, 'Forever Amber', p. 73.

88 T. Haddaway, 'Comic dialect', in Colls and Lancaster, *Geordies*, p. 88.

89 M. Hunt, www.screenonline.org.uk/film/id/792296/index.html (accessed 15.8.09).

90 A. Plater, *Guardian* (6 November 2004). See also S. Friesner, 'Travails of a naked typist: the plays of C.P. Taylor', *New Theatre Quarterly*, 4: 33 (February 1993).

91 Recorded interview with Val McLane, 18 June 2009. .

92 Ibid.

93 Ibid.

94 *Daily Telegraph* (10 September 2007).

95 Recorded interview with Val McLane, 18 June 2009.

96 K. Armstrong, 'Letting all the flowers bloom', *Northern Review*, 7 (1998), pp. 52–58.

97 www.amber-online.com/exhibitions/the-filleting-machine-1981 (accessed 10.6.10).

98 For an affectionate account of Common see L. Wilkes, *Tyneside portraits: studies in art and life* (Newcastle: Frank Graham, 1971). The Common Trust based in Newcastle has published numerous pamphlets on Common and stages events about his work.

99 For an account of the development of Bloodaxe see R. Price, 'A look back at the Bloodaxe Books at 16', *Northern Review*, 1 (1995), pp. 95–101.

100 Moreover these efforts are difficult to contextualise in the absence of a broader scholarly history of women in the north east. There are a number of worthy studies including E. Knox, 'Keep your feet still Geordie Hinnie', in Colls and Lancaster, *Geordies*, pp. 92–113, and specialist studies such as M. Callcott, 'Dr. Marion Phillips Labour MP, Sunderland 1929–31', *North East Labour History Society*, 20 (1986), pp. 9–14; K. Price, 'What did you do in the war, mam? Women steelworkers at the Consett iron company during the second world war', *North East Labour History Society*, 20 (1986), pp. 14–30; M. Williamson, '"I'm going to get a job at a factory": attitudes to women's employment in a mining community', *Women's History Review*, 12: 3 (2003), pp. 407–421; and P. Lynn, 'The influence of class and gender: female political organisation in County Durham during the interwar years', *North East History*, 31 (1997), pp. 43–65; D. Neville, *To make their mark: the women's suffrage movement in the north east of England 1900–1914* (Newcastle: Centre for Northern Studies, 1997). A feminist reading of north east culture can also be found in B. Campbell, *Goliath: Britain's dangerous places* (London: Methuen, 1993). It must be noted that this is a selection rather than a comprehensive list.

5

Northern Arts: institution building and the cultural region 1946–84

In the spring of 1946, delegates of statutory and voluntary organisations interested in the arts gathered at the Royal Station Hotel in Newcastle to listen to the inaugural address of the first North Regional Conference by Mary Glasgow, secretary general to the Arts Council and a native of Newcastle upon Tyne. The delegates then made their way to the council's offices in Bessie Surtees House on Newcastle's Quayside for the main part of the conference. The conference covered a range of issues pivotal to British cultural policy after the Second World War, including housing the arts, art in schools, music and the importance of art to what was prosaically termed 'the man in the back street'. Representatives were primarily drawn from curators, librarians and directors of major museums, but there were also a few managers from companies such as Reyrolle and Co., as well as Parsons, the Tyneside turbine manufacturers.[1]

The influence of Glasgow in driving forward popularising initiatives such as the art centre movement, about which Keynes, the council's first chairman, remained deeply circumspect, has been well documented.[2] At the same time, at the Newcastle conference, her continued commitment to the late chairman's dictum that 'every part of England be merry in its own way' was reflected in the distinction she made between the work of a government department and the Arts Council, 'not bound to distribute its work evenly throughout the country; it wanted to work in an unequal way – to be free to build wherever there were signs of a firm foundation'.[3] Applied to the ambition to stimulate interest in art in the community this philosophy elicited the somewhat awkward compromise during the conference discussion that 'everyone had the right to enjoy what he liked and those who wanted a better type of art must try to induce the Man in the Back Street also to want something better'.[4] Helen Munro, Arts Council regional director for the north of England, gave positive feedback from her region, describing feverish efforts by members of the Teesside Arts Guild, also present at the conference, to promote their activities in the face of competition from newly established art centres in the area.[5]

On the other hand, the fears expressed by delegates over the position of smaller working-class communities, and mining villages in particular, appear to have been warranted. Rooted in the voluntaristic traditions of the 1930s local art scene, two young actors and members of the People's Theatre in Newcastle decided to form a travelling theatre company to stage productions in the region's remote mining villages after the Second World War. Inspired by Joan Littlewood's work in Middlesbrough, Mollie Simmonds and Roger Trafford successfully approached the Arts Council to help finance this venture.[6] Littlewood was touring the north east at this time, with sponsorship from the Arts Council, British Council and BBC Radio Newcastle. She would later describe the north east as a stimulating creative environment in a manner that recalled the 1930s, when the region, and in particular mining communities, had provided a fruitful site for both the documentary film movement and the Mass Observation initiatives.[7]

The Trafford Players' fortunes were mixed. Their production of *Rapunzel* in the working-class town of Consett in 1949 was poorly attended, whilst on the same tour there was an enthusiastic audience of 140 people for the production of Bernard Shaw's *The Man of Destiny* at Monkseaton Grammar School, in a middle-class coastal suburb.[8] The echoes of earlier initiatives in cultural improvement are noteworthy. Mollie Simmonds, a socialist after the Second World War, had been a member of the Bensham Settlement on Tyneside during the 1930s, which had been established at a time of frenetic national preoccupation with cultural improvement of urban and industrial areas. In developing their theatre group the Trafford Players drew upon their earlier experience of the settlement, which was posited on the idea of moral renewal through art, and their involvement with the Newcastle People's Theatre, which they sought to develop with support from the newly established Arts Council.[9] This small example indicates that the transition from voluntary to public patronage of the arts often facilitated a continuity of ambition amongst institutions such as the People's Theatre and the settlement movements stretching back to the inter-war years and beyond.

It is equally important to acknowledge that the Second World War represented a break with both the voluntaristic tradition of cultural improvement, as well as the private patronage of the arts. The most important post-war development was the growth of state sponsorship of the arts following the creation of the Arts Council in 1945. The Arts Council of Great Britain was preceded by the creation of the Council for the Encouragement of Music and the Arts (CEMA) in 1939, a wartime organisation for the sponsorship and dissemination of art that would boost national morale.[10] Although an outgrowth of wartime initiatives to popularise the arts, the Arts Council was often characterised by efforts to distinguish its policies from the popularising CEMA. This feature derived much from John Maynard Keynes's short lived but important role as chairman of the Arts Council between 1945 and 1946. Keynes was foremost a world-leading economist, but his personality and education also played an important part in shaping early British cultural policy. His argument for full employment was complemented by a belief that this condition would create an environment conducive to deriving pleasure from art. But for Keynes, a leading member of the inter-war 'Bloomsbury circle', aesthetic enrichment was not a task for government intervention.[11] His commitment to elite high culture and his disdain for amateurism informed his belief that government and arts funding should remain separate. For some commentators this distinguishing feature of British cultural policy was also its strength. Uninhibited by government intervention, British cultural policy made great strides in national culture after the Second World War: 'Public subsidy [without government intervention] served to make the culture of the British more international and liberated'.[12]

Aside from Keynes, there were individuals who shared the wider European enthusiasm for increasing participation in, and widening access to, the arts. Prominent dissenters from the Keynesian line included William Emrys Williams, a leading adult educationalist and founding member of the Arts Council, as well as the Arts Council's first director of publicity, Ivor Brown, and Mary Glasgow, the council's first secretary general.[13] Glasgow also made little secret of her disdain for the nineteenth-century inheritance of private patronage.[14] Her ambition to broaden the public contribution to arts sponsorship was realised following the 1948 Local Government Act, which gave local authorities one-eighteenth of a penny rate for culture. In Newcastle this prompted the decision by the local authority to form a committee in 1950 to encourage cultural activities in the city. The Special Committee for the Encouragement of Cultural Activities took its cue from the Arts Council in emphasising that it would not promote 'entertainment' but support 'musical, artistic and cultural activities'.[15] However, the first municipal efforts to encourage musical activity of 'suitable' quality were hampered by the crucial absence of that vital cultural institution, the symphony orchestra.

The focus of this discussion is the history of Northern Arts, the Arts Council of Great Britain's regional board that was to become the blue print for regional cultural policy nationally. As with broadcasting, the historical context for Northern Arts was the development of new national cultural institutions after the Second World War, but particularly the Arts Council of Great Britain. The history of this process in specific cities or regions has yet to receive comprehensive attention and it is acknowledged that the field of international cultural policy research could be enriched further by local and historical perspectives.[16] It is important to emphasise that whilst the early north-eastern public arts patronage was mobilised by both the creation of the Arts Council and the 1948 Local Government Act, the momentum and energy for sustaining a wider regional cultural policy in the north east was posited upon the desire to rectify a major cultural deficit. Michael Hall, a north-easterner who had been studying music in London, returned in 1956 full of determination to supply the north east with its own orchestra. His letter to Newcastle Council's Special Committee for the Encouragement of Cultural Activities, soliciting help with establishing an orchestra, was taken seriously and extended an ongoing discussion of culture in the city to arts subsidy in the region.[17]

Elsewhere in the country, Arts Council efforts to improve popular sensibilities had by this time foundered in the face of changing consumer behaviour and taste.[18] But in the north east this initiative endured thanks to institutional developments leading to the creation of Britain's first regional arts council in 1961. In 1960 Councillor Edward Fletcher, a veteran of the Spanish Civil War, chairman of the Labour Party in Newcastle during the 1950s, and the Labour MP for Darlington after 1964, submitted a memorandum on 'the case for a regional arts council' to the Newcastle Committee for the Encouragement of Cultural Activities.[19] Following an initial discussion in Sunderland, Tyneside was proposed as the first area for the new institution, and shortly afterwards collaboration over funding for the arts was extended to Teesside and Wearside.[20] Northern Arts' regional boundaries quickly came to the attention of the Arts Council of Great Britain, as well as the Northern Economic Planning Council. In 1964 the association was asked by the Arts Council to extend their area to coincide with the boundaries of the Northern Economic Planning Board and Council. From 1967 Northumberland, Durham, North Riding and the whole of Cumberland and Westmoreland were incorporated and title was changed to 'Northern Arts Association'.[21] It is interesting to note that both the development council boundary and the parameters subsequently adopted by Northern Arts broadly coincided with Fawcett's early twentieth-century delineation for the province of the North. This serves to reinforce how this early geographical recommendation became embedded not only in government administrative boundaries, but also in both planning and cultural infrastructure by the second half of the twentieth century.[22]

In 1961, with Dame Flora Robson as president and Lady Crathorne, Lady Ridley, Viscount Lambton and Dr D. C. Bosanquet as vice presidents, the association certainly appeared to provide a continued platform for elite patronage of the arts. On the other hand, as a consortium of local authorities brought together to help address the fact that the north east possessed no regional orchestra, this outstanding impediment revealed the limits of traditional arts patronage in the area. In its early years, Northern Arts' representatives frequently complained about the unwillingness of local firms to endorse or support cultural activities, and comparisons were made with cities such as Liverpool, where the Liverpool Philharmonic was sustained by funding from local industrial companies.[23] This lack of patronage for classical musical culture forced Michael Hall, the founder of Northern Sinfonia, to engage musicians from 'the remnants of the Yorkshire Symphony Orchestra … and the Manchester and Liverpool freelance pool'.[24]

These difficulties encouraged Northern Arts to cast the net wide in the effort to secure funds for Northern Sinfonia. In 1963 Northern Arts supported Trades Union conferences in Newcastle and Middlesbrough to encourage support for the arts where audiences were addressed by Arnold Wesker from Centre42. That year Northern Arts' membership comprised 40 trades unions, 50 local authorities, 40 other organisations, 30 industrial representatives and 700 individual members whose contributions enabled it to offer the Northern Sinfonia Orchestra a £6,000 loan to help meet their £12,000 deficit. These initiatives did not go unnoticed: at the third annual general meeting of the Arts Council Nigel Abercrombie recommended that Northern Arts be the model for arts funding in the rest of the country.[25]

That Northern Arts became the template for regional arts funding nationally warrants further consideration. The north east's fledgling arts association preceded the decision by the Arts Council of Great Britain to develop regional cultural policy. This took shape with the creation of a new post of chief regional officer, a position taken by Nigel Abercrombie in 1968.[26] Eric White, who was assistant secretary to CEMA from 1942 and literature director to the Arts Council from 1966 to 1971, noted that bringing together all the local authorities and county boroughs that were to make up Northern Arts was unprecedented: 'this was a completely new style of arts association. There was no question of confining it to a federation of local arts centres, clubs and societies, as in the Midlands and South West. It was intended to exercise a wide range of powers to encourage the arts in the region'.[27]

One explanation for the north east's distinctive approach to cultural policy may be found in the political regionalism that reached its pinnacle during the 1960s. White singled out Arthur Blenkinsop, MP, as seminal to securing the support of the region's political community for this venture. Basil Bunting, writing in his capacity as president of Northern Arts during the 1970s, also emphasised Blenkinsop's role in the creation of Northern Arts: 'when Arthur Blenkinsop first began to stir things up in this part of the world he founded a magazine, a short lived one … to which I was invited to contribute … that invitation was the first hint I heard of a movement which became Northern Arts'.[28]

Blenkinsop was Northern Arts' first acting secretary, but he was foremost a politician and was Labour MP for Newcastle East between 1945 and 1951, and represented South Shields between 1964 and 1976.[29] A 'dedicated socialist' and 'old boy of Newcastle Grammar School', Blenkinsop, like so many cultural activists of his generation, had been a member of the People's Theatre in Newcastle during the 1930s. Together with his wife he also played a leading part in founding the Youth Hostel Movement in the north and remained a key figure in the Rambler's Association until his death in 1979.[30] A close friend of Sir Charles Trevelyan, Blenkinsop fits the character type of left-leaning cultural improver and politician that emerged during the inter-war years. Their marriage of cultural improvement and socialist politics was given strength by institutions such as the Newcastle People's Theatre, host to contemporaries with similar political and cultural ideals and sponsored by 'progressive' regional elites such as the Trevelyans. Blenkinsop's part in drawing together the regional authorities that were to make up Northern Arts was undoubtedly assisted by his knowledge of and anchoring in the region's progressive cultural community. Equally important was his prominence in the white-collar managerial union APEX, which sponsored his political career, and provided a ready-made network of regional political contacts to tap in his role as secretary of Northern Arts.

The complementary interests of cultural activists and politicians in the region were also exploited to the full by Frank Atkinson, who was later able to draw upon the gathering sense of regional awareness in the north east to secure support for Beamish Museum.[31] Thus whilst the initial impulse had been to pool regional resources for arts funding, the institutional realisation of Northern Arts, and its quickly growing profile beyond the region, owed much to the economic and political discourse of regions during the 1960s. When the director for the Scottish Arts Council, Ronald Mayor, visited the north east in 1966, he described the organisation as the 'cynosure of Great Britain'. Mayor concluded that the success of Northern Arts was due to the peculiarities of the region, which, in contrast to Scotland, supported 'a large compact population, a number of large urban areas adjoining each other, each vying with each other for the edge in some form of superiority or other, but very much the same kind of urban area or city with the same kind of people'.[32] The urban dynamics of the north east and the dominance of these cities by northern Labourism undoubtedly played a part in facilitating support for a project that became anchored in the language of economic modernisation. Equally important, however, was the initial attraction to the project of Labour politicians such as Blenkinsop, but also T. Dan Smith, as well as Fletcher, who all brought with them the experience of cultural radicalism, voluntarism and left theatre of the 1930s, and applied it to the ambition to construct new cultural facilities in the north east.

This feature was given further weight by the Labour government's appointment of Jennie Lee as Minister for the Arts following the 1964 election.[33] In 1965 Lee's first white paper on support for the arts encouraged cooperation between local authorities on a regional basis in a manner that had been anticipated by the North East Association. Blenkinsop, having left the association for full-time political life following the 1964 general election, was keen to promote the innovations of the north east in parliament, describing the successful collaboration between seventy local authorities, representatives from industry, the unions, higher education and the media as: 'sufficiently important for us to look to its development over the country as a whole … This method of trying to link local authorities with industry and with trade unions on as wide a basis as possible is valid for the country as a whole'. Remonstrating from the opposite side of the House, Nicholas Ridley, MP for Cirencester and Tewkesbury and a member of the Northumberland aristocratic dynasty, complained about the 'extraordinary habit of having a trade unionist, a housewife and every sort of representatives on these associations', describing the regional 'Little Emrys' as biased against private arts. Defending his political ally and north east compatriot, Fletcher argued at length that their innovations had 'transformed the attitude to the arts in the north east'. This prompted the Conservative MP for Tynemouth, Dame Irene Ward, to point out sharply that Northern Arts collaboration with Labour-led councils, particularly in Newcastle, had sanctioned the demolition of the architecturally and artistically significant Eldon Square. The north east Labour MPs were nevertheless backed by Jennie Lee, who concurred that the additional subsidy to the north east from the Arts Council was justified in respect of their 'pioneering work'.[34]

On the other hand, it also needs to be acknowledged that the 'unique' level of regional collaboration mobilised by Northern Arts may also have been a product of a wider sense of disenfranchisement from national or metropolitan culture. Echoing the experience of regional broadcasting, the new regional cultural policy institution evolved, and carried political consensus with it, as a response to being 'at the end of the national queue'.[35] Whilst the director of the Scottish Arts Council magnanimously applauded Northern Arts' organisational innovation, their annual report noted resentfully in 1968 that the northern region, trying to serve a population larger than Wales and Israel, received only a fraction of the Arts Council direct grants enjoyed by Scotland.[36] In articulating the need for additional support from businesses and local authorities, Northern Arts pinpointed cultural centralisation as a major factor: 'owing to economic and technological factors, London has become the centre for television, radio, recording, film making and publishing which increasingly dominate levels of pay and the availability of musicians, actors, directors and writers'.[37]

Since the north east was the 'region furthest from London', institutions such as the Tate or Covent Garden were 'denied by distance to all but a privileged few from the North'. Therefore the motivation for Northern Arts assuming a leading role in the development of regional arts associations nationally was also rooted in the familiar ambition to secure a 'fair deal for the North'. This is not to detract from their innovations: along with the Lincolnshire Association, Northern Arts spearheaded the 1967 Standing Conference of Regional Arts Associations.[38] But it is essential to recall that these efforts were underpinned by a desire to enhance access to metropolitan culture on the one hand, and to compensate for the local lack of patronage for classical music on the other.

The tenuous affinity between regional politics and regional culture, rooted in the initial overlapping interests of left-leaning politicians and progressive intellectuals, appeared to have reached a pinnacle in 1972, when the modernist poet and regionalist Basil Bunting was elected president of Northern Arts.[39] In that year vice presidents included Arthur Blenkinsop, Barbara Hepworth, Anthony Jelly of Tyne Tees, and T. Dan Smith, with the Duke of Northumberland remaining as the organisation's patron.[40] With a poet and regionalist as president – Bunting had written already in 1953 of the need in the north for a 'paper' to represent 'the very northern point of view and to remind the north that literature exists' – Northern Arts certainly appeared to be responsive to cultural regionalism.[41] Bunting's appointment would nonetheless reveal a growing tension within Northern Arts between those committed to supporting vernacular culture and others who were beginning to articulate with increasing confidence the virtues of importing metropolitan culture to the creative 'wasteland' of the north.

That competing interests were mobilised by the Northern Arts project had become apparent already by the early 1960s. Politicians such as Blenkinsop tapped the wave of enthusiasm for regional planning in helping to establish a role for the new arts association, and therefore sought to draw on national directives in both planning and cultural policy. In an early interview he stated that it was the organisation's ambition to fulfil a role for culture which the North East Development Council was achieving for industry. One journalist in the *Economist* wrote that the NEDC and the new regional arts council were together 'trying to dispel the impression that the region consists largely of slag heaps and grime'.[42]

In 1965 the chairman of the Arts Council described the regional councils as 'essential in order to offer a freedom of choice and provide a cultural corrective to the uniformity of mass culture'.[43] There is little evidence to suggest that Northern Arts officials were uncomfortable assuming the role of 'cultural correctors'. Whilst the emergence of a regional arts bureaucracy may have been organic to the north east, the new regional organisations were undeniably perceived by the Arts Council as effective vehicles for the dissemination of 'legitimate' national culture, echoing the conclusions of more recent analyses that regions were not recognised as *producers* of culture before the 1980s.[44] Northern Arts' increasingly patrician approach to regional culture was to become apparent in the discussion of the literature panel's policies during the 1960s.

In 1961 Northern Arts admitted that they were largely ignorant of the quality and quantity of the region's cultural talent. This prompted them to make the appointment of an arts officer to conduct an audit of arts in the region. The officer, Sandy Dunbar, director of Northern Arts from 1963 to 1969, had been assistant secretary of ICI Wilton Works before he was persuaded by Lady Crathorne to become the secretary of the association's Teesside Liaison Committee. Reflecting on his appointment Dunbar noted that 'compared with the massed, managerial ranks of ICI, NEAA was tiny, but it had a wide network'.[45] His first audit as arts officer concluded that opportunities for writers in particular were limited. Scarce facilities for publishing or public debate were compounded by the inadequacies of regional sound and television broadcasting: 'BBC sound and TV [local] programme time is negligible while Tyne Tees Television mainly use other networks and have no theatre group of their own'.[46] In response to these findings and hoping to boost literary activity, Northern Arts began publishing its own journal, *North East Arts Review*, in 1962. The first issue featured an illustration by the 'pitman painter' Norman Cornish as frontispiece and included a short story by the recently returned writer and regional enthusiast Sid Chaplin. The publication's explicit regional focus was curtailed following a decision by Northern Arts to replace the review with *Stand* after three years. A literary magazine edited by Jon Silkin in Leeds, *Stand* was not northern in origin but began as a London poetry magazine in 1952.[47] The decision to cease the review reflected the growing consensus, particularly amongst members of the literature panel, that the region would be better served by importing talent with an established national reputation. And the initial impulse to establish a regional magazine that could fulfil a social function, 'providing a sense of belonging to the region and giving writers an additional outlet', proved to be short lived as the organisation was increasingly characterised by efforts to bolster the north east's cultural palette with metropolitan imports of 'national' significance.[48]

Jon Silkin was born in London in 1930 into a talented literary and political family. But by the 1960s, having come to the north east via Leeds, Silkin had acquired a northern persona, and was later remembered for his laboriously short-ened 'a'.[49] This gesture nevertheless co-existed with deep-seated scepticism about vernacular culture. In 1967 one prominent local newspaper began promoting the idea of a 'cultural renaissance' in the north east. With the publication of an anthology of poems by Tom Pickard, Bunting's young protégé, a new novel by Catherine Cookson, another new novel about the Durham Gala by David Bean, originally a Londoner but settled in Whitley Bay, a début novel about growing up on Tyneside by David Boll and the latest contribution from Edward Grierson, the Newcastle *Journal* identified 'the long awaited flowering of north east talent which it was hoped might accompany the regional consciousness we have heard so much about in the last five years'.[50] This claim prompted a lively discussion of vernacular authenticity and its revival. Sid Chaplin was an enthusiastic promoter of the region as a site flourishing with vernacular literary talent.[51] By contrast Silkin remained obdurately sceptical about both the cultural renaissance and the very notion of a clearly identifiable north east culture: 'whilst the north east has its own individuality, it is certainly difficult to maintain that it possesses an immediately identifiable culture, any more than does the West Country, Cumberland or Liverpool'.[52]

As editor of *Stand* it also seemed clear that Silkin was underwhelmed by vernacular literary culture. In 1966 the magazine had invited contributions from within the north east which Silkin later described as 'hugely disappointing', with limited submissions in dialect 'and very few that had even chosen regional sub-jects'.[53] We should hesitate before taking such views at face value, particularly in the light of the resurgence of interest in both popular dialect writing under the auspices of Frank Graham's publishing venture as well as the embrace of

Table 2 Northern Arts literature expenditure 1964–9 (£s)

	1964/5	1965/6	1966/7	1967/8	1968/9
Northern Arts *Review/Stand*	585	1,770	1,777	1,760	2,150
Morden Tower	100	450	720	994	650
BBC/NEAA Play Company	750				
Writer's Award		1,950			
Poetry Library				100	330
Young writers/poets				244	70
Poetry fellowships				1,000	1,500
Other poetry readings	100	60	240	71	300
Other magazines	50	50	155	103	300
Other projects		194			200
	1,585	4,404	3,085	4,272	5,500

Source: Tyne and Wear Archives Service, D. 4341, Literature Panel Minutes, 1964–9

local idiom by the Morden Tower group. Moreover Silkin's main interests lay in 'established' poetry and prose: he was a leading authority on First World War poetry. By the early 1970s *Stand* was being circulated largely outside the region, its north east content limited.

Silkin's response to vernacular culture did not impinge upon his flourishing relationship with Northern Arts, and his impervious stance may well have impressed members of the literature panel. In 1965 he was appointed as an advisor to the panel and by 1969 *Stand* received nearly 40% of the literature panel's expenditure.[54]

By the end of the decade poetry was absorbing the largest proportion of monies, whereas earlier initiatives, such as the 'Writer's Award' and the 'BBC/NEAA Play Company' were short lived. In justification of this feature Northern Arts pointed towards the organisation's pivotal contribution to the development of a poetry scene on Tyneside:

> This boom has placed Tyneside on the poetry map as firmly as Liverpool in the early 1960s … This new awareness and increased audience has been particularly significant among young people … Finally Northern Arts, by maintaining a broad outlook and being prepared to support a number of ventures from their earliest beginnings has contributed to the development of a comprehensive 'scene'.[55]

The Morden Tower poetry group had been in receipt of Northern Arts expenditure since 1964 when it had been awarded a small grant of £100. This rose to £994 it 1967/8 but funding to Morden Tower declined in direct proportion to the increase for *Stand*.[56] Famously described by Allen Ginsberg as a kind of 'medieaval tackroom', the tower, reached by a dark cold alley which had the remains of the city wall on one side and the kitchen entrances of Newcastle's chinatown on the other, had a widespread reputation for unconventional forms of poetry reading. It was certainly well out of view of the city's more prominent cultural and architectural landmarks. Its smells, sounds and darkness still make Back Stowell Street a 'psycho geographer's' delight.

Unsurprisingly there were some in the city who remained unsympathetic to the nascent Newcastle poetry scene and in 1964 Tom Pickard had been refused money from the Newcastle Council Cultural Activities Committee. Their hostility was utilised to great effect by Bunting in his widely acclaimed poem 'What the Chairman Told Tom'.[57]

> Poetry? It's a hobby.
> I run model trains.
> Mr Shaw there breeds pigeons.
> ***
> Nasty little words, nasty long words,
> it's unhealthy.
> I want to wash when I meet a poet.
> What you write is rot.[58]

Northern Arts did support the tower by covering the travelling expenses and paying a fee to visiting poets. Connie Pickard recalls visiting 'the Arts Council tiny office in the Bigg Market Chambers. Sandy Dunbar was quiet but this other fellow didn't like us. They were mainly concerned with things like the Sinfonia'.[59] The Pickards were paid a few pounds for organising events and by the early 1970s Connie was receiving £9 per week for running the venue. This support did come with condition; Northern Arts insisted that that the tower's activities were to be managed by a committee chaired by a member of the university literature department. In the early years Claude Rawson, who was supportive of the poetry being developed by the tower poets, chaired the committee which included the Pickards, Richard Hamilton and Bunting. These early years are viewed by Connie Pickard as a golden age. 'Claude Rawson was terrific and supportive and he did our expenses for us … became our de facto administrator … he was very positive.'[60]

In 1965 Bunting read his epic poem *Briggflatts* in the Morden Tower for the first time.[61] Written on his daily rail journey to his position as financial journalist for the *Evening Chronicle, Briggflatts* was well received by poets in America at the time of its publication.[62] The Atlantic poetry connections brought the Morden Tower to the attention of Northern Arts from 1964. In 1968 Basil Bunting was appointed to the two-year Northern Arts poetry fellowship at the universities of Durham and Newcastle; however, over the next few years the institutional goodwill towards the Morden Tower dissipated. Rawson had moved on to Warwick

University and his place was taken by Robert Woof, the distinguished Wordsworth scholar and friend of Jon Silkin and Tony Harrison. Connie increasingly felt surrounded by poets and administrators who were unsympathetic to the poetry world of Pickard and Bunting: 'Basil was a friend of Pound and Pound was a fascist … You really hoped you'd get some help from the University but they just couldn't see beyond the fact that Pound was a fascist and I would say well what about Louis Zukofsky and they would say well even some fascists have Jewish friends'.[63] The poetry tradition at Morden Tower founded by the Pickards and Bunting was strongly influenced by American trends, particularly the Objectivists, and they increasingly found themselves at loggerheads with the mainstream of British poetry dominated by the 'Movement'.[64]

In 1973, Connie Pickard, by now largely responsible for organising readings at the tower, and her husband and poet Tom, were invited to a meeting with representatives of the literature panel, then chaired by Sid Chaplin. Some consternation was expressed because only fourteen readings had taken place against the stipulated subsidy for twenty. Whilst it was suggested privately that the tower may have 'had its day', Northern Arts remained anxious to be associated with the international interest it had generated. Later the same year Pickard wrote from America with the following request:

> I can't afford to subsidise Morden Tower with my energy when it should be injected with a large amount of money to give it room to flower … I'd need to have an assistant, office space, travelling expenses, office expenses etc. (£3,500–4,500). The *American Poetry Review* (a new poetry newspaper conceived on a gigantic scale: circulation 50,000) wants to do a feature on the Tower including photographs – statements from poets as well as our experiences in reviving it – pity if it has to be a retrospective-period piece.[65]

But 'the employment of Pickard as a "poetry impresario"' remained an unacceptable proposition, and in 1975 after the breakup of their marriage and the loss of their bookshop Connie's request for an increase in her weekly payment was rejected and she was forced to abandon her role as organiser and concentrate on her work as a television researcher. The literature panel decided to replace Connie Pickard with a new organiser and the following year it was recorded with satisfaction that the tower's activities 'were at a much higher level than previously' and the newly appointed Bob Lawson confirmed the 'success' of the organised readings, with the caveat that the occasions continued to attract a 'number of egocentrics and empire builders'.[66]

Meanwhile, support for *Stand* remained unflagging. In 1973 Northern Arts increased the editorial fee to Silkin, bringing the total grant for *Stand* to £3,090. Defending their decision, the literature panel drew attention to the magazine's growing international profile, and emphasised its importance as 'the only major arts activity exported from the region on a national and international level'.[67]

The ongoing support for *Stand* was also closely connected to the construction of Northern Arts' own version of its accomplishments: 'this magazine had been established in Newcastle by the initiative of Northern Arts and therefore it should continue to be a funding priority'.[68] In 1976, having grown tired of what he perceived as the stifling influence of a growing art bureaucracy dominated by Arts Council directives, Basil Bunting resigned his position as president of Northern Arts, having made clear his commitment to a 'light touch' art management. He was increasingly frustrated by the climate of 'fear of criticism and too much attention to respectability' which pervaded the organisation. Perhaps with half an eye to Tom Pickard he argued that the new public sponsorship should not shy from 'keeping company, now and then, with young men in torn jeans and long hair, who treat authority with rudeness and whose notions of book-keeping are chaotic or even disingenuous'.[69]

Despite Bunting's pleading for the individual artist and the organisation to adopt a policy 'to let a thousand flowers blossom', resources continued to be concentrated towards the safe havens of Northern Sinfonia and *Stand*. It is difficult to conclude other than that institutions prefer to deal with institutions, rather than the potentially unpredictable individual artist. Bunting's views may have embarrassed some but the organisation's longstanding commitment to compensate for the historic cultural deficit of the region inevitably resulted in the lion's share of resources being devoted to bodies such as Northern Sinfonia. What then was the contribution of Northern Arts to shaping the cultural region during the 1960s and 1970s? Was the institution's claim to have sustained the Tyneside poetry scene really justified? The official rhetoric was consistently posited upon a rejection of vernacular culture and particularly its association with industrial heritage. Yet the international acclaim secured by poets including Pickard and Bunting saw a renaissance of poetry that was celebrated and acknowledged by poets such as Lawrence Ferlinghetti. The new poetics which emerged from the region during the 1960s were heavily influenced by American modernists and Beats, particularly in the use of vernacular and everyday speech.[70]

Should the resilience of the Morden Tower group, and the associated disdain, so eloquently articulated by Bunting, for metropolitan arts directives, be seen as evidence of a cultural region that was impervious to the allure of mainstream culture? By the early 1970s Bunting and his supporters were confident in the strength of the poetry movement which they had established, and heartened by the international acclaim showered upon them, and they looked with incredulity at Northern Arts' increasing strategy of 'parachuting in' representatives of metropolitan culture. On the other hand, could the cultural regionalism of those who remained committed to vernacular integrity be read as a symptom of an alienated and circumscribed territorial culture?[71] Or could it be that this new development of the vernacular tradition simply sat uncomfortably with Northern Arts' original remit to improve middle-class cultural infrastructure?

We turn now to consider the relationship between Northern Arts and its local political partners. Despite its national recognition as the model for collaboration with local government, between 1961 and 1979 Northern Arts was unable to generate unanimous backing within the area under its jurisdiction. Whilst the organisation had never claimed that its boundaries represented anything other than a financial remit, the remarks of the Scottish Arts Council director in 1966 revealed an external perception that Northern Arts reflected a shared sense of belonging in the area. The development of regional arts councils after 1945 may have contributed to a growing elision in official discourse between the regional institutional boundaries and territorial culture. This tendency has been noted in the north west, where the regional descriptor was transferred from bureaucratic conventions, including the regional arts council, to popular culture such as literature associations.[72]

However, the external perception of north-eastern cultural cohesion, which Northern Arts helped to generate, was rarely mirrored by internal consensus. Historic divisions within the 'Tyne Tees' area, for instance, remained enduring. A map produced for Northern Arts in 1969 showed clearly that the artistic facilities supported and provided by the association were concentrated on Tyneside.[73] This had been a problem for the organisation from the outset and Blenkinsop reported in 1961 that certain corporations regretted the emphasis on the Newcastle area and the apparent isolation of Teesside. Moreover, one of the early criticisms of the *North East Arts Review* was that it lacked material from the Teesside area.[74] By the end of the 1960s 90% of the total literature expenditure for Northern Arts was devoted to supporting projects, people and publications existing within a fifteen-mile radius of Newcastle, and concern was once again expressed over the lack of literary activity in Teesside.[75] In 1973 anxiety over the lack of visual arts provision in the area prompted the unusual decision to provide 'special consideration' to applicants from Teesside with the caveat that 'artistic considerations are not jeopardised'.[76]

Perhaps unsurprisingly local government in Middlesbrough made little financial contribution to Northern Arts during the 1970s. By the end of the decade the Northern Arts director David Dougan had come into open conflict with Durham County Council over their unwillingness to sponsor Northern Arts.[77] Dougan had been appointed director in November 1969 and he initially enjoyed the support of the majority of the region's local authorities.[78] However, the growing recalcitrance of local politicians in Durham was undoubtedly prompted by the clear evidence for a Newcastle-centric approach to the distribution of resources: Dougan memorably spoke at length to an audience in County Durham detailing the extent of expenditure in other parts of the region. But their reticence was perhaps also heightened by the publication in 1976 of the long-awaited Gulbenkian-funded *Support for the Arts in England and Wales*, which concluded that local authorities should be the principal patrons of future arts funding.[79] This reflected the devolution of funding responsibility to regional arts associations during the 1970s, which had been a part of the 1966–70 Labour government's art policy, in no small part a response to Northern Arts' argument for enhancing the powers of the regional arts boards. During the 1970s the proportion of Arts Council funding to regional arts associations increased by 7%; however, as we have seen, this did not always reflect a willingness to respond with increases in local government contribution.[80]

The north east, with its early initiatives in regional collaboration, should have been well positioned to capitalise on this moment of institutional devolution. Nevertheless, reticence towards the support for Northern Arts was not confined to the larger authorities, and neither was it an exclusive feature of the 1970s. Throughout the 1960s there were frequent complaints over the poor representation from smaller local authorities and establishing its regional profile caused Northern Arts great difficulties from the outset.[81] Despite its consensual rhetoric, Northern Arts struggled to elicit a broad regional backing, both in terms of the geographical spread and in persuading commercial bodies to contribute to the association's activities. Two years after the creation of the association, Owen Brannigan, the locally born distinguished baritone singer, writing in his capacity as president, complained that

> a small number of authorities – almost all in Northumberland – have refused to contribute. We should like in particular to draw attention to the position of Gosforth UDC and Whitley Bay B.C. as outstanding examples of authorities who have resolutely refused to contribute to our association or directly to any individual projects we support.[82]

Paradoxically, whilst acknowledging the difficulties of loyalty to Manchester and Scotland in Westmoreland and Cumberland respectively, the proposals in 1967 to extend the western boundary of Northern Arts, roused *less* hostility to the institution than had been witnessed within the counties of Northumberland and Durham.[83] In fact, the most strident opposition to the association actually came from within Tyneside, inverting Putman's argument that central cultural imperialism in regions has chiefly been opposed by peripheral areas. Moreover, the role of Northern Arts, as a potential arbiter of conflict in the regional arena, is highly dubious.[84] Northern Arts produced its own conflicts and in so doing revealed the fragility of regional cohesion upon which it was allegedly based. Equally, the hostility evoked by the institution could also be read as a measure of a strong territorial affiliation. Again this can be usefully contrasted to the north west, where the regional descriptor was adopted more readily since there was no comparable historical legacy or discussion over what a 'north west' institution should consist of.

The 1970s have been identified as representing a shift in the 'politics of culture' characterised not only by the devolution to regional arts boards but also by a change in the aesthetic parameters of the Arts Council. Stuart Laing has written that 'the second half of the decade … was marked by the replacement of fringe and experimental work with community arts as the main terrain for debate over the aesthetic boundaries within the council'.[85] The creation of the new Community Arts Panel in 1975 has been acknowledged as a challenge to both the consensual political base upon which the Arts Council had been precariously balanced since the post-war settlement, as well as to the centralised structure of British cultural policy. This was because community arts frequently incorporated an explicit political content, often resting uneasily with the Arts Council's commitment to prioritising 'high' artistic standards, and also because it was anchored in the enhanced regional arts boards (the first community arts board was set up as a sub-committee of the Arts Council's first full regional committee in 1975).[86]

The autonomy and radical potential of community arts in the regions was nevertheless quickly eroded. From the mid 1970s Northern Arts supported a substantial growth in community arts activities. This growth was partly the product of strategies by various agencies, including the Manpower Services Commission, to use art and culture as a vehicle for job creation schemes. One activist complained that by the late 1970s community arts had been transformed into 'welfare arts'.[87] The growth and administration of community arts was often *ad hoc* and uncoordinated and added to the expanding administrative burden of the association. Whilst the early stages of the community arts movement were largely based upon individual activists, by the late 1970s there were complaints that the movement had become institutionalised and the autonomy and potential for political radicalism was curtailed by increasing institutionalisation – a complaint that expresses similar concerns to those voiced by Bunting in his 1976 presidential address.

The election of a Conservative government in 1979, and the quickly changing economic and political landscape, was bound to have an impact upon Northern Arts and its activities. There was also another important shift taking place in the administration of public arts sponsorship and this was generational. In 1984 Peter Stark replaced David Dougan as the director of Northern Arts. He was the first director to have a background exclusively in arts management. In contrast to Dougan, who began his career as a journalist and broadcaster, Peter Stark represents a new generation of arts bureaucrats and managers who did not undertake work in arts management alongside their principal career, as was the case with politicians such as Blenkinsop, or those including Dougan for whom the entry into arts bureaucracy represented a distinct career shift.

Born in the upper-working-class/lower-middle-class Newcastle suburb of Heaton, Stark, like Blenkinsop, was a former pupil of the Royal Grammar School

Fig. 7 People's Theatre Newcastle

and a member of People's Theatre during his youth. Stark grew up in Lesbury Terrace, close to the People's Theatre Art Centre, of which he was a member. The theatre had relocated in 1962 to the former premises of the Lyric Cinema, with the help of sponsorship from, amongst others, the Trevelyans and Northern Arts. As we have seen, the People's Theatre and the Trevelyans' patronage had been important factors in bringing together the first wave of cultural policy makers in the north east. Despite these similarities with many leading figures in the local arts world, Stark was the embodiment of a radical new managerial approach to regional arts and under his stewardship Northern Arts underwent a major restructuring.[88]

By the age of fifteen Stark, who describes himself as one of the '*we've got to get out of this place*' set, had lost his accent. Despite the obvious allure of the 'People's', university took Stark out of the region to Leeds – 'I thought I was going to the Midlands' – in 1966. Going to read sociology at the 'Red University' at that time 'meant I didn't end up doing much sociology'. But here he met and engaged with a group of young men and women immersed in student politics. Cultural affairs secretary to the student union during Jack Straw's presidency, he would also share the lead roles with Alan Yentob in the University Theatre Group, which enjoyed four months at the West End playing Max Fischer's *Chinese War* directed by Mike Waring. As well as experimental drama and student politics Stark was by now re-entering the world of traditional singing, but by the late 1960s was forced to sing Yorkshire and Lancashire 'as I couldn't re-find my accent'.[89]

Although aware of the North East Arts Association, and vaguely inquisitive about it, his entry into the world of arts management came with the creation of the Birmingham Arts Laboratory in 1968. Alone in Birmingham and working as an assistant lecturer in English and General Studies, Stark stumbled across an advert eliciting support for the new Arts Lab in a copy of the *International Times*. Mark Williams, the organiser of the new lab, modelled self-consciously on the London and wider network of arts laboratories, happened to be a school friend of Stark's.[90] Subsequently Stark entered what he described as a 'hippy world' which his youth at the Royal Grammar School had not afforded him. But as a 'responsible hippy' he quickly assumed the role of administrator and gave up his teaching job to devote his time to the new Birmingham Arts Lab. Clearly this experience was vital to his later career as an arts manager, but it raises a pertinent question: how could Stark and his contemporaries survive undertaking what was essentially unpaid, if highly creative, labour? With no private benefactors, no Trevelyans and no Spence Watsons, they did what it was possible to do in those days: 'I give up teaching and I go on the dole. And for a year I took the dole and we built Birmingham Arts Lab'.[91] This experience proved to be seminal. As a twenty-two-year-old 'responsible hippy' with a third class degree in sociology from the 'Red University' Stark was appointed to the New Activities Committee of the Arts Council of Great Britain in 1969.[92]

The notion of a generational-shift is heightened by the response of the existing tier of arts managers, such as the chairman of the West Midlands Arts Association, who wrote to the Arts Council during the late 1960s to establish the identity of this 'Stark fellow' who had been invited to set up the Birmingham Arts Festival: 'Does the West Midlands Arts Association no longer enjoy the confidence of the Arts Council?'[93] This experience was not unique to Stark but was shared by others and this era is described as one which generated a critical mass of very young cultural managers and administrators who were drawn further into, and exclusively interested in, the management of the arts. Together with his now business associate Brian Debnam, Stark was amongst the first students to take the pioneering diploma course in arts administration at the Polytechnic of Central London. The course offered a placement at John Fox's Welfare State International. Founded in 1968, Welfare State was an artist-led umbrella predicated upon the idea of 'art for all'. It pioneered the use of street theatre, music and sculpture in a manner that was considered 'revolutionary' during the late 1960s.[94] As John Fox's first administrator with Welfare State, Stark was by this time on the Experimental Drama Committee and the Experimental Cultures Committee of the Arts Council. This early experience was complemented by contact with Elizabeth Sweeting of Oxford Playhouse, the external examiner for the arts administration diploma. Sweeting, acknowledged as 'a founding mother of the new profession of arts administration', subsequently helped Stark to secure the position as the director of the Southwell Park Arts Centre.[95] With a sixty-room Edwardian mansion to convert into an art centre as his brief at the age of twenty-four, this era was a baptism of fire for the young arts administrator.

Stark was also to be closely involved with the regional devolution of arts management that took place during the 1970s but, as yet, his connections to Northern Arts were not formal. In part this reflected the generational shift; the common perception of Northern Arts during this time was still that it remained preoccupied with funding the symphony orchestra. On visits to the north east Stark was more at home in the bohemian Handyside Arcade, talking to Tom and Connie Pickard and attending Newcastle Arts Lab events, than he was with the Northern Sinfonia. But his national network brought a growing awareness of regions through the New Activities Committee's regional remit which he co-ordinated. Moreover, as a founding member of the Community Arts Committee, Stark was also part of the decentralising impulse identified by Laing as coinciding with the shift from an experimental to a community agenda during the 1970s. This milieu and its young managers were seen as a challenge to the Arts Council 'canon'.

By 1973 Stark had allied himself with the 'community arts field', a move which brought him into contact with the new generation of regional arts association activists such as Peter Booth, Geoff Simms and Pat Abrahams who sought to capitalise on the findings of the Redcliffe Maude Report on arts funding in order to enhance the power of regionally based institutions. The growing momentum of the regional arts boards had already brought the 'north east' model to national attention, especially its early emphasis upon a strong partnership with its local democratic base as opposed to the original model of the funding predicated upon an 'art form based approach'. However, under the directorship of David Dougan, Northern Arts by the second half of the 1970s was often in conflict with local authorities and the organisation increasingly looked to the Arts Council as their major source of funding. Paradoxically Northern Arts became highly skilled in securing resources from the council at the same time as local funding declined. This was a reversal of its much vaunted pioneering regional funding formula. Stark notes that the organisation prior to his arrival was 'driven by its art officers who picked their own committees and its purpose in life was to asset strip the Arts Council. And they were very good at it … inventing schemes, getting money devolved to the regions, they were geniuses at it'.[96]

The context of a shifting political landscape, and in particular the growing threat to the metropolitan county councils, prompted the new generation of regional arts directors to expand the horizons of their arts funding strategy further. Keith Armstrong, a community arts worker, suggests this era precipitated the transition from community to 'welfare art' as agencies such as the

Manpower Services Commission began to acknowledge the arts as a potential measure to tackle youth unemployment – described by another community worker as 'teenagers painting walls'.[97] The involvement of local government was strengthened and in some cases renewed with the appointment of local arts officers, a post pioneered in the north by Gateshead following the appointment of Ros Rigby as the first local authority arts development officer in the early 1980s.

Peter Stark was appointed the director of Northern Arts in 1984 and this was to be a homecoming in more ways than one. By the early 1980s, having finished running Southwell Park and struggling to find a suitable paid position, Stark began to long for the place that he had been so desperate to leave as an eighteen-year-old university student: 'and there's only one job in the world that I want'.[98] This job became available in 1984 following Dougan's appointment as head of the National Craft Council.

Convinced of the need for radical change in regional arts boards, Stark initiated strategies to regain the confidence of local government. In 1984 the rhetoric of Northern Arts was still that of a responsive grant-giving body, but according to Stark, 'Northern Arts was a medieval baronetcy …'. Driven by the art officers, who were extremely successful in their attempts to devolve money from the Arts Council, this strategy was, as Stark recognised, dependent upon an ever diminishing national pot of which the north had by now arguably received its 'fair deal'. The first major change was to restructure Northern Arts as a 'non profit distributing company with the protection of corporate status' and in 1986 Northern Arts Association ended, to be replaced by Northern Arts Ltd.[99] Stark realised that the voluntarist basis of their previous arrangements was incompatible with an organisation that by now employed many people and handled large sums of money. But restructuring and developing a new corporate identity posed a threat to the often *ad hoc* decision-making systems to fund community art projects. Armed with the rhetoric of democratic accountability Stark pushed through a structure of funding that was responsive to local government and not organised in terms of art forms as had previously been the case: 'and in the area of local arts development I said sorry we are not going to continue funding independent local community arts because if after five years you've not convinced democratically elected politicians what you are doing locally is of value to their community then, sorry, you don't have validity'.[100]

These views were made public in his policy document entitled *Changing Landscapes*, which led to the creation of new local arts development agencies from 1986 to take responsibility for art in local authority areas. As Stark saw it this shift from an 'art form based approach' to one that was spread more equitably across the region's local authorities was one of his chief innovations. Unsurprisingly such strategies roused hostilities amongst the existing community arts officers, whose projects were henceforth phased out and whose 'full time workers were induced to turn "free lance"'. The new era of Northern Arts management initiated complaints, resonating with a longstanding tension in the institution, that Northern Arts had little interest in 'home-grown skills' and suffered from the 'national disease' of importing a 'cultural diet of high profile national companies and exotic festival fodder'.[101]

But Stark insisted that changes were pivotal to the survival of Northern Arts during the turbulent years of the 1980s.[102] Armed with the new structure, Northern Arts was in fact able to capitalise upon developments that could otherwise have been extremely detrimental. For instance, following the abolishment of the Tyne and Wear Metropolitan Council, Northern Arts, as a limited company with corporate status, was able to benefit from the 'free money', the 'redistribution funds', which flowed from this to complete the first local arts development agency network, and 'basically do a whole load of deals on the handshake with chief execs or leaders of councils which really expanded the arts economy of the north east'.[103]

Undeniably the shift heralded by the arrival of a new generation of arts managers and bureaucrats embodied by Stark was decisive for Northern Arts. This would also be significant to the rapidly changing cultural landscape of the north east. In the culture-led regeneration of the region's urban riversides Northern Arts would play a decisive role in the creation of flagship cultural projects that came to be seen as landmarks of the region's transition to a post-industrial society. Speculating on the possibility of Northern Arts' survival without such a change in personnel and without the transition to corporate status is an exercise in counterfactual history that is beyond the scope of this discussion. Nevertheless, the discontinuity that the emergence of a new generation of arts managers and bureaucrats represented allows us to reflect upon the longstanding tension within the institution, between vernacular and metropolitan culture. Whilst he complained of culture arriving by parachute, Armstrong also regretted that the new structure was turning 'activists into professionals'.[104]

Stark's reforms had brought Northern Arts full circle: the organisation started off as an exercise in 1960s style corporatism. Blenkinsop and Fletcher's vision for new structures of public patronage for the arts meshed with George Brown's innovations for the economic planning of regions. Stark's arrangement, with its strong emphasis upon the involvement of local politicians, is closer to the ideas of Blenkinsop and Fletcher than the free-floating grant-awarding body that had evolved during the 1970s. Stark was not a professional politician, but his long apprenticeship in arts management had driven home the importance of working closely with political partners. Blenkinsop and Fletcher's was as much a political initiative as it was cultural and was part of a shift in the political climate of the 1960s. Northern Arts by the mid-1980s was keenly sensitive to local politics *and* was increasingly responsive to the market-oriented dictum of central government.

The wish of Keynes and Glasgow to establish a structure that was 'at arm's length' from political interference could not be realised. The ambition to bring art to the 'man in the back street' was an equally difficult objective, even more so when he and she were more at home with the region's vernacular cultural forms. Sandy Dunbar and his tiny team were well aware of these countervailing forces in the early 1960s. But what of the cultural landscape itself; how did Northern Arts impinge on or influence this in the new era of corporate restructuring? Was it any more responsive to Bunting's argument to let a 'thousand flowers blossom', particularly local ones, than the first generation had been? Judging from the often repeated complaints that there was a preoccupation with 'exotic festival fodder' it appears that the later generation of arts managers were more concerned about the parlous state of home-grown talent than their predecessors had been. However, this complaint needs to be set alongside the argument that the most successful symbol of culture-led regeneration, the Sage Music Centre in Gateshead, was both anchored in, and responsive to, a deeply rooted appreciation of the vernacular past.

Notes

1 Arts Council of Great Britain, *Report of the first north regional conference*, May (1946), p. 12; N. Vall, 'Bringing art to the "man in the backstreet": regional and historical perspectives of labour and the evolution of cultural policy in Europe 1945–75', *Labour History Review*, 75: 1 (2010), pp. 30–43.

2 Weight, 'Building a new British culture', p. 173.

3 Arts Council of Great Britain, *Report of the first north regional conference*, p. 12.

4 Ibid.

5 Helen Munro, 'North region parish notes', n.d., c. 1946, cited in Weight, 'Building a new British culture', p. 172.

6 TWAS, Box 4333, Northern Arts records, 'Middlesbrough Little Theatre development: housing the arts', June 1976, p. 2. During the early 1950s, a dozen local amateur dramatic societies raised £59,000 to build the first post-war architect-designed theatre in Britain.

7 J. Littlewood, *Joan's book: Joan Littlewood's peculiar history as she tells it* (London: Methuen, 1994), pp. 195–6; J. Corner (ed.), *Documentary and the mass media* (London: Edward Arnold Publishing, 1986).

8 The Monkseaton Grammar School, Parents' News Sheet, November 1949. Thanks to Mollie Simmonds for providing this source.

9 For the north east see Vall, '"Polishing the pitmen"', pp. 163–180. For a wider account of the settlement movement see A. F. Davis, *Spearheads for reform: the social settlements and the progressive movement 1890–1914* (Oxford: Oxford University Press, 1967); J. F. C. Harrison, *Learning and living 1760–1960: a study in the history of English adult education* (Aldershot: Gregg Revivals, 1994); J. Rose, *The intellectual life of the British working classes* (New Haven: Yale University Press, 2001).

10 F. M. Leventhal, '"The best for the most": CEMA and state sponsorship of the Arts in wartime, 1939–1945', *Twentieth Century British History*, 1 (1990), p. 295.

11 A. Light, '"Lady talky": *Bloomsbury ballerina: Lydia Lopokova, imperial dancer and Mrs John Maynard Keynes* by Judith Mackrell', *London Review of Books* (18 December 2008), pp. 17–20.

12 A. Brighton, 'Consumed by the political: the ruination of the Arts Council', *Critical Quarterly*, 1: 48 (2006), p. 2.

13 Weight, 'Building a new British culture', p. 161.

14 Weight, 'Building a new British culture', p. 172.

15 In 1958 amongst the organisations in receipt of money from the committee were: the Newcastle Glee and Madrigal Society; Northumberland Orchestral Society; Newcastle Bach Choir; YMCA; Choral Society, Cathedral Choral Society; North East Musical Tournament; People's Theatre; Newcastle Photographic Society; Newcastle Society of Artists and the Federation of Northern Arts Society. TWAS, MD/NC/94/22, Special Committee for the Encouragement of Cultural Activities, Corporation of Newcastle upon Tyne, General Minute Book 20, 11 July 1958, p. 65.

16 A. Lindgren, 'Varför inrätta kulturnämnd? Lokal kulturpolitik i två kommuner', *Historisk Tidskrift*, 128: 2 (2008), p. 179.

17 Griffiths, *Northern Sinfonia*, pp. 3–4.

18 Weight, 'Building a new British culture', p. 178.

19 *Northern Echo* (3 July 1976), p. 4.

20 TWAS, MD/NC/94/22, Special Committee for the Encouragement of Cultural Activities, Corporation of Newcastle upon Tyne, General Minute Book 20, 27 July 1960, pp. 294–297, 320–322, 353–354, 376–385, 442.

21 TWAS, Northern Arts Records, D. 4347, NEAA, Annual Report, 1964–5; Northern Arts Annual Report, 1970/71.

22 Fawcett, *Provinces of England*, pp. 19–23 highlights the ways in which various governments implemented his delineations as administrative regional boundaries.

23 TWAS, Northern Arts Records, D. 4346, North East Association for the Arts, Annual Report 1963–4.

24 *Guardian* (14 December 1959), in Griffiths, *Northern Sinfonia*, p. 4.

25 *Northern Arts Annual Report*, 1970/71 (Newcastle, 1970), p. 2.

26 E. W. White, *The Arts Council of Great Britain* (London: Davis-Poynter, 1975), pp. 243–245.

27 Ibid.

28 Newcastle Library Local Studies Collection, L706, *Basil Bunting's presidential speeches*, published by the Northern Arts Gallery for the 1977 'Current British Arts Exhibition'.

29 A. Blenkinsop, *Enjoying the countryside* (London: Fabian Research series no. 265, 1968).

30 *Evening Chronicle* (25 July 1975), p. 14.

31 There was also an important cross-over between these two organisations: Atkinson was the chairman of the Northern Arts visual arts panel in 1970, Northern Arts Annual Report, 1970/71.

32 Newcastle Library Local Studies Collection, L706, Northern Arts, December Arts Diary and Gallery Guide, 1966.

33 L. Black, ' "Making Britain a gayer and more cultivated country": Wilson, Lee and the creative industries in the 1960s', *Contemporary British History* 20: 3 (2006), pp. 323–342.

34 Hansard 1803, Commons sitting, Government support for the Arts, 27 April 1965, vol. 711, cols. 231–295.

35 See Chapter 3 on television above.

36 Northern Arts Annual Report, 1968/7, p. 6. In that financial year Scotland received £630,000 to serve a population of 5.2 million as compared to under £200,000 for Northern Arts to service 3,200,000 people.

37 Ibid.

38 Ibid.

39 C. Simms discusses Bunting's political regionalism and membership of the Campaign for the North in 'A glimpse of the "Inly-Working North": a meeting of the Campaign for the North', *Northern Review* 6 (1998), pp. 69–71.

40 TWAS, Northern Arts Record, Minutes of the Management Committee, April 1974, Bound Volumes. In 1974 it was decided that Smith's name be dropped from the list of vice presidents.

41 Basil Bunting cited in B. Lancaster, 'Editorial', *Northern Review* 1 (1995), p. 1.

42 *The Economist* (13 October 1962), cited in *Northern Arts: our first 25 years, 1961–86* (Newcastle: Northern Arts, 1986), p. 5.

43 TWAS, Northern Arts Records, Bound Volumes Minutes of the 5th AGM, 1965.

44 Casey, Dunlop and Selwood, *Culture as commodity.*

45 Northern Arts, *Northern Arts Thirtieth Anniversary, 1961–1991* (Newcastle: Northern Arts, 1991), p. 2.

46 TWAS, Northern Arts Records, D. 4347, NEAA, Annual Report 1963.

47 *North East Arts Review* 1 (1962–4), p. 1.

48 TWAS, D. 4341., Regional magazine. A feasibility study. Northern Arts 1969.

49 M. Standen, 'Obituary: northern by choice, Jon Silkin 1930–1997', *Northern Review* 6 (1998), p. 75.

50 David Bean was later to become a member of the Northern Arts literature panel, Northern Arts Annual Report, 1970/71.

51 Newcastle *Journal Weekly Review* (27 May 1967).

52 Ibid.

53 Ibid.

54 TWAS, Northern Arts Records, Bound Volumes, Minutes of the Executive Committee, 7 January 1965.

55 TWAS, D. 4341, Northern Arts Records, Literature Panel Minutes, 1968/9.

56 See Table 2. TWAS, Northern Arts Records, D. 4346, North East Association for the Arts, Annual Report, 1964/5.

57 R. Cadell (ed.), *Basil Bunting: the complete poems* (Oxford: Oxford University Press, 1994), p. 122.

58 Ibid.

59 Recorded interview with Connie Pickard, 27 August 2009.

60 Recorded interview with Connie Pickard, 27 August 2009.

61 Pickard, 'Work in progress 1', p. 43.

62 D. Cavanagh, 'Notice: Buntingology', *Northern Review* 3 (1996), pp. 69–73; N. Everett, 'Bunting's Briggflatts', in Colls, *Northumbria*, pp. 314–334.

63 Recorded interview with Connie Pickard, 27 August 2009.

64 Ibid.

65 TWAS, Northern Arts Records, D. 4328, Minutes of the Literature Panel, 9 April 1973. *Stand* was later to relocate to Liverpool when it received an offer of a higher subsidy.

66 TWAS, Northern Arts Records, D. 349, Literature Panel Minutes, 5 May 1975; 1 July 1975; 1 March 1976; 9 April 1979.

67 TWAS, Northern Arts Records, D. 349, Literature Panel Minutes, 24 January 1977.

68 TWAS, Northern Arts Records, D. 4328, Minutes of the Literature Panel, 9 April 1973.

69 Northern Arts, B. Bunting, *Presidential Address*, November 1975.

70 Cavanagh, 'Notice', pp. 69–73.

71 M. Keating, 'Rethinking the region: culture, institutions and economic development in Catalonia and Galicia', *European Urban and Regional Studies*, 8 (2001), p. 220.

72 Walton, 'Imagining regions', pp. 289–303.

73 TWAS, Northern Arts Records, D. 4346, North East Association for the Arts, Annual Report, 1969.

74 TWAS, Northern Arts Records, Bound Volumes, North East Association for the Arts, Minutes of First General Meeting, 1962.

75 TWAS, Northern Arts Records, D. 4341, Literature Panel Minutes, April 1969.

76 TWAS, Northern Arts Records, D. 4353, Visual Arts Panel Minutes, 4 July 1973.

77 TWAS, Northern Arts Records, D. 4336, Management Committee Minutes, Director's Report.

78 TWAS, Northern Arts Records, Northern Arts Annual Report, 1970/71.

79 S. Laing, 'The politics of culture: institutional change in the 1970s', in B. Moore-Gilbert (ed.), *The Arts in the 1970s: cultural closure* (London: Routledge, 1994), p. 43.

80 Ibid.

81 TWAS, Northern Arts, D. 4339, Report of the Organisation Sub-committee to the Executive Committee, 17 July 1969.

82 Both Gosforth and Whitley Bay were distinctive middle-class areas with strong local Conservative political traditions. It is interesting to note that Gosforth and Whitley Bay are two middle-class enclaves whose insularity from the remaining, mainly working-class part of the conurbation shocked the 1938 Royal Commission and underlined the animosity shared by Gosforth and Whitley Bay towards the core of the industrial zone. D. Goodfellow, *Tyneside: the social facts* (Newcastle: Co-operative Printing Society, 1942).

83 TWAS, Northern Arts, Bound Volumes, Minutes of the Executive Committee, 19 January 1967. Fawcett, *Provinces of England*, pointed out the strong connections between the north east and its western neighbours.

84 R. Putman, *Making democracy work: civic traditions in modern Italy* (Princeton, NJ: Princeton University Press, 1993).
85 Laing, 'The politics of culture', p. 44.
86 Ibid.
87 K. Armstrong, 'Whither community arts', *Northern Review*, 2 (1995), pp. 95–103.
88 This analysis of the rise of the professional arts bureaucrat is informed by H. Perkin, *The rise of professional society: England since 1880* (London: Routledge, 1990), pp. 436–455.
89 Recorded interview with Peter Stark, 18 June 2009.
90 The London Arts Lab was founded by Jim Haynes and became the model for others in the regions.
91 Recorded interview with Peter Stark, 18 June 2009.
92 The New Activities Committee was established in response to the expanding number of grant applications from organisations such as the Arts Labs and its purpose, as articulated by Lord Goodman, was to decide 'whether in all this froth and foment [sic] there is something worthy of public subsidy from public funds', Goodman, 1970, cited in S. Hope, 'Draft contextual analysis chapter: the economics of socially engaged art', September 2008, www.welcomebb.org.uk/ (accessed 16.8.09).
93 Recorded interview with Peter Stark, 18 June 2009.
94 www.welfare-state.org/pages/aboutwsi.htm (accessed 16.8.09).
95 *Guardian* (11 December 1999).
96 Recorded interview with Peter Stark, 18 June 2009.
97 Armstrong, 'Whither community arts?', p. 97.
98 Recorded interview with Peter Stark, 18 June 2009.
99 *Northern Arts Thirtieth Anniversary, 1961–1991* (Newcastle: Northern Arts 1991), p. 9.
100 Recorded interview with Peter Stark, 18 June 2009.
101 Armstrong, 'Whither community arts', p. 101.
102 Whilst the Conservative government did not abolish the Arts Council, an acknowledged inheritance of the post-war Labour settlement, this was a precarious time for the organisation, particularly with the appointment to the Arts Council in 1980 of Alistair McAlpine, treasurer of the Conservative Party, whose attitude echoed Nicholas Ridley's strident opposition to public subsidy of the arts during the 1960s, Hope, 'Draft contextual analysis chapter', p. 39; http://hansard.millbanksystems.com/commons/1965/apr/27/government-support-for-the-arts. (accessed 17.8.09).
103 Recorded interview with Peter Stark, 18 June 2009.
104 Armstrong, 'Whither community arts?', p. 100.

6

Riverscapes

In some areas, including some of the most deprived urban centres such as Newcastle/Gateshead or Walsall, culture-led regeneration, largely drawing on lottery funds, has contributed to the revival of whole communities.[1]

In 2004, the Arts Council of Great Britain revealed their commitment to a cultural policy with wide-ranging social and economic ambitions. This appeared to be a decisive break with the cultural inheritance that had cast a long shadow over the development of British cultural policy since the Second World War. In his capacity as founding chairman of the Arts Council in 1946 John Maynard Keynes had conceived an arts policy that would operate at 'arm's length' from the government, letting diversity flourish in national culture, refraining from intervention, and especially avoiding involvement in the fraught question of regional imbalances. But in 2004 the Arts Council's confidence in culture-led regeneration reflected a growing consensus regarding both the capacity and purpose of art as an economic stimulant and generator of social well being.

Although the efficacy of cultural regeneration has given rise to a certain degree of scholarly debate, by the millennium the north east appeared to be meeting the criteria for successful culture-led regeneration, and its inclusion in Arts Council publicity material comes as little surprise.[2] The now well-known markers of urban regeneration were all in place: Millennium Bridge, Baltic and the Sage Music Centre in Gateshead. There were equally notable developments on the banks of the Wear and Tees: in 1998 the National Glass Centre opened in Sunderland on the former site of the J. L. Thompson and Sons Shipyard alongside the city's new riverside university campus, and on Teesside an audacious plan for 'Middlehaven', a completely new urban centre on the banks of the Tees, was being developed.

It is pertinent to recall that the north east had been described by metropolitan arts officials as a 'cultural desert' after the Second World War.[3] But by the last decade of the twentieth century academics, journalists and commentators were enthusiastically promoting the area's cultural renaissance and its role in the transformation from an industrial region to a post-industrial society with 'flagship' cultural institutions. The national and regional press added to the sense of a dramatic and triumphant transformation with headlines that described rising phoenixes and boundless cultural achievements: 'YES IT's NEWCASTLE: from Coal Hole to City of Palaces' and 'Birth place of the Cultural Revolution'.[4] Amongst some architects and developers the hyperbole has been quite astonishing: one commentator memorably identified culture as a critical element in reversing Sunderland's 'downfall', which he alleged had been precipitated not so much by deindustrialisation, but by much earlier misfortunes:

> The old Anglo-Saxon *Sundered Land* actually refers to the land separated by the River Wear from the monastic estates of Monkwearmouth to the north … It was this unintentional severance from the mainstream … that perhaps contributed to Sunderland's downfall. Things are happily changing now … Culture is of course a critical element in helping to achieve this.[5]

The success of northern *grand projets* appeared to underscore the claims of those who had continued to champion increased resourcing for publicly funded cultural and arts institutions, especially when consideration is given to the north east's poor cultural infrastructure in the immediate post-war years. In 1945 the region was the only English region without a full-time orchestra, the last to acquire a television transmitter and had the least number of theatre seats per thousand inhabitants in the United Kingdom.

If we stand on the banks of the rivers Tyne and Wear and survey the visual transformation of these landscapes we might surmise that they provide irrefutable testimony to the efficacy of culture-led regeneration. A dramatic example is provided by the Hilton Hotel in Gateshead on a former industrial site that was reclaimed for the development of a public art project in the 1980s. But to what extent has this transformation been the result of a conscious plan? The task for this chapter is not to enter the debate about the viability of the arts economy; rather its importance lies in understanding the role of the past in shaping these initiatives. In addressing this question the aim is to separate the rhetoric and hyperbole of the politicians, arts officers, developers and architects from the reality of what has often been a very haphazard process. This will serve to develop an understanding of the late modern cultural region, particularly in the light of the current shift in the appraisal of the regeneration of these areas.[6] Whilst the task for this chapter is not to interrogate the economic premises of regeneration, the existence of this debate makes it important to ask what the wider relevance of flagship cultural institutions is. Are they part of, and integral to, a sustainable cultural region? Or are they merely monuments to the new arts bureaucrats who have flourished in the era since 1945?

In understanding the role of the past in these developments we might do well to recall that the Arts Council's recent reference to the revival of communities through cultural regeneration is not unprecedented and in actual fact strikes a chord with much earlier discussions about the region. The underlying idea that economic benefits could accrue from cultural improvement had been present amongst politicians and industrialists in the north east since the 1960s. Perhaps it is unsurprising that many of those involved in the strategic regional policy during the 1960s made the transition readily to free-market urban regeneration. The north east has been described by one critic as 'the land of one hundred quangos'.[7] Is it therefore possible that the increasingly centralised approach to institutional development was accepted readily in a region where local control over cultural institutions had historically been weak?

The 1980s have often been viewed as the point of departure for a new emphasis in cultural policy upon public private partnerships in supporting 'flagship' cultural projects that would contribute to overall urban image improvement. This phase is often contrasted to an earlier policy strategy that was principally driven by concern to widen access to culture and increase participation.[8] But in the north east the view that culture could be the handmaiden to future economic development could be discerned in earlier plans for regional economic improvement. Equally the cultural policy of the 1960s did not confine itself to questions of access and participation, but clearly had an eye to the question of economic planning. As we have seen, the cross-over between regional cultural and economic planning was at its height during the 1960s. Local politicians tapped the growing enthusiasm for regional planning in helping to establish a role for the new arts association, and sought to draw on national directives in both planning and cultural policy. In marketing the organisation they actively promoted the ambition to fulfil a role for culture which the North East Development Council was achieving for industry. In turn, representatives of bodies such as the Northern Economic Planning Council were convinced that correcting the north-eastern cultural deficit would assist the process of economic development: 'The Northern Region must not only offer factory sites and supplies of labour, but also show that it is an area of growing artistic endeavour with high cultural standards ... past preoccupation with industrial development ... has left little room for the development of cultural services'.[9]

By the late 1960s politicians such as Arthur Blenkinsop and those who succeeded him had effectively persuaded the regional business community that Northern Arts were fully committed to the economic modernisation project. But given that the remit of Northern Arts was still essentially confined to arts policy, the appetite for cultural policy amongst the business community remains noteworthy.[10] The arguments made by the planning council were repeated elsewhere, and the rhetoric of these institutions points towards the belief in a reciprocal and mutually beneficial agenda: 'the NEAA has pioneered a new concept of regional help for all the arts and is the largest of its kind in the country. Its membership includes firms, trade unions, foundations, art societies and individuals as well as 72 local authorities'. Despite mobilising such wide-ranging interest groups, the scale of the task facing the arts association was also acknowledged: 'artists in general, and those who promote, manage or administer the arts, need help if cultural standards in the region are to keep pace with economic development'.[11] As well as reinforcing the distinctive and pioneering qualities of Northern Arts' strategy, the evidence suggests that the region's cultural deficit was viewed as an obstacle to wider economic progress. And whilst no explanation was provided for this surprisingly rounded perspective upon economic development, the undercurrent of this discussion was the growing fear that the failure to retain externally recruited managers for 'branch plant' businesses would threaten the wider modernisation of the region's economy, which relied heavily upon a strategy of importing both firms and personnel.

Successive Northern Arts directors subscribed to and reiterated this view. 1968 was described by the representatives of the North East Development Council as a 'bad year' in which rising unemployment was coupled with growing anti-development-area sentiments, perpetrated both by the national press and at Westminster. In this climate Northern Arts tried to shore up their relevance to the regional modernisation project by emphasising the economic benefits to be realised by addressing the north east's cultural deficit:

> Many progressive firms believe they should help make the community attractive to expensively recruited personnel. After all, what is the point of spending £600 to recruit or move an expensive keyworker from London to the North, if he leaves in six months because the area lacks cultural facilities which he or his wife or his children are used to? ... With imaginative sponsorship the arts themselves can be good business.[12]

Perhaps it is therefore possible to view the era after the 1980s as an extension of a much longer campaign to improve the culture of the north east. In the twentieth century this crusade of cultural improvement stretched back to the inter-war years and reached its zenith in the context of 1960s regional planning. Whilst cultural policy's architects and institutions may have changed, reflecting the transition from voluntary improvism during the inter-war years to state-led cultural policy after 1945, which carried through to the more recent market-led approach, the long standing efforts to sustain and import middle-class cultural infrastructure remained remarkably resilient.

Although the national arts policy, as it merged after 1945, produced a distinctive hybrid in the north east between arts and economic planning, since the 1980s cultural policy has nevertheless operated in an entirely different context. The rise of a consumer and service based economy and the associated bifurcation of culture and economic development has produced many unprecedented features. The changing economic landscape of the 1980s informed the restructuring of Northern Arts' funding system and led to an increasing focus upon the development of large, high-profile arts projects which we return to examine in the concluding chapter. But the region's changing cultural landscape, and particularly the growing commercial and creative interest in the former industrial riversides, reflected influences beyond the sphere of national arts policy. In addition, the rise of a corporate cultural policy coincided with new forms of urban governance in the shape of the urban development corporations, which were central government initiatives. In turn the regeneration of the riverside areas which they orchestrated reflected the Conservative government's appetite for regeneration models imported from the USA.[13] Once the regeneration of an urban riverside area was successfully realised in London, there seemed to be no reason why the same logic could not be applied to the nation's ailing industrial conurbations.[14] But the allure of the American model was not restricted to Whitehall officials. Alistair Balls, the chief executive of the Tyne and Wear urban development corporation, had prepared for his new job by visiting American regeneration sites including Boston, Pittsburgh, New York and Philadelphia, returning to the north east convinced that such 'successes' could be repeated in this region. The chief executive of the Teesside Corporation also referred to international models with the hope that riverside regeneration would result in a leisure facility to 'rival Copenhagen's Tivoli Gardens'.[15]

With this in mind we need to acknowledge that culture assumed a more central position in urban and regional development from the late 1980s. The impression of a discontinuity was heightened in the national context, and in the north east, because this shift coincided with the radical overhaul of urban governance. The emergence of the urban development corporation during the 1980s was reflected in a growing preoccupation with public private partnerships to secure funding for the regeneration of 'flagship' sites, and explicit marketing campaigns to improve the image of ailing urban environments.[16] In the north east this shift reflected the creation of two urban development corporations in 1987. On Tyneside the Tyne and Wear Development Corporation's redevelopment areas were located within *four* of the five district councils which made up the former Tyne and Wear Metropolitan Council area. They had control of twenty-seven miles of riverside and planned for the development of four flagship sites: Newcastle East Quayside, Royal Quays in North Shields, St Peter's Riverside and Sunderland Docks.[17] Likewise the Teesside Development Corporation was created in 1987 and covered the largest area of any similar agency in the country. As with other cases, notably Cardiff Bay, it has subsequently been suggested that public art was integral to their portfolio of developments, and thus they came to be seen as spearheading the ground-breaking culture-led regeneration of the industrial riverscapes.[18] But does the evidence support this assertion?

The contribution of the development corporations to culture-led regeneration must also acknowledge the wider political context. The new development corporations have since the 1980s been regarded as a turning point in the history of twentieth-century local politics and accelerating the decline of urban governance. They were established under the 1980 Planning Act and tasked with securing the regeneration of their designated areas. Their powers were wide-ranging and they could 'generally to do anything necessary or expedient', including commissioning works of art, for the purposes of regeneration.[19] Most important and controversial, the development corporations possessed a fast-track compulsory purchase order capacity. Thus they could effectively by-pass the traditional planning procedures in purchasing and clearing sites for regeneration. This facilitated the transformation of the industrial riversides, but it undeniably also had a profound impact upon inner-city politics. With the development corporations in place the existing urban governments were left with planning departments that were effectively circumscribed; their jurisdiction was henceforth confined to inner-city areas and the idea of planning for wider urban development was severely restricted.

It is widely acknowledged that the development corporations were part of the central government agenda to weaken truculent Labour city councils. Michael Heseltine had argued vociferously that local (Labour) council failings had forced the Conservative central government to assume responsibility for these new areas of urban governance. Heseltine has also been credited with persuading recalcitrant Labour councils towards the benefits of cultural regeneration after he inaugurated the 1984 Garden Festival in Liverpool, an event that allegedly presaged the building of the Millennium Dome as well as stimulating the growing appetite of central government for a radical overhaul of the northern industrial cities.[20] Gateshead was to host the Garden Festival in 1990 and this event came to be seen as pivotal to the subsequent culture-led regeneration of Baltic Quays.

Critics of this era of urban governance have noted that it often produced overbearing and highly 'welfarist' interference in local affairs. Following a visit to the North Shields Meadowell Estate in 1991, the site of widespread social unrest and violence, Heseltine stridently blamed North Tyneside Council, led by Stephen Byers, for the blight that afflicted the area: 'You go and see what Meadowell looks like … the place has been abandoned … used as a sink by local authorities. … We are forced to bring in more and more central government programmes to make good the deficiencies'.[21] Equally, the development corporations often reinforced the impression that they were responsive to the Conservative government agenda, despite their 'non-governmental' status. In describing its strategy the Teesside corporation drew explicitly upon central government rhetoric, even adopting Margaret Thatcher's motto that 'where you have initiative, talent and ability, the money follows' as its slogan.[22] In 1991 the board members of the Tyne and Wear corporation provided further evidence of government control. In a private discussion of their attempts to secure additional government funds the director of finance admitted that, in practice, *suggestions* from the Department of Environment were equivalent to *instructions*.[23] Given the adversarial nature of development corporations in the context of the

Labour-dominated political landscape, and the corporation's propensity for by-passing or circumventing local democracy, commentators in the north east have noted that despite opposing the creation of the new agencies some representatives of north east's Labour elite were quick to accept seats on the board of organisations that were acknowledged as the prime minister's preferred instrument for clipping the wings of dissenting outposts.

Defending their involvement, individuals such as Joe Mills, Labour Party regional chairman and member of the board of the Tyne and Wear corporation, argued that their presence was necessary in order to ensure the development of an 'appropriate' economic strategy for the industrial north east: 'I made absolutely clear. I would be consulting with all councils in the area ... fortunately the board is made up of what I would call northern nationalists who realise the strength of local councils and realise they're in a Labour area'.[24] Thus the regional political elite may have found a new voice following the arrival of the urban development corporations. Equally, the surprisingly cordial relations have also been read as evidence of continuity: in the north east the dialogue between Labour politicians and the new quangos also appears to have been facilitated by a pre-existing and historical democratic deficit in local politics.[25] In their contemporary assessment of the area's regeneration experience Peter Hetherington and Fred Robinson referred to Joe Mills's involvement in the regional quango as a form of 'damage limitation', intended to *prevent* a London Docklands style development from being steamrolled onto Tyneside.[26] Even Alistair Balls, the chief executive of the Tyne and Wear corporation and the man who was openly influenced by the US regeneration model, claimed initially that he recognised the distinctive features of the north east economy and would not try to emulate London Docklands in this fragile territory.[27]

The allure of the London model was nevertheless quickly apparent.[28] By 1991 Balls acknowledged that 'the corporation had prepared its vision in 1988 for Tyne and Wear largely on the basis of a property-led regeneration programme'. Moreover, the parlous state of the region's industrial assets was emphasised in order to underscore the appropriateness of this approach. The negative aspects of a deindustrialising culture were frequently emphasised, the corporation's site being described as characterised by 'decaying industrial and commercial areas' with 'large public sector housing estates' abutting to these sites and displaying 'classic symptoms of urban decline and social deprivation'.[29] Writing in 1992, David Byrne reflected that the initial 'opposition' to the property-led model proved to be short lived, and in the end these bodies contributed to the accelerating pace of industrial decline.[30] Moreover, whilst their official plans included commitments to public housing and community consultation, private briefings with the Department of Environment revealed that the corporation board were often at pains to reassure ministers that social housing subsidy was to be a minimal feature of future developments.[31]

The new development corporations' strategic preoccupation with securing private inward investments and its emphasis upon commercial activities has prompted others to look for continuities with nineteenth-century approaches to urban management. In her study of the regeneration process in Middlesbrough, Friberg noted that during the nineteenth century much of industrial Teesside evolved upon a greenfield site and businesses could largely locate where they wanted without restrictions from pre-existing interests. Paradoxically these were strikingly similar circumstances to the powers that were bestowed upon the development corporations almost a century later. Despite their ambition to be regarded as the architects of a new market economy, in some respects they actually reinforced aspects of the twentieth century's legacy in the north east. Although hailed as agents of enterprise and private inward investment these organisations were in reality heavily reliant upon public funds. Between 1987 and 1996 the Teesside corporation received government grants of £354 million and generated other income of £116 million through the sale of property and land. Its strategy to attract private investments reached a figure of £1.1 billion. With these resources it brought 1,300 acres of derelict land back into use and created over 12,000 new jobs.[32] Their Tyne and Wear counterpart had raised private-sector investments in excess of £950 million by 1991 resulting in the creation of 23,000 jobs (according to their own figures). However, the agencies' own success narrative needs to acknowledge that they were forced to seek additional government funds in 1991, in order to realise the plans for the four 'flagship' projects. After some negotiation the board managed to secure an extra £2 million over their baseline, but not without some cost to their status and prestige. During these negotiations government ministers had expressed concern that 'extra resources do not appear to create extra regeneration, merely bringing forward existing schemes'. In his private notes the corporation's financial controller wryly commented, 'the argument could be that we are only pouring money in and awaiting the market to pick up (found us out!) i.e. the Teesside approach'.[33] Thus the national (especially from Westminster) image of the north east as heavily reliant upon the public purse was not fundamentally altered by the arrival of these new agents of urban regeneration.

Both the north east development corporations produced prolific marketing material and it is worth considering how the conurbations were profiled given our interest in their role in the changing cultural landscape and image of the area. In contrast to the state-led reconstruction initiatives that evolved after 1945, the question of attracting further funds became a much more central concern during the 1980s and was emphasised at the expense of developing a cohesive vision for the new urban future.[34] The Teesside corporation emphasised a few striking flagship sites as a lure to bring in further money. This raises questions about the extent of the conscious commitment to the notion of the economic and or social benefits of culture and the arts, and reinforces the impression that the evolution of the culture-led regeneration project in the north east should be extrapolated from the historical legacy of these quangos.

However, a distinguishing feature of development corporation policy has been the emphasis upon waterfront developments that have become integral to the discourse of the new culturally vibrant north east. Of striking postmodernist design these include commercial and residential buildings, festival retailing and visitor attractions, often based on site-specific history, that have all been constructed with dramatic riverside or ocean-front locations since the arrival of the urban development corporations during the 1980s. Many of these developments have been marketed and promoted in a manner that emphasises the maritime, rather than the industrial, significance of these areas.[35] For example, the first commercial buildings of Terry Farrell's master plan for East Quayside were named after the waterfront's historical legacy: Copenhagen House was the first in this series of commercial office buildings. Further down river in North Shields an old dockland area was transformed into a 'festival shopping' style outlet mall with the 'historic' name of 'Royal Quays'. The Tyne and Wear Development Corporation's flagship development for Sunderland at the mouth of the Wear is a national glass centre which places a strong emphasis upon the glass-making tradition dating back to early medieval times. In 1994 the Teesside corporation's plan for the regenerated Hartlepool dockside 'theme park' was opened to the public; 'a no-expense spared recreation of an eighteenth century dock' created in just twelve months within walking distance of a new US style mall, 'Jackson Landing', it was surrounded by 1,000 luxury private homes boasting 'ocean frontage'.[36]

Whilst the reason for the changing narrative of these areas, from industry to property development, culture, tourism and art, was in effect structural (without the fast-track CPO capacity it is unlikely that such dramatic changes in land use would have been realised), external influences also played a part.[37] Although the use of the region's waterfronts as the star attractions of development corporation achievements has often been seen as evidence of the north east appetite for, and efficacy in, executing cultural regeneration, these developments drew heavily upon American precedents where the primary thrust of regeneration was not anchored in a commitment to social and economic renewal through art and culture.

In Europe the Spanish cities of Bilbao and Barcelona spearheaded the culture-led regeneration model characterised by waterfront redevelopment and an emphasis on boosting the provision of visual and performance art spaces in these areas.[38] These 'success stories' initiated during the 1980s drew inspiration from developments in American cities that had begun in the previous decade. In Britain, the appetite amongst architects and politicians for the 'American model' remained especially strong – Teesside's development of Hartlepool Docks was explicitly influenced by such models – and it is worth considering examples such

as Boston, Massachusetts, often cited as the pioneer of successful urban regeneration.[39] Although it needs to be emphasised that the redevelopment of Boston
was not an attempt to revive a flagging industrial city, it was the first major
example of what has later been called festival shopping. This development provides evidence of how the transfer and application of the model for success in
a British site compares to the historical evolution of this process in its 'host'
location.[40] From the 1970s onwards the Boston model of urban regeneration
has been characterised as pioneering a type development that since the 1970s
combined residential regeneration, economic strength (particularly in the financial services), tourism, luxury retailing, visitor attractions, culture and art and
the preservation of historic city centre buildings.

James Rouse, the American developer whose company was the first to use the
term 'shopping mall' in the 1950s and invented what is now dubbed festival
shopping at the Faneuil Hall Marketplace Boston in 1972, casts a strong shadow
over British urban redevelopment schemes of the last two decades. Rouse began
his career as an urban reformer closely involved with public-sector housing schemes
initiated by Eisenhower's government in the early 1950s. He moved towards a
development model that was based on planned communities and shopping centres
and was solely financed by private capital. He has been credited with devising
the term 'urban renewal' and his formula consisted of striking architecture and
a new style of retailing that he claimed put the fun back into shopping. His
city centre developments were often cited as key to rising property values and
he became a major advocate of modern capitalism's superiority over the state in
delivering renewal.[41] The success of Faneuil Hall and festival shopping resulted
in Rouse rolling out the concept across a number of sites in the US including
a similar development in Baltimore and Jacksonville Landing and Miami's
Bayside. When the (purposely named) 'Jackson Landing' opened in Hartlepool
in 1996, it was heralded as a breakthrough in US-style retailing and attracted a
number of international brands. Likewise the development of Royal Quays in
the dock area of North Shields was opened in the same year with claims to be
'one of the first outlet centres in the country'. And whilst they were never realised,
the original plans for the regeneration of the Newcastle/Gateshead Quayside area
were clearly influenced by the idea of festival retailing as pioneered by the Rouse
Company. In Gateshead the initial plans for the regeneration of what was to
become the site of BALTIC had incorporated the development of office blocks,
luxury flats and retailing, to be funded by a London-based development
company. The plans for the flagship art gallery on the site of the former Baltic
Flour Mills only evolved after 1993 once funding for the first programme had
fallen through.[42]

Rouse's deeply held faith in the efficacy of his model delivered by the private
sector found an audience in 1980s Britain, where 'rolling back the state' was
a popular slogan in Conservative Party and business circles. In the United

States the model was seen as a panacea for the problems of the 'rustbelt' in the northern states and it is not surprising that historic or potentially historic locations in the north of England were seen as ripe for a Rouse-style development. Perhaps it is understandable, in a British context, that the appetite for this model has not been strongest in cities with a nationally recognised architectural and cultural heritage. Rather rundown northern sites such as Hartlepool and Tyneside have seen the adoption of the festival shopping concept tied to the *creation* of kitsch historical culture. These areas, many of them former docks, shipyards and major industrial transport amenities, were a tabula rasa for the transfer and application of a model that promised to deliver a post-industrial landscape.[43]

Whilst the 'historic quay' at Hartlepool has since become a symbol for the revamped town and recognised by the Imperial War Museum through the allocation to the 'world-class' marina of HMS Trincomalee, *old* Hartlepool sat uneasily with these developments. In his obituary of Reg Smyth, the creator of Andy Capp, Mark Adlard, award-winning writer and Hartlepool resident, speculated wryly about the prospects of a statue commemorating the internationally recognised cartoon character next to the Trincomalee.[44] But as we have seen the difficult relationship of the developers to 'old Hartlepool' was not restricted to the 1990s era of cultural improvism: the North East Development Council's report for 1968 referred to Andy Capp as part of the ongoing attempt to recruit new managers to the region:

> Where are you Andy? To us, Andy's the greatest. We'd love to meet him. Andy Capp was born and bred in the north east, and he helps us reminisce about the past. But Andy wouldn't recognise the old place now. New towns, new roads, new factories, new housing estates, luxurious new hotels, a new drive that's putting the region right ahead in terms of expansion and development. Andy would hate it. We think you'd like it.[45]

Thirty years later in the era of the urban quangos it would appear that, notwithstanding the appetite for American retail concepts, little had changed. Although less candid about their intention to bury the industrial past, the representatives of the new development corporations actively promoted the region's pre-industrial heritage in their future visions. On South Tyneside the Tyne and Wear corporation funded the Bede Heritage Centre in Jarrow. The reclaimed site was intended to incorporate the 'recreation of an Anglo-Saxon village and farm, sculpture park, craft workshops and housing' in the hope that this would stimulate and 'justify a hotel and conference centre'.[46] This development involved a consistent underplaying of the industrial vernacular past, particularly on Tyneside, where the rhetoric of the new quango connected the riches of medieval Northumbria directly to the corporation's aspiration for entrepreneurial success in the post-industrial era.

Elsewhere the industrial legacy was harder to ignore. In a press interview, the chairman of the Teesside corporation acknowledged that industry must play a part in any future vision for Teesside:

> seated behind the wheel of his black BMW, Ron Norman, chairman of the Teesside Urban Development Corporation, aims his cigar at the chimney of the ICI chemical plant, towering above the high-level road leading into Middlesbrough. 'See that?' Norman asks. 'If it were up to me I would hang a ruddy great sign on that chimney saying: this is Britain's most successful company, proud to be on Teesside. We can't hide something like that, so we've got to be positive about it'.[47]

Based on their funding and marketing rhetoric it would appear that before 1991 these agencies were principally concerned with property regeneration and festival retailing, and that art, culture and heritage were late, and less enthusiastically championed, additions to their portfolio of developments. Indeed, judging from Hartlepool and Jarrow it remains difficult to conclude other than that the principal application of transatlantic models can be seen in an appetite for kitsch history and new offices. This is unsurprising if we look more closely at the dynamics of the Boston model, where cultural institutions were never explicit in the plans for redevelopment. On the other hand, Boston had an already established range of arts institutions, and a unique collection of pre-served nineteenth-century residential areas was undeniably complemented by access to, and evidence of, strong cultural infrastructure – even the local baseball ground, Fenway Park, is regarded as a national monument. The wider idea of art and the arts economy also remains applicable to the US cases of urban regeneration. The regeneration of the harbour areas in Boston included the construction of residential 'artists' lofts right alongside the World Trade Center exhibition facility; clearly developers and architects in the US were well aware of the link between the so-called avant garde lifestyle, bohemian consumption and rising property values.

The notion of rising property values anchored in middle-class lifestyle and employment has undeniably been crucial. If culture-led regeneration is acknow-ledged, as it has been in more recent critical appraisals, as integral to a wider ambition to stimulate a middle-class consumption model then clearly the north east's development corporations were responsive to this impulse. Regeneration of flagship sites such as the East Quayside in Newcastle, and in particular the building of new law courts, was posited on the belief that this would generate demand for restaurants, 'shops, wine bars and offices' and more widely open opportunities for up-market consumption.[48] The consortium chosen to develop the East Quayside, arguably the most significant site in the region, was made up of Stanley Miller Holdings, a long-established local building and property company, Shearwater Property Holdings and a marketing team fresh from

Liverpool's Albert Dock. Their plan had all the hallmarks of a Rouse waterfront development, their publicity made direct reference to Rouse's famous Baltimore Harborplace and the centrepiece was to be 'Central Square', devoted to festival shopping.[49] Interestingly there is no reference to public art in their publicity material, which reflects a similar uninterest in art as the Tyne and Wear Development Corporation in 1991, when the commitment for arts sponsorship was confined to £195,000 per year for the Bede Heritage Park.

Whilst early plans did not appear to consider art or the question of public engagement as particularly crucial, by 1998 the regeneration of the Newcastle 'riverside promenade' had won a Civic Trust award, and the scheme itself, designed by Terry Farrell, had led to the commissioning of several works of public art that were considered to be 'integral to the aesthetic appeal of the area'.[50] The appointment of Terry Farrell, the Newcastle born and educated, internationally acclaimed architect, to design the 'master plan' for Newcastle's East Quayside development raises issues worthy of consideration. The abandonment of the festival shopping initiative caused by the collapse of the developer during the early 1990s financial crisis forced the corporation to change its strategy for the Quayside, away from a consumer-led development to one based upon commercial property. Farrell, who had encountered postmodernist architecture whilst a graduate student at the University of Pennsylvania, where he met Robert Venturi, amongst others, subsequently established his reputation with a number of major commissions, including the striking waterfront developments of the MI6 headquarters on London Southbank and the Embankment Place structure on the north bank of the Thames.[51] Farrell's waterfront interests can be traced back to his early student essay on the planning of Lytham St Anne's. Highly critical of Wilfred Burns's 1960s central Newcastle development, Farrell was anxious to project an architectural style that was playful rather than brutal. Farrell knew these sites intimately from his childhood and he had a close affinity with the area: his works in Newcastle, including the Centre for Life, were often former sites of childhood memories. It is of course a legitimate criticism of the development corporations that their budget for public art was small and that their interest in the history of the area was superficial. But in their defence it could perhaps also be argued that the buildings themselves were 'public art' and that the employment of an internationally acclaimed architect represented an attempt to combine commercial advantage with cultural/artistic sensibility.

Moreover the regeneration of the East Quayside provided the most palpable evidence to support the claim that art policy, and in particular public art, 'became a vital element in most of TWDC's plans' as the decade progressed.[52] In 1993 the centrepiece of the second 'Tyneside International' was the retrospective by the New York video and performance artist Vito Acconci situated in the then derelict CWS building. Perhaps this strategy, like the later construction of the Hilton Hotel on Bottle Bank, can also be used to underscore the efficacy of culture-led regeneration: whilst the performance hardly attracted any visitors the building now houses a luxury hotel, a process which reflects the link between the emergence of the area as a commercially profitable space and 'what is thought to be the desirable, socially exclusive world of "Art"'.[53] Local history has also played its part in the regeneration game. Works such as *River Tyne*, by the sculptor Neil Talbot, a representation of the Tyne carved into the retaining wall by the Wesley memorial, were commissioned by the development corporation in 1996. Incorporating '30 miles of landmarks in a 100-foot stretch', the carving presents a narrative of the region's development from Roman settlement to industrial development, including landmarks such as Thomas Bewick's birthplace, George Stephenson's cottage, Vicker's factory, Jarrow monastery and Tynemouth priory. Nearby is a carving by the same artist commissioned in 1996 entitled *Keelrow*. This work explicitly references the area's historical significance for the community of keelmen who crewed the boats discharging coal into sea-going colliers during the eighteenth century.[54]

With these commissions had the leaders of the development corporation embraced an industrial past that they had otherwise actively played down? In addressing this question it is important to recall that most of the works were commissioned around or after 1992, a year that saw many local authorities and development corporations responding to the Arts Council initiative promoting 'percentage for art' legislation which stipulated that a proportion of budgets for new construction should be set aside for decorative purposes. Given the ambiguous legal status of these recommendations it is also possible to critically evaluate this public art strategy, particularly in the absence of any evidence that the quangos were intrinsically or more broadly committed to commissioning public art.[55] The use of public art by development agencies has been regarded as integral to corporate influence over the urban regeneration process. Arts councils, it is alleged, also applauded the use of public art in association with the property boom principally because it provided a new market for art and arts management. In the US the public art in urban regeneration strategy has also been read as the triumph of corporate power and the ambition to create an environment rich in cultural capital for investors. The central feature of this strategy is short-term corporate gain and it has been compared to similar approaches in British sites, including Cardiff Bay and London Docklands. Whilst this approach to art in urban regeneration tends to favour recognisable international artists, engagement with 'local' culture and heritage can also benefit the 'corporate model', where features such as the Boston Freedom Trail, or the Tyne and Wear Development Corporation's commissioning of art about the keelmen, are interpreted as form of corporate colonisation of local history.

However, other north-eastern riverside sites appear to offer opportunities for alternative analysis. The focal point for Tyne and Wear Development Corporation's redevelopment of Sunderland Docks was the National Glass

Centre, which opened in October 1998. It was the first major building to open in the UK funded by a Capital Arts Lottery award.[56] The location of the site commanded much publicity: the new building was realised as part of a Europe-wide architectural competition and was erected on the banks of the Wear, where the contraction of shipbuilding was still a recent and significant local experience. National journalists were quick to make connections between the Glass Centre and the area's history of glass making, which dated back over 1,000 years, and more broadly it has been suggested that the city's approach to culture-led regeneration should be distinguished from the corporate model.[57] In contrast to Newcastle, this was 'not a central business area masquerading as a cultural or civic centre'. Drawing upon evidence from St Peters Riverside, Malcolm Miles emphasises that the former industrial area was reconstituted as a housing area and university campus, rather than a business park. In 1989 an art project was initiated in the area by the Artists Agency, which had been established in Sunderland with a regional remit to 'broaden people's creative sensibilities'.[58] Their 1989 feasibility study had canvassed the local community and found it to be receptive to the idea of using art to promote community identity. But the Artists Agency did not seek funding from the development corporation; rather the riverside 'sculpture trail' was characterised by collaboration between agencies such as schools, community groups and churches. They employed a local artist, Colin Willbourne, to work in residence and the project has been regarded as a more organic and locally led example of cultural regeneration than those witnessed in Cardiff Bay, London Docklands or arguably Teesside with its future proposals for Anish Kapoor's *Tees Valley Giants*.[59]

On balance the relationship between new forms of quasi-governmental urban management that evolved during the late 1980s and the evolution of culture-led regeneration as an approach interested in the promotion of the creative and visual arts appears rather tenuous before the arrival of new funding sources aimed specifically at cultural projects in the 1990s. The development corporations remained chiefly interested in property-led regeneration and had a shared interest in importing American retail concepts. Engagement with the 'percentage for art' strategy came late in the day and the evidence that there was serious consideration of the social or 'moral' benefits of the arts is negligible. Perhaps this is unsurprising given that these bodies were working to a very constrained brief and also since they presided over the financial crisis of the early 1990s, which put paid to many of their initial property-led schemes. However, these transformations using striking postmodernist architecture; glossy facades; the re-creation of riverside promenades and the subsequent boom in bars, restaurants nightclubs, etc., has added to the sense that these agencies contributed to the 'cultural renaissance' of the industrial riverscapes. In view of this impression it is important to note the evidence that the development corporations had little appetite for engagement with the emerging arts and cultural industries that were located either within or adjacent to their area. This, it could be argued, delayed the renaissance of important run-down areas by more than a decade.

The idea of a 'cultural quarter' is not new. During the late 1980s Newcastle Council launched the 'Theatre Village' project which was to be located in the run-down western end of the city centre. The focal point was to be the refurbished Tyneside Theatre on Westgate Road, which was close to the Newcastle Arts Centre and Dance City, a contemporary dance academy. The area's potential was enhanced by its proximity to the city's chinatown. A regional music centre was also to be part of the scheme. The project was never realised, foundering on disputes with the development corporation over a site for the music centre and a change in policy within Newcastle Council's controlling Labour group.[60] The concept of the 'quarter' still persists: Newcastle has since attempted to create a cultural quarter clustered around the Hancock Museum, University and theatre. This is part of a grander realignment of the city's cultural flows devised by Terry Farrell. Others have pursued similar schemes, with Middlesbrough developing a 'Boho Zone' adjacent to the new headquarters of Cleveland police.

In Newcastle's inner east end another quarter emerged which was rooted within the local, young, often radical, cultural community. The lower Ouseburn area directly abuts the former Tyne and Wear Development Corporation East Quayside site. Originally part of Byker, the lower Ouseburn, a tributary of the Tyne, was developed as an industrial area from the seventeenth century thanks to its proximity to the Tyne coal trade; it also supported a significant glass and pottery industry. Lime Street forms the centre of the area, a street that runs from below Byker Bridge to the Quayside. The street is dominated by the Cluny, a former flax mill (latterly a whisky warehouse) designed by John Dobson in 1848. Most of these concerns had declined by the second half of the twentieth century and by the 1980s the Ouseburn area was beset by dereliction and high levels of river pollution. During this time the area was identified by Newcastle City Council as a site for environmental improvement to be financed by the Department of Environment Urban Programme.[61] In setting out its vision for the future the council-led plan drew explicitly upon the area's industrial past. The strategy paper projected future potential by referring to its central position in the narrative of regional industrial development. The site's significance as the home of regional sporting heroes such as Clasper was underlined; equally the history of the keelmen in nearby Sandgate was deployed as evidence of the area's cultural significance. Charleton's 1885 account of Newcastle recorded that 'just above the bridge the keels may be seen lying and delivering coal into carts … In the cold water, too, we see ragged people with baskets and bags, wading and groping with their hands for the coal which has fallen over board'.[62] Thus the industrial inheritance was exploited in describing the area's potential as an 'attractive and stimulating environment which will bring visitors, residents, jobs and investment into the valley' and this document emphasised the capacity for

Fig. 8 The Cluny warehouse

development that drew upon and engaged with the past. Acknowledging the terrible environmental conditions, the report found that the area still retained 'many fascinating aspects of Tyneside's history ... local characters, housing cheek by jowl with heavy industry, river life, cinema and art'.[63]

These plans, however, were to be realised in an area that was already seeing the early signs of regeneration. 36 Lime Street is one of the Ouseburn valley's most enduring success stories. Described in the promotion of 'NewcastleGateshead' as a 'hive of creative enterprise', the conversion of the Cluny warehouse by Michael Mould to house artists and to serve as a base for his community theatre company, Bruvvers, is often seen as a point of departure. Arguably this initiative has served as a catalyst for the subsequent development and marketing of this area as a cultural quarter, a process that was consolidated with the opening in 2005 of the Seven Stories children's book centre in the converted warehouse adjacent to the Cluny.[64] Mould is nonetheless reticent about positioning himself in the history of riverside cultural regeneration, emphasising that his initial interest in the Cluny was unrelated to the council's plans for environmentally improving the area. Having moved to Newcastle during the 1970s to work for the Northern Stage he was living in Byker when the issue of accommodating the newly formed theatre company was becoming a pressing concern: 'I ended up in Byker and lived and worked there but we were always in temporary accommodation and the council were going to knock it down … and we were always looking for somewhere permanent for the theatre company to live but we just kept being shifted'.[65]

Initially Bruvvers had purchased a disused cinema adjacent to the Byker Wall, but this building was obtained by the Tyne and Wear Metropolitan Council to make way for the Byker by-pass. In an era of frenetic slum clearance and a still expanding programme of urban road construction Mould found that many potential theatre spaces were being demolished. But not so in the Ouseburn, which served no major population and where arterial road access was unlikely to be required. However, Bruvvers' transition to the Ouseburn was also influenced by the area's significance as a magnet for countercultural activity: 'I knew it because of the Byker City Farm was next door and was started by groups of hippies in the mid 1970s and we became involved in that and in Byker Phoenix and running the farm and co-ops and *that movement*'.[66]

Next to the city farm was a large and beautiful unoccupied old warehouse designed by John Dobson, available to be purchased for £30,000 in 1982. Mould had always wanted a building of some vintage for the theatre company and had explored the possibility of buying former warehouse buildings on the Newcastle Quayside, including the current site of the Wetherspoons pub and the Malmaison hotel. In 1982 the entire building which now houses Malmaison, a four-star hotel incorporating 'luxury spa', could have been purchased by a representative of the cultural left for £90,000. But this was beyond the reach of the Bruvvers and Mould was to use the proceeds from the sale of a house in Walker 'that we squatted and it just came into my possession' to fund half the cost of purchasing the Cluny. The remaining funds came from Mould's brother, the actor Roy Marsden.

Whilst the city's first Ouseburn strategy acknowledged the presence of artists as illustrative of the area's potential for further development, Mould insists that the work of the theatre company and the progress towards the refurbishment of the Cluny took place without political intervention. But the presence of a critical mass from the cultural left coalescing in this bohemian area, frequenting pubs and supporting community projects such as the city farm, is acknowledged as a decisive factor. The local pubs in semi-abandoned areas such as the Free Trade enjoyed spectacular river views and became a magnet for students, academics and cultural workers. Moreover, Tyne Tees studios were situated nearby in a converted warehouse on City Road and *The Tube* was launched at the studios for Channel 4 in the same year that Bruvvers purchased the Cluny. Whilst there was no formal connection between the Cluny and Tyne Tees, there was an informal cross-over between those working in television and theatre. Bruvvers maintained close links with Live Theatre and the Amber Films collective, whose founder, Murray Martin, was instrumental in the campaign to preserve many of the historic buildings on Newcastle's Quayside. But it remains important to recall that the subsequent transformation of the area as a marketable cultural quarter could not have been anticipated during the 1980s. As Mould reflected, local politicians were generally bemused by the clutch of 'artists' inhabiting these dilapidated buildings in an area designated as an 'industrial zone': 'the council-lors used to call us the loony Cluny in the 80s when it [Newcastle] was still a Labour council and it was still the old guard Labour and we were asking them for bits of money to do parts of the building up … This was an industrial zone, I'm sure they haven't changed it'.[67]

The relationship to the city council was to change as 'culture' moved up the local and national policy agenda. The appointment of Paul Rubinstein during the 1990s as head of culture and economic affairs signalled the city's growing acknowledgement of the 'culture as economic driver' argument and reflected government encouragement to all British cities to bid for the 'Capital of Culture' award following the success of Glasgow in 1990. But the acceptance of the Cluny and its incorporation into a Labour-led cultural policy strategy also reflected the personal contacts that Mould and others in the area sustained.[68] For the city farm, the institution that pioneered the Ouseburn area as a poten-tial 'urban village', this shift proved to be less beneficial. During the mid-1990s local government subsidy for the project was withdrawn on the grounds that the farm was located on land contaminated by industrial waste, but Mould infers that this reflected a growing desire to focus upon cultural projects eligible for major funding grants and palatable for inclusion in the preparation for the Capital of Culture bid, and it would appear that the city farm was simply 'too smelly' for the new cultural policy.

Though uncomfortable with the idea that his projects can be incorporated within a regeneration agenda which may have undermined the Ouseburn as a site of local community engagement, Mould's initiatives have nonetheless endured, and perhaps also benefited from the growing enthusiasm for the area as a cultural quarter. However, funding for the project was always scarce and the renovation of the building in 1999 cost £100,000, half of which was pro-vided by the Ouseburn Partnership. This voluntary organisation was created in 1995 and granted £2.5 million under the Government Single Regeneration 3 scheme to 'to carry out a programme aimed to make the Valley a more attrac-tive place to live, work and spend leisure time and involving its communities of interests'.[69]

Although Mould is clear that there was no relationship or direct dealings with the urban development corporation, the development of the Ouseburn valley during this time occurred against the backdrop of the overhaul of the East Quayside area, which shares a boundary with the land surrounding the Ouseburn river. Initially the development corporation's interest in the Ouseburn valley was principally strategic. As Mould recalls: 'they bought loads of the land and property in the Ouseburn so they could move people from the Quayside, where they had CPO'd them … they built the pigeon crees on the hill … to get rid of all the pigeon crees on the Quayside. So it was like a penal colony'.[70]

Thus the contested and overlapping interests that characterise the physical and cultural regeneration of the riverside location are clearly apparent. The development corporation's strategy of purchasing surplus buildings in the area inhibited the wider spread of a grassroots cultural development as characterised by the Cluny: 'all the land that's opposite this belonged to the corporation, which remained sterile and couldn't be developed'.[71] And when the area started to be recognised as a site where property value could accrue the development corporation refused to sell any of the riverside sites, a policy which may well have stopped in its tracks an organic, cultural regeneration of the valley.

Equally, the contribution of artists to this process of urban gentrification is ruefully acknowledged by Mould. Buying the building in 1982 ensured the survival of Bruvvers, a small community group that, like Live Theatre, struggled to obtain funding as an itinerant body. Whilst the renovation took nearly twenty years to realise, the purchase of the building convinced funders such as Northern Arts and Newcastle City Council of the company's qualities and intentions: 'although we didn't turn it into a beautiful palace it was there and you could see that there were studios and all sorts of different people working there. So they were more inclined to give us grants for our works'.[72]

Of course this funding culture and the purchase of the building brought Mould closer to a kind of regeneration strategy, posited on rising property values, about which he remains deeply circumspect: 'it's history isn't it … Paris and New York, they are interesting places to be, the jazz, the cafes and these sorts of movements and then gradually *they* move in and *we* shift out, the problem is that there aren't any interesting places, there are no old buildings left now, they're all lofts and apartments'.[73] On the other hand this process does not appear to have changed Bruvvers' approach to community theatre, which remains determinedly of the cultural left, with stories of struggle and revolution woven through most of their productions. However, Mould is clear that cultural regeneration's increasing focus upon 'flagship' institutions has had an impact upon the availability of venues for small-scale theatre work. Gateshead, often hailed as the pioneer of successful culture-led regeneration, is singled out as reflecting this shift: 'they now put most of their money into their big things. We used to do regular tours of the smaller Gateshead venues funded by the arts team and now they don't put any of their money into that sort of thing'.[74]

On balance it is important to recall when confronted with the current marketing of the Ouseburn as a successful cultural quarter that this process began because it offered cheap buildings and because many of those involved lived nearby in bohemian Heaton and Byker, frequenting pubs like the Free Trade and the Ship. There was no coherent vision for culture-led regeneration: the artists moved there purely and simply because of access to cheap, dilapidated, 'romantic' property. Equally the development of the Ouseburn reinforces further the haphazard nature of the development corporation's approach to cultural regeneration, with the organisation appearing to oscillate between viewing it as a low-value area, of use in the displacement of tenants and pigeons, to acknowledging it as a riverside location with the potential to evolve as a 'little Venice' on Tyneside. Moreover the experience of the Bruvvers reveals the impact of a growing political preoccupation with large flagship institutions upon smaller, grassroots cultural developments. As Mould reflects: 'There aren't very many survivors. I mean Live Theatre is hardly popular art any more, they have a beautiful palace on the Quayside'.[75]

The discussion of cultural regeneration since the 1980s has revealed a number of overlapping and competing influences. Changes in urban governance during the 1980s re-focused regional and national attention on the industrial riverscapes but the development corporations were not particularly interested in cultural regeneration as a concept relating to economic and social renewal through the arts. Rather these agencies were principally oriented towards the US retail, especially the festival shopping-led model of urban regeneration. Evidence of these influences is obvious: festival shopping malls have often been a pivotal component of the rebranding of river or ocean fronted sites in many of the region's conurbations. Although the development corporations appeared to engage with the 'percentage for art' initiative during the 1990s, evidence for a thoroughgoing engagement with the arts was negligible. Equally, the refurbishment of these areas, and particularly the use of 'playful' postmodernist architecture and design, has often come to symbolise the successful cultural renaissance of such areas. But development of the now highly marketable Ouseburn cultural quarter was in some respects curtailed by the development agency's preoccupation with accruing increased property values.

Many aspects of the region's industrial inheritance, such as poor-quality social housing and blighted areas away from central waterfronts, did not feature in the corporation strategy. 'Heritage', however, could be harnessed in a playful postmodernist style to add 'colour' to some key, highly profitable developments. Moreover, in many respects the development corporations were agents of both economic and cultural continuity. For all the rhetoric of new enterprise their economic legacy is less than convincing and the financial difficulties they experienced may also have reinforced the external perception of the region as over reliant upon the nation's purse. This era also sustained the agenda of 'improvement', shared across regional economic and arts boards from the 1960s, which emphasised the importance of nourishing and stimulating middle-class consumption and lifestyle. Nevertheless, major change did arrive in the 1990s. The Gateshead Garden Festival, with its notable emphasis upon public art as a tool for redefining a blighted landscape, was more than a straw in the wind. Lottery and Millennium funding for art and cultural projects of a scale previously unimaginable prompted commentators to increasingly use the term 'culture-led regeneration'. Ironically the major beneficiary and highly successful player in this new funding landscape was the town of Gateshead, long the region's poor relation and the only large urban area to escape the clutches of the development corporations.

Notes

1 www.artscouncil.org.uk/regions/press_detail.php?id=349&rid=1 (accessed 16.6.09).

2 During the 1990s a series of studies emerged advocating the mutually beneficial relationship between private and public agencies, galleries, festivals and events in stimulating the recovery of stagnant urban economies, notably: F. Bianchini and C. Landry, *The creative city* (London: Demos Papers, 1995) and Bianchini and Parkinson, *Cultural policy and urban regeneration*. In its turn this literature has given rise to critical appraisals of the 'cultural sector', including Casey, Dunlop and Selwood's *Culture as commodity?*, which criticises the economic benefits of the cultural sector. Others, notably D. Massey, *For space* (London: Sage, 2005), as well as P. Chatterton and R. Hollands, *Urban nightscapes: youth cultures, pleasure spaces and corporate power* (London: Routledge, 2003), refer to the exclusion of the local population from such strategies, particularly with reference to former industrial conurbations such as Manchester and Newcastle. E. Belfiore and O. Bennett, *The social impact of the arts: an intellectual history* (Basingstoke: Palgrave Macmillan, 2008), have focused upon the intellectual roots of cultural policy. Recently J. Vickery, 'The emergence of culture-led regeneration: a policy concept and its discontents', *Centre for Cultural Policy Studies, Research Paper* 9 (2007) suggested that the 'cultural' dimension within urban regeneration emerged during the 1990s and was most visible in urban design and public art. He has further pointed out that this was taken to a new level under New Labour, and that the emergence of culture-led regeneration promoted a view of culture, under the stewardship of Chris Smith, that was 'unquestioningly positive' and capable of creating 'unproblematic modes of engagement with leisure, training, job creation and industry' (p. 57). www2.warwick.ac.uk/fac/arts/theatre_s/cp/publications/centrepubs/ccps.paper9.pdf (accessed 24.6.10). As has been shown, the Arts Council also appeared willing to subscribe to this highly instrumental view of culture as a driver of social *and* economic improvement.

3 D. Dougan, *Northern Arts: the people of the north* (Newcastle: Northern Arts, 1974).

4 M. Sighart, 'Grim up North? It's an urban myth from Leeds to Glasgow', *The Times* (26 May 2005); R. Christiansen, 'Birthplace of a cultural revolution', *Daily Telegraph* (2 January 2006); S. Steward, 'YES … IT'S NEWCASTLE!: from coal hole to city of palaces', *Daily Telegraph* (10 May 2003).

5 I. Banks, 'Art on the front line: a cultural revolution in Sunderland', *Art and Architecture Journal*, 64 (2005–6), p. 20.

6 S. Miles, '"Our Tyne": iconic regeneration and the revitalisation of identity in NewcastleGateshead', *Urban Studies*, 42: 5–6 (2005), pp. 913–926; T. Leunig and J. Swaffield, *Cities unlimited: making urban regeneration work* (London: Policy Exchange, 2008).

7 Office of the Deputy Prime Minister: Housing, Planning, Local Government and The Regions – Written Evidence. Memorandum by Councillor Chris Foote-Wood, Vice Chair, North East Assembly (RG 21), 6 March 2006.

8 Bianchini and Parkinson, *Cultural policy*, p. 2.

9 Department of Economic Affairs, Northern Economic Planning Council, *The challenge of the changing north: a preliminary study* (London: HMSO, 1966) part 1 paragraphs 167–175.

10 Members of the Northern Economic Planning Council included T. Dan Smith in his capacity as chairman, the director of the North East Development Council, the mayor of Middlesbrough, labour movement representatives such as D. F. Edwards, the area secretary of the Electrical Trades Union, the district secretary of the Confederation of Shipbuilding and Engineering Unions, and representatives from the region's principal industrial employers such as the managing director of Hawthorn Leslie as well as regional elites and landowners including the Earl of Lonsdale, but few company owners from either Wearside or Teesside were represented. Northern Economic Planning Council, *The challenge of the changing north*.

11 Ibid.

12 Northern Arts Annual Report, 1967/8, p. 5.

13 R. Brandes Gratz, 'Cities reborn, new world lessons', *Guardian* (30 October 2002).

14 C. Knevitt, 'The Phoenix is ready to rise', *The Times* (23 April 1987). The architecture correspondent reported that the public private partnerships in cities including Newcastle, Manchester, Sheffield and London Docklands had a remit to 'repeat the successful American formula of urban regeneration which revived places such as Baltimore and Boston'.

15 P. Davenport, 'Selling the future down the river', *The Times* (3 August 1987).

16 Bianchini and Parkinson, *Cultural policy*, p. 2.

17 TWAS, TW00IX, Box 7202, Letter from Gordon Ramsay, Director of Finance and Business Development, to John Owen, Esq., Department of Environment, 10 April 1991.

18 J. Beach, 'Introduction', in P. Usherwood, J. Beach and C. Morris (eds), *Public sculpture of north east England* (Liverpool: Liverpool University Press), p. xxii.

19 www.englishpartnerships.co.uk/udcs.htm (accessed 8.5.09).

20 J. Meades, 'The curse of Bilbao', *Independent on Sunday* (29 April 2007).

21 P. Davenport, 'Heseltine accuses Labour of creating sink estate – Meadowell Estate, North Shields', *The Times* (14 November 1991).

22 F. Robinson, M. Lawrence and K. Shaw, *More than bricks and mortar? Tyne & Wear and Teesside development corporations: a mid-term report*, Department of Sociology and Social Policy, University of Durham (1993), p. 25.

23 TWAS, TW00IX Box 7202, Memorandum from the Financial Controller to Director of Marketing, 19 March 1991, subject, Corporate Plan.

24 F. Robinson, *Post-industrial Tyneside* (Newcastle upon Tyne: City Libraries and Arts, 1988), p. 207.

25 K. Shaw, 'The politics of private public partnerships in Tyne and Wear', *Northern Economic Review*, 19 (1990), p. 3. This could also be viewed as a form of regionalism which Aronsson has referred to as 'cultural mapping in a national framework'. Aronsson, 'The old cultural regionalism', p. 254.

26 Shaw, 'The politics of private public partnerships', p. 3.

27 Davenport, 'Selling the future down the river'.

28 S. Cameron and J. Doling, 'Housing neighbourhoods and urban regeneration', *Urban Studies*, 31: 7 (1994), pp. 1211–1223.

29 TWAS, TW00IX Box 7202, TWDC Corporate Plan, 1991, p. 11.

30 D. Byrne, 'What sort of future?', in Colls and Lancaster, *Geordies*, p. 46.

31 TWAS, TW00IX Box 7202, TWDC notes on meeting with DoE, 15 January 1991.

32 *The operation and wind up of Teesside Development Corporation*, Report by the Controller and Auditor General HC 640 Session 2001–2002: 27 February 2002, p. 1.

33 TWAS, TW00IX Box 7202, Gordon Ramsay's notes on meeting with the DoE, 15 January 1991.

34 Teesside Urban Development Corporation, *Tees-side: initiative, talent and ability* (Middlesbrough: Teesside UDC, 1989).

35 G. Milne, *North East England 1850–1914: the dynamics of a maritime-industrial region* (Woodbridge: Boydell, 2006), argues that the north east's industrial rivers have been on the 'town boosters' agenda since the 1960s, when it was believed that community cohesion was dependent upon sustaining the rivers as a unifying force. The idea of reorienting the focus of Tyneside to the Tyne was also closely connected to the T. Dan Smith era of regionalist politics and built upon his understanding of a modern functional city-region. Milne notes that in contrast to the strategy of the 1960s, the boosterist agenda of the late twentieth century was primarily anchored in the rivers as a 'visual rather than transport amenity', p. 207.

36 'Renaissance in the north', *Independent II* (27 July 1994).

37 Robinson, Lawrence and Shaw, *More than bricks and mortar?*, p. 25.

38 D. Dodd, 'Barcelona: the making of a cultural city', in M. Miles, T. Hall and I. Borden (eds), *The city cultures reader* (London: Routledge, 2000), pp. 177–183.

39 H. L. Wolman, C. Cook Ford III and E. Hill, 'Evaluating the success of urban success stories', *Urban Studies*, 31: 6 (1994), pp. 835–850.

40 D. Judd and S. Feinstein (eds), *The tourist city* (New Haven: Yale University Press, 1993), p. 161.

41 The most critical account of Rouse is N. Dagen Bloom, *Merchant of illusion: James Rouse: America's salesman of the businessman's utopia. Urban life and urban landscape* (Columbus, OH: Ohio State University Press, 2004).

42 *Gateshead Post* (7 September 1989); *Gateshead Post* (8 February 1990).

43 For a sympathetic study of Rouse and his theories see J. Olson, *Better places, better lives: a biography of James Rouse* (Washington: The Urban Land Institute, 2003).

44 M. Adlard, 'Obituary: Reg Smythe', *Northern Review*, 7 (1998), p. 79.

45 North East Development Council, Annual Report, 1967/8.

46 Tyne and Wear Development Corporation, Corporate Plan, 1991, p. 41.

47 Davenport, 'Selling the future down the river'.

48 Ibid.

49 *Newcastle Quayside Developments PLC Brochure* (Newcastle: Newcastle Quayside Developments PLC, 1990).

50 Usherwood, Beach and Morris, *Public sculpture*, p. 105.

51 T. Farrell, *Place: a story of modelmaking menageries and paper rounds* (London: Laurence King Publishers Ltd., 2004), p. 279.

52 Beach, 'Introduction', p. xxii.

53 P. Usherwood, 'Art on the margins', in Colls and Lancaster, *Newcastle*, p. 262.

54 Beach, Morris and Usherwood, *Public sculpture*, p. 109.

55 TWAS, TW00IX Box 7202, Tyne and Wear Development Corporation Draft Corporate Plan 1991–1995, 3 January 1991. The plan included no formal discussion of arts sponsorship.

56 *BALTIC: the factory* (Gateshead: BALTIC, 2002), p. 148.

57 *Independent II* (27 July 1994).

58 *BALTIC*, p. 124.

59 M. Miles, *Art space and the city: public art and urban futures* (London: Routledge, 1997), p. 76.

60 Recorded interview with Peter Stark, 18 June 2009.

61 Newcastle upon Tyne Planning Division Development Department, *Ouseburn heritage*, n/d [1989], p. 2.

62 Charleton, *Newcastle Town* (1885) cited in *Ouseburn heritage*, p. 14.

63 *Ouseburn heritage*, p. 2

64 D. Whetstone, *NewcastleGateshead: the making of a cultural capital* (Newcastle: ncj Media, 2009), p. 57.

65 Recorded interview with Michael Mould, 15 June 2009.

66 Ibid. Emphasis added.

67 Ibid.

68 Rubinstein and Mould were regulars at the Free Trade pub and also knew each other through Northern Arts, where Rubinstein was director in 1999.

69 Draft Ouseburn SRB3 forward strategy, www.newcastle.gov.uk/cab2001.nsf/ allbykey/BBEA73B0D676BA6080256B660038F799/$FILE/RR3.03%20app2.doc., p. 1 (accessed 24.6.10).

70 Recorded interview with Michael Mould, 15 June 2009.

71 Ibid.

72 Ibid.

73 Ibid. Emphasis added.

74 Ibid.

75 Ibid.

7

Coda: Gateshead

Gateshead has long been overshadowed by its neighbour Newcastle on the opposite banks of the Tyne. In the sixteenth century much of the south bank of the river was owned by the Corporation of Newcastle and almost incorporated into its jurisdiction. The north bank boasted fine merchant buildings, the Guildhall and two Georgian churches. Moreover, the Quayside was a social epicentre that attracted revellers from the surrounding coalfield.[1] The Gateshead side of the river became the largest area for chemical production in Britain during the nineteenth century and was one of the most blighted urban landscapes in the country.[2] From Dr Johnson's 'Dirty lane leading to Newcastle' to Priestley's assertion that 'Gateshead had been designed by an enemy of the human race' the town had suffered from a bad press, and had long functioned as a poor, working-class, industrial suburb of Newcastle. Its housing and health conditions were amongst the worst in Britain from the early nineteenth century onwards. With few wealthy patrons and a diminutive middle class, Gateshead entered the twentieth century ill prepared for the coming economic decline. The arrival of a Labour council in the inter-war years gave a hint that the town was not without hope. The ambitions of the council's public housing programme of the 1930s provoked an angry response from central government which resulted in the suspension of the house building programme.[3] What amenities Gateshead possessed were well tended; Saltwell Park, recently awarded the title of Best Park in Britain, is testimony to more than a century of nurturing the town's major communal asset and the Beacon Lough estate is one of inter-war Britain's finest municipal housing developments. Key social indicators, however, demonstrate that Gateshead experienced more than its share of the region's economic decline.[4]

Gateshead has recently been distinguished amongst British towns as an indisputable case of 'culture-led' regeneration.[5] This is remarkable given its centuries-long experience of backwardness relative to its northern neighbour. Baltic and Millennium Bridge opened in 2004 and are the flagships of the region's culture-led regeneration project. The Gateshead Quays also boasts a Norman Foster-designed international music centre, the Sage, and the most recent addition to this portfolio is the Hilton Hotel, dramatically positioned on the steep riverside bank close to Sage and the Tyne Bridge. Other regional developments in public art were dwarfed by Gateshead's initiatives, both in terms of physical scale and wider impact, following the erection of Gormley's *Angel of the North*, now Britain's most recognisable work of public art, next to the A1 in 1998.

The Hilton Hotel is perhaps most suggestive of Gateshead's peculiarity in the regional context. The site formerly occupied by the Richard Harris sculpture *Bottle Bank* has often been seen as emblematic of Gateshead's cultural regeneration strategy. The positioning of an international hotel on a former industrial site that was cleared to facilitate a public art project has led some to argue that this is clear and unequivocal vindication of the 'culture as economic driver' argument, as well as endorsement of the broader efficacy of culture-led regeneration: 'Richard Harris's 200ft. long sculpture featuring a series of arches above a walkway at Bottle Bank was completed in 1986. Some 20 years later it made way for the NewcastleGateshead Hilton whose presence on the site would have seemed unbelievable a quarter of a century ago'.[6]

This is also a reversal of developments on the Newcastle Quayside, where initiatives in public art were largely additions to, or adornment for, the construction of new residential and commercial developments. But for others Gateshead's developments represent something more intangible than the efficacy of culture-led regeneration. They are also anchored in a '*rooted* local identity': 'and therefore represent something far more significant than the inevitable end product of cultural commodification'.[7] The notion of cultural regeneration as connected to local identity invites us to consider the wider issue of the cultural region. Why and how did this development acknowledge a local identity with roots to the past and what has been the significance of the developments spearheaded on the southern banks of the Tyne for the wider notion of the north east as a culturally cohesive unit?

In view of the complex and haphazard nature of cultural regeneration elsewhere in the region we need to ask how far Gateshead's distinctive approach was the product or culmination of a self-conscious strategy. Many developments were initiated prior to the late 1980s. Gateshead was the only authority within the Tyne and Wear area to remain outside the development corporation remit, and as a borough, to retain control over, and responsibility for, all planning for the riverside areas. Thus the narrative of its regeneration cannot be tied as explicitly to the radical overhaul of local government associated with the urban development corporations.[8] Moreover the point of departure for Gateshead's cultural regeneration strategy has often been linked to sport, and particularly athletics, rather than arts policy. Opened in 1955, Gateshead stadium attracted international attention in 1974 when Brendan Foster, the distance runner and founder of the Great North Run, broke the 3000m record on the stadium's newly laid tartan synthetic running track. At the time Foster was also Gateshead Council's sport and recreation manager and whilst the connection between sport and arts policy might seem tenuous, this has been seen as a crucial starting point for Gateshead Council's regeneration narrative. David Whetstone, arts and culture editor of the Newcastle *Journal,* recalls that Foster had made public his ambition to break the record prior to the event, which memorably drew a crowd of 10,000 people. This moment of sporting history raised the area's profile nationally and internationally, helping to convince local politicians that Gateshead should no longer languish as a cultural backwater of Newcastle. In this respect a strategy of using big events to attract publicity and boost the image of the area can be traced to the success of athletics during the 1970s.

The next flagship in Gateshead's regeneration was the development of the MetroCentre retail facility. Located on land designated as one of the country's early enterprise zones in 1981, the first part of the 'mall' officially opened in 1986. The MetroCentre was politically significant also: 'coming after the national miner's strike, Prime Minister Margaret Thatcher was happy to point out in 1987 that 4,500 jobs had been created'.[9] This was followed in quick succession by Gateshead's successful application to host the Garden Festival in 1990.[10] Drawing upon the lead taken by Glasgow and Liverpool, the success was viewed as a major coup for the town. It secured £37 million worth of investment (£33 million from the Department of Environment) and enabled the environmental improvement of toxic former iron, coke and railway workings located on the riverside into a site that famously incorporated a Japanese Garden sponsored by KOMATSU. The significance of the festival should not be downplayed; at least as far as the regeneration narrative is concerned, 'it was the road that proceeded towards the *Angel of the North* which benefitted from the lottery money and thereafter to the Baltic'.[11] Interestingly the emphasis assigned to sport is shared by others working with arts policy in Gateshead, including Anna Pepperall, arts officer to Gateshead Council since 1985. She recalls that public art as urban renewal grew from the success of Gateshead stadium and the expertise in sport as well as the growing reputation of athletics influenced by sporting personalities such as Brendan Foster and Steve Cram. The development of the Metro Centre followed by the successful bid for the Garden Festival in 1990 can be seen as indicators of a policy mindset amongst councillors that sought to realise grand ambition. This tenacious local political culture is not without historical precedent in Gateshead.

Whilst terms such as 'regeneration' were used in conjunction with projects that evolved after the Garden Festival, it is important to note that the pre-history of public art initiatives emerged during the 1970s. In 1986 Gateshead Council launched the Riverside Sculpture Park on the derelict stretch of land west of the Tyne Bridge. The park supported work by a range of internationally recognised artists and sculptors including Richard Harris, Andy Goldsworthy and Colin Rose. Richard Harris's project had initially been offered to Newcastle City

Council, where it was rejected.[12] Therefore the Gateshead initiatives often reflected a broader pattern where its distinctive approach to cultural regeneration evolved because the local authority was responsive to ideas that had been rebuffed elsewhere in the region.

However, the 'journey towards the Angel' also evolved as a strategy to tackle the problem of industrial contamination. The scheme to environmentally improve land contaminated by former iron and chemical workings had been started by Gateshead's planning department during the 1970s. Initially conceived as a strategy to 'green' the former slum areas, by the 1980s the ambition to use the area as a site for 'art in public places' had begun to take shape. The impetus for this approach came initially from the planning department but also from personnel within libraries and the arts. In 1984 Ros Rigby was appointed as arts officer in Gateshead, the first arts officer to be appointed by a local authority in the north east. This formed the basis for a partnership with Northern Arts, whose visual arts officer Peter Davies played an important role in the development of Gateshead's arts policy. Davies was already acknowledged for his 'art in public places' initiatives in Grizedale Forest, Cumbria. In 1977 Northern Arts supported the Grizedale Forest project which allowed 'a number of emerging sculptors to work in a challenging "non-art" environment'. According to Beach this approach was continued in the north east as a response to a gallery culture that was not especially receptive to contemporary art. These initiatives were therefore also intended to create an audience for contemporary art.[13] In Gateshead, Patrick Conway, chief librarian in the 1980s, was especially receptive to these developments and, echoing Peter Davies, began to speak of the possibilities for an 'urban Grizedale' in the town. Representatives from Gateshead Council's Libraries, Arts and Shipley Art Gallery Committee were also enthusiastic about the idea of 'Art Outside the Gallery', principally because the town had no suitable gallery venues for such works. Coupled with the initiatives of planning officers determined to widen the remit for environmental improvement, this collaboration provided the platform for Gateshead's development of the riverside sculpture park.[14]

It is difficult to say how far such embryonic initiatives can be interpreted as conscious attempts to engender the indisputable culture-led regeneration for which Gateshead became renowned. Pepperall suggests that the terms 'urban renewal' and 'environmental improvement' were the 'buzz words' during the 1980s and that a shift towards the regeneration agenda occurred after the Garden Festival in 1990. The early public art initiatives are viewed as discrete, local projects, influenced neither by national or international agendas. After all, public art was anything but a 'vote winner' in an area with high unemployment and widespread poverty and Pepperall acknowledges that 'the last thing people actually wanted or needed was items of public art'.[15] Thus the contrast with the development corporation's sponsorship and commissioning of public art is pronounced. In Gateshead this strategy predated both the commercial and residential regeneration of Gateshead Quays; the MetroCentre, Gateshead's explicit response to the central government regeneration agenda, was planned and built with no acknowledgement of the 'percent for art' agenda and with no obvious adornment or engagement with public art.

Whilst Gateshead Council avoided involvement with the development corporations, it nevertheless sustained a cordial relationship with Northern Arts and perhaps this goes some way to explaining the town's distinctive approach to cultural regeneration. The council had established an 'Art in Public Places Committee' during the 1980s to realise a formal process for the structure of public arts and this resulted in the invitation of Northern Arts officers to present ideas to the council. Whilst many on the council found their approach rather too patrician and remained opposed to importing ideas from Northern Arts, the sculptures known as 'the big five' (Richard Harris's *Bottle Bank*, Richard Cole's *Windy Nook*, Andy Goldsworthy's *Cone*, Richard Deacon's *Once Upon a Time* and Mike Winstone's *Sport's Day*) reflected Northern Arts' input. For Pepperall the sentiment within Northern Arts was that 'Gateshead *should* have these pieces of work'. With the exception of *Sport's Day*, which was installed in the town centre, these pieces all occupied riverside sites or areas of industrial reclamation. The extent of Northern Arts' input was nevertheless often tempered by the existence of a particularly independent ethos in local politics: 'Gateshead have always wanted to do things from the inside … [W]ith Art in the Riverside they appointed an external visual arts officer to run that programme and … have always been resistant to having people tell us what to do'.[16] This local political tenacity is widely celebrated and has been used as a counterpoint to the idea that the road from athletics in the 1970s to the *Angel* and Baltic by the millennium was the product of external cultural management. As Mick Henry, leader of Gateshead Council since 2002 and a councillor from 1986 reflects, 'Who was responsible for the Angel, the Sage and Baltic? The answer is nobody. It was organic. It came from officers and members talking and working together'.[17]

Erected in 1998, Gormley's *Angel* has since become one the country's most recognisable pieces of public art. Building on the 'art in public places' initiatives of the 1980s, Gateshead's councillor Sid Henderson had identified the site at Eighton Lodge, above the former pit head baths of the old Teams Colliery, as the location for a 'landmark sculpture' in 1990. The following year Northern Arts made a commitment to funding the research and initial costs of the work. The wider funding arrangements reinforce Gateshead councillors' assertion that after the Garden Festival they became 'expert at the bidding game': the *Angel* was paid for by the Arts Council Lottery Fund, European Regional Development Fund, Northern Arts and local business sponsorship.[18] Unsurprisingly the 'landmark sculpture' has been used as further evidence of the efficacy of culture-led regeneration, with some suggesting that it paved the way for the successful bids to regenerate Gateshead Quays and that the 6,000 jobs created and £1 billion invested 'would have taken longer to generate – and might not have come at all' without the *Angel*.[19] Running counter to this is the view that such investment did not check a downward spiral in the wider social and economic development of Gateshead:

> The consequences of all this activity have been mixed. Between the 1991 census and the 2001 census, Gateshead's population fell by more than 5%. The proportion of its residents without work or qualifications or access to a car has remained stubbornly high by national standards. Away from the quayside, the town looks little different – spread out, slightly under-populated, well-kept but a little worn.[20]

The town boosters' exuberance surrounding the launch of the *Angel* has also prompted academic appraisal. For instance, Usherwood has written that the adoption of the northern prefix reflected the local (especially broadcast) response to the sculpture as a monument to post-industrialism:

> Some, including many of the press present at the inauguration, have wanted to see the Angel as a comment on the demise of mining and shipbuilding industries which were once so essential to Tyneside's economy; to see it as a kind of phoenix rising from the ashes of the area's post-war industrial decline. However, this again must be regarded as problematic … since it was Hartlepool rather than Tyneside where the sculpture was fabricated, and all traces of the old Teams Colliery on which the Angel stands were systematically obliterated before the sculpture's erection.[21]

His reservation over the *Angel* as a 'witness to place' rests upon his understanding of the piece as sculpture. The *Angel* was not conceived as a 'monument' and its capacity to stimulate or consolidate a regional or local identity should be extrapolated from its location or broader significance to the area's past: it is now correctly celebrated as an 'almost anonymous part of the landscape'.[22]

Local arts officers have contested this view, stating that the piece was indisputably site-specific and drew upon Gormley's response to the area's past: 'yes Gateshead [council] had located that site, and it was the former colliery, the pit head baths, but Gormley absolutely loved that idea of the sculpture being located above the ground where men had worked below it'.[23] Like Anthony Caro, who had also been invited to submit a proposal for the site, Gormley appreciated the resonance of the site's industrial past as well as recognising the prominence of the location. The vision's audacity was reflected in the escalating discussion and also in the wider response to the project as a challenge to the hierarchy of Tyneside's cultural landmarks. As Pepperall reflects, 'at the time somebody said "it could become as famous as the Tyne bridge" and I saw that as an extremely inflammatory thing to say at the time … when it was really difficult and tense'.[24]

The strong local, academic and media response to the audacity and scale of the
Angel has prompted some to see a formative chain beginning at Eighton Bank
and ending at Gateshead Quays. But in some respects, the evolution of Gateshead
Quays was a much more prosaic development than the grand narrative from
the *Angel* would lead us to believe.

The Baltic Flour Mills had long been recognised for its imposing architectural significance. In 1959 the Port of Tyne Authority described it as a notable
feature of the riverside scene, which it dominated thanks to the distinctive
character of its architecture and impressive size. Spillers Mill on the Newcastle
Quayside was similarly acknowledged for its striking presence.[25] During the
1950s the Baltic Flour Mills employed approximately 350 men and women; it
closed in 1973 with a loss of nearly 200 jobs when part of the complex was
demolished.[26] By 1989, the core building, used in the intervening years as an
EEC grain store, provided the platform for Gateshead Council's plan for a
multi-million-pound redevelopment scheme and the following year a £20
million proposal incorporating office blocks, luxury flats and retailing had
been passed by Gateshead planning department.[27] Despite the proximity to
the riverside public sculpture trail, the initial plans for the redevelopment,
which originated with a London-based development company, did not include
public art or wider engagement with the urban art programme a few hundred
yards upstream.

These initial plans fell through following the collapse of the development
company in the midst of the early 1990s financial crisis and although local politicians were later to claim responsibility for the idea to convert the building as
an art space, it is difficult to ascertain exactly where or whom the first impulse
came from. In 1991 Northern Arts had published a consultation document which
detailed its ambition to achieve new facilities for visual arts and music on Tyneside.
There followed a widely documented conversation between Peter Stark and Bill
McNaught of Gateshead Council in which Stark memorably said, ' "Central
Tyneside" is not codeword for Newcastle … If Gateshead, out of everything
that it's done in the visual arts could find a building for the contemporary visual
art centre nothing would give me more pleasure'. McNaught would later
publicly acknowledge Northern Arts' initiative in recognising the potential of
Baltic with the qualification that 'the idea of converting the building was
conceived by Gateshead Council'.[28] There has been less noticeable discussion
of the apparent switch from an earlier plan for a property and commercial led
development to one that could be connected to the growing cultural regeneration
project that followed the success of the *Angel.* Rather in the momentum that
gathered with the approach of Year of the Visual Arts in 1996, local politicians
in Gateshead were increasingly making a link between the town's initiatives and
the potential of culture-led regeneration. According to Councillor Sid Henderson,
mayor of Gateshead, 'It is widely recognised that the arts play a major role, not

only in terms of quality of life but also economic development. Gateshead's policy of promoting visual arts and the establishment of a facility such as Baltic clearly underline this view'.[29] The collaboration between Northern Arts and Gateshead Council resulted in a successful bid to the Arts Council of Great Britain which awarded the project £33.4 million from the National Lottery for the conversion of the former flour mills into an art space. The project was awarded a further £1.5 million per year in revenue funding for the first five years. Baltic opened its doors to the public in 2002 with a range of displays intended to reflect its operational concept as an 'Art Factory'.[30]

The gathering momentum of Gateshead's riverside regeneration threw into sharp relief developments on the northern side of the river. Andrew Dixon, regional executive director of Northern Arts, suggested that the defining moment in realising the Baltic site was Northern Arts' decision to pursue the 'bird in the bush' rather than the 'bird in the hand' of the Co-operative building on Newcastle Quayside.[31] The lukewarm response of the regional capital to the cultural regeneration agenda has been widely acknowledged. In 1997 one national newspaper exploited the prominence of longstanding urban rivalries, noting that 'long in the shadow of its northern neighbour' with its plans for the visual arts, Gateshead would soon be in a position to demonstrate its 'innate superiority'. Peter Stark, by then special projects advisor to Gateshead Council, was reluctant to endorse inter-regional cultural rivalry: 'the South Bank is an easy cliché … this will be much more, with people living and working alongside each other in an urban village. It defines a new cultural confidence in the north east'.[32] Nevertheless, it needs to be acknowledged that his work for Gateshead, and the subsequent evolution of Baltic, Millennium Bridge and the Sage Music Centre, are the star attractions of culture-led regeneration in the north east. Sight must not be lost of the fact that so much ended up on the Gateshead side because of the difficult relationship between Northern Arts and the development corporation and their competing visions for the regeneration of industrial riverscapes.

After leaving his post as director of Northern Arts in 1990 Stark was enlisted by Jeremy Beecham, the leader of the then Labour Newcastle City Council, to develop a plan for the millennium project. Working with Tony Pender, who had established a regeneration consultancy with offices in Newcastle in 1985, Beecham put forward a proposal which involved development of the area now occupied by the Terry Farrell designed Centre for Life as well as the land adjacent to St James's Boulevard, incorporating a dance and visual arts space, planned to be connected to the newly revitalised 'historic' central Grainger Town area and Theatre Village. TWDC was strongly opposed to the plan and in the political upheaval that followed Beecham's retreat from the leadership of the council, Alistair Balls managed to secure support for his alternative vision of a millennium project with the International Centre for Life as the centrepiece:

and suddenly the site that was going to be the site for the music centre wasn't available for the music centre anymore, namely the site that is now the International Centre for Life … Tony and I were shafted in a meeting and then it was not going anywhere except I had this idea about what the millennium bid should be and the answer to me seemed so very blindingly obvious that it needed to *build bridges*.[33]

Stark took the building bridges idea to the North of England Councils Association (ANEC) and promoted a project to construct new crossings for 'all the rivers and becks of the region'. Couched as a fusion of arts and sciences, anchored in local heritage and promoting a forward-looking vision, the project received the backing of ANEC's chairman, John Bridge. Echoing his commitment to an arts policy that was responsive to the democratic base of the region and that shared cultural resources equitably, Stark's proposal audaciously demanded funding for thirty bridges, 'at least one for every local authority'. Unsurprisingly the Millennium Commission were more cautious. Nevertheless the commission agreed to the principle and suggested a modified project that would fund six bridges and one new 'landmark' crossing over the Tyne. Stark's previous experience with Northern Arts had taught him that convincing the regional authorities to share funding for a landmark project centred on Tyneside would be mired by regional rivalries and was about to discard the project when he received a phone call from Gateshead Council inviting him to contribute to the development of Baltic. He agreed with the proviso that he could bring with him the project proposal to build a new bridge across the Tyne. Under Stark's stewardship, a proposal to the Arts Council for both capital and revenue funding for Baltic was written in a manner that emphasised the pivotal need for the bridge and, in turn, the bid to the Millennium Commission to fund the bridge hinged upon the success of Baltic. Gateshead Council, drawing upon its growing reputation for successfully 'playing the bidding game', was an active participant in the 'ratchet game: we said to the Millennium Commission don't give us the money for the bridge unless you can persuade the Arts Council to give us money for Baltic and vice a versa'.[34]

The decision to locate the new music centre adjacent to Baltic on the Gateshead Quays was also a surprisingly haphazard development. In September 1996 at a Labour Party conference held in Newcastle, the Northern Labour Group voted against plans for an international music centre in Newcastle. In response to the apparent political stalemate, Peter Hewitt, the director of Northern Arts, instituted a region-wide tender for the site. Stark, working with Gateshead on the millennium project, had helped to identify the site adjacent to Baltic. Gateshead Council submitted a bid based upon what is often described as a 'world-class' location. They were awarded capital funding for the project from the Arts Council, European Regional Development Fund, Gateshead Council and the regional development agency OneNorth East. The Sir Norman Foster-designed 'landmark' music centre opened in December 2004. Although this development was historically fortuitous, Stark nevertheless credits Gateshead with a resolute commitment to the project that weathered considerable storms: 'It was Gateshead's rock steady hand' that secured the confidence of the Arts Council'.[35]

The opening of Baltic, Millenium Bridge and Sage understandably provided an opportunity for further journalistic superlatives on the regeneration of Tyneside, ranging from the wildly amusing, *'The Tyne, it is a changing'* to endorsement from the *Northern Echo* ('the jewel in the region's cultural crown') and the more caustic insiders' critique of the regeneration game, 'All fur coat and no-knickers'.[36] The architects of these projects nevertheless remain convinced of their efficacy and local resonance: 'Newcastle/Gateshead is now a confident driver for an experience based cultural region. That could all have just been left [after losing the Capital of Culture bid to] Liverpool like to kind of fade away but … there is a genuine short break destination here and it was always there but it had to have central Tyneside as a believable base'.[37]

Baltic was also quickly endorsed in the literature advocating cultural regeneration of former industrial sites and it has been suggested that along with comparable projects in Malmö and Dresden, it provides a successful example of an industrial heritage deployed to promote a new identity based on art and culture.[38] Equally it has been read as part of an international tendency to redefine industrial sites by converting them into art 'spaces'.[39] The criteria for success and the evidence that Baltic, and the underpinning Art Factory concept, have deployed a local industrial heritage are nevertheless unclear. In the years following its launch under the charismatic leadership of Sune Nordgren, Baltic has not been without critics, particularly once the details of its costly commissioning policy came to light. After all, the project had initially been well endowed by comparable flagship project standards. In addition to receiving £46 million capital funding from Lottery and private sources, unusually, it also received revenue funding for the first five years. The growing sense that Baltic was unsympathetic to local heritage, and that its curators had little interest in forging connections between the institution and its local environment, was exacerbated by publicity surrounding the Swedish director's revelation of his daughter's unfavourable reaction to the area (she had reputedly 'likened Tyneside to Beirut') in his introductory lecture.[40] Others have noted that despite Baltic's position as a centrepiece of Gateshead's commitment to cultural regeneration, the Art Factory was clearly uncomfortable about its relationship to this narrative and often commissioned art that was highly critical of the wider regeneration of the area.[41] Among other critical voices, Brian Sewell argued in the London *Evening Standard* that the COBRA exhibition was 'too sophisticated' for a Tyneside audience. The cost and direction of Baltic's commissioning policy also produced consternation amongst Gateshead councillors who had an otherwise demonstrable enthusiasm for contemporary art dating back two decades.[42]

Whilst it is clearly too soon for historical evaluation of these developments, they nevertheless resonate with many of the themes that have been central throughout this discussion. Arguably one of the most important factors in the construction of the new music centre was the need to provide a home for Northern Sinfonia. This reinforces the historical context for these developments. The north east's connection to, and innovative intervention in, national cultural policy after the Second World War was mobilised to support the creation of a regional symphony orchestra. At the end of the millennium the region's 'jewel in the cultural crown', situated in what has been termed 'United Nations land' adjacent to the Tyne, was a music centre to house the orchestra that had initiated regional cultural policy in the north east. The red threat of cultural improvism is very strong: Stark is clear that a cultural policy ethos of bidding for *grands projets* was mobilised in the north east because of a deficit of large cultural institutions, a deficit which had mobilised the creation of Northern Arts decades earlier. But the road to the Sage has not been straightforward. The venue planned as an Arts Council-funded regional music centre was originally destined for Newcastle. The first plan for Gateshead Quays was for festival shopping and office blocks. Had it not been for the collapse of this proposed development in the early 1990s, could Gateshead Quays have been just another of the region's, now struggling, 'US-style' outlet malls?

And what of 'local identity'? The evidence that the culture-led regeneration pursued by Gateshead was assisted by a long tradition of local political imperviousness to external pressures is strong. But beyond that the anchoring of this process in a wider sense of place rooted in the past is rather tenuous. Indeed in some respects the process could be viewed as contributing to a growing fragmentation and alienation of the local population as reflected in the near collapse of the nearby town centre as a coherent urban space, as well as the evidence that alongside increases in participation in 'the arts' there has been little evidence of wider economic regeneration.[43] Equally, how does the vernacular region that was promoted as different and distinct by impresarios ranging from Tyne Tees' Black Brothers to Scott Dobson and Bunting correspond to the new urban landscape promoted by the cultural regeneration project?

Certain aspects of cultural regionalism may have been strengthened by de-industrialisation. Scott Dobson's 'Geordieland' continued into the 1970s, giving rise to the BBC television show *Geordierama* in 1974. Six years later the beleaguered north east was reflected in *Auf Wiedersehen Pet* and whilst the visual landscape was provided by a German construction site, Clement and La Frenais' use of dialect was more tenacious than any of the earlier 'Geordie' incarnations that had enjoyed a national audience. Vernacular popular culture and especially music and broadcasting have also flourished since the 1980s. The north east became a site for popular broadcasting beyond the region during the early 1980s, thanks in part to the input of the charismatic and widely acknowledged creative talent of Andrea Wonfor, the creator of the cult Channel 4 programme *The Tube*, broadcast from Tyne Tees studios in Newcastle between 1982 and 1987. The Sunderland-born musician Dave Stewart recalled playing a session at *The Tube* in 1983 at a time when Tyneside was at the cutting edge of music television: 'I remember we did a *Tube* session and there was us and Tina Turner and a load of people on the show and we were going, "oh wow-there's Tina Turner"'.[44]

Wonfor's contribution to the survival of the broadcasting region during the 1980s is widely acknowledged, particularly for the children's BBC production *Byker Grove*, allegedly based on her idea and characters she knew.[45] For a time under her stewardship it appeared that the vision of a broadcasting region meshing with regional culture, as envisaged by Briggs as early as 1975, was close to realisation. But the flourish was shortlived. *The Tube* suffered as much from its thorny relationship with the ITA as from the difficulty of enticing nationally recognised acts to the north. For example, Madonna's record company would not pay her travel expenses to Newcastle for her appearance early in her career.[46] Moreover the challenges of the culturally peripheral region also produced some unfortunate representations of vernacular popular culture, particularly in broadcasting. During the 1990s Wonfor commissioned a new series for Tyne Tees. *Quaysiders* showcased the newly revamped Newcastle Quayside and featured the lives of Newcastle United players and their 'WAGs'. Despite pioneering an idea that would later find lucrative success with the internationally popular *Footballers' Wives*, Wonfor's Newcastle series did not enjoy similar accolades. One commentator described it as 'hilariously poor, seeming to revolve around the lives of a couple of Toon footballers and some lasses who fancied them … it looked as though they were making it up as they went along. The network wasn't impressed'.[47] The failure of *Quaysiders* for many challenged the idea that cultural success would follow major infrastructural investment – in this case the dramatically transformed riverscape. Lancaster went so far as to argue that the decline of local television production capacity drained talent away from the region and made future 'built' broadcasting less likely to succeed.[48] In the long run the brief renaissance of popular broadcasting which was initiated by *The Tube* may have exacerbated the underlying sense of the region as disenfranchised from mainstream metropolitan culture. Melvin Bragg would memorably articulate the notion of the frustrated cultural region in 1997: 'if you don't live in or make it in London you are somehow second rate. This acts as a depressant and is expressed as irritation amongst those who stay'.[49]

Some stayed, if peripatetically and remotely. And perhaps there have also been glimpses of the old in the new. In 2005 the Sage Gateshead staged *The ballad of Jamie Allan*, a libretto by Tom Pickard celebrating the life of the eighteenth-century border gypsy 'piper, serial army enlister, deserter, horse thief, and jailbird'. In her review of the opera Murphy hailed the new institution for being appreciative of a past of 'tougher times'. The Sage has certainly quickly

Fig. 9 The Sage Music Centre, Gateshead

endeared itself to the regional community with its catholic approach to music and performance. The regional folk music scene has always been tenacious. Like folk music generally, a strong self-help ethos, a disdain for the inauthentic, which often meant the same as commercial, and the creation of a network of informal venues characterised the regional folk scene.[50] This rich tradition benefited from the arrival of Folkworks, a regional folk music agency established by Ros Rigby and Alistair Anderson in 1988. Their administrative skills combined with the wealth of regional talent have seen the emergence of arguably England's richest folk culture.[51] Appreciating its importance, Newcastle University established Britain's first performance-based folk music degree programme. Folkworks joined forces with Sage, becoming a partner of the new organisation and providing a regional home for northern folk music, including the establishment of an important archive. The role of history is central to contemporary music from Pickard's *Jamie Allen* to Katherine Tickell's celebration of Northumbrian pipes and the Unthank's exploration of the tough side of past industrial life.

The success of the Sage is widely acknowledged and arguably, unlike its next-door neighbour, it deserves 'factory' status. Can art and culture, however, fill the gap left behind by the disappearance of older forms of production? Can the 'experience economy' haul the region out of its longstanding position of relative backwardness? Cultural institutions, new waterfront architecture and a sense of being 'on the map' may serve to uplift the regional spirit but this is a qualitative assertion that is too intangible to quantify. It remains inescapable that recent decades have witnessed an attempt to draw to a close the physical and cultural legacy of industry. Nowhere was this more palpable than in the most dramatic physical transformation of the region's urban riversides to be realised since the arrival of the industrialised riverscapes during the eighteenth century. Throwing off the mantle of heavy industry, the architects of the regeneration process perceived the alternative potential of the rivers, as conduits of commerce, consumption, prosperity and innovation.

What part has this process played in the shifting notion of the cultural region? In 1989, one of the first 'post-industrial' assessments of the regeneration process reflected ruefully that 'fashionable nightlife and glitzy shopping' had replaced 'coal and ships' as the region's dominant descriptors. In the midst of deindustrialisation the 'production model', and the muscular tradition of work that it represented, continued to resonate in the academic and media response to regeneration. But during the 1990s the prevailing attitude shifted, helped in no small part by a new generation of arts managers, many with roots in the cultural left, who consolidated their vision for a cultural region allied to the 'consumption model'. What has changed is the role of art and culture in the broader regional agenda. When Blenkinsop and Fletcher strove to establish a regional cultural programme and organisational structure in the 1960s they shared the same ambition as their contemporaries in the regional development agency: the improvement of culture in England's most proletarian region to make the area more amenable to the middle classes. Culture was to be the handmaiden of industry, making the region an attractive destination for inward industrial investment. Today, for many, culture is the economy.

Notes

1 Lancaster, 'Sociability and the city' pp. 319–41.
2 W. A. Campbell, *The old chemical industry on Tyneside* (Newcastle: Newcastle University, 1964) offers the best overview of this major industry before its departure to Teesside in the early twentieth century.
3 B. Lancaster, 'Introduction', in B. Lancaster (ed.), *Working class housing on Tyneside* (Newcastle: Bewick Press, 1994), p. 3.
4 H. Mess, *Industrial Tyneside* (London: E. Benn Ltd., 1928).
5 Jonathan Vickery compares developments in Gateshead to those in Birmingham and Coventry, suggesting that in the Midlands culture has been allied to a broader framework for urban development, whilst Gateshead's culture-led regeneration has been focused more specifically upon the arts. Vickery, 'Culture-led regeneration', p. 22.

6 D. Whetstone, *NewcastleGateshead: the making of a cultural capital* (Newcastle: ncj Media, 2009), p. 13.

7 C. Bailey, S. Miles and P. Stark, 'Culture-led regeneration and the revitalisation of identities in Newcastle, Gateshead and the North East of England', *International Journal of Cultural Policy*, 10: 1 (2004), p. 63.

8 Gateshead Council rejected the invitation to join the development corporation and this was accepted by the government in part because they had already begun acquiring land on the riverside for development purposes; moreover the presence of the MetroCentre in the country's first designated enterprise zone persuaded Conservative ministers of Gateshead's proactive approach to regeneration.

9 Whetstone, *Newcastle/Gateshead*, p. 11.

10 K. Stansfield, 'Gateshead Garden Festival strategy', *The Planner* (1 June 1990), pp. 12–13.

11 Recorded interview with David Whetstone, 27 May 2009.

12 *BALTIC*, p. 122.

13 Beach, 'Introduction', in Usherwood, Beach and Morris (eds), *Public sculpture*, p. xxi.

14 Recorded interview with Anna Pepperall, 27 May 2009.

15 Ibid.

16 Art on the Riverside was set up in 1995 and managed through TWDC who, perhaps spurred by the earlier success of Gateshead's public art initiatives, presided over what was described as 'the largest programme of public art in the UK'. http://www.northtyneside.gov.uk/pls/portal/NTC_PSCM.PSCM_Web.download?p_ID=29046 (accessed 29.6.10)

17 Whetstone, *NewcastleGateshead*, p. 11.

18 Ibid., p. 26.

19 Ibid., p. 28.

20 Andy Becket, 'Can culture save us?', *Guardian* (2 June 2003).

21 Usherwood, Beach and Morris, *Public sculpture*, p. 59.

22 P. Usherwood, 'Wrestling with the Angel', *Northern Review*, 6 (1998), pp. 45–51.

23 Recorded interview with Anna Pepperall, 27 May 2009.

24 Ibid.

25 Gateshead Libraries, BALTIC press cuttings archive, *Port of Tyne Official Handbook* (1959).

26 *Gateshead Post* (28 April 1950).

27 *Gateshead Post* (7 September 1989); *Gateshead Post* (8 February 1990).

28 Ibid.

29 Gateshead Libraries, BALTIC press cuttings archive, 'Arts Council Chairman backs plans for major art development', Gateshead Metropolitan Borough Council, News Release, 28 March 1994.

30 *BALTIC*, p. 180.

31 Andrew Dixon cited in *BALTIC*, p. 138.

32 *Guardian* (28 June 1997).

33 Recorded interview with Peter Stark, 18 June 2009.

34 Ibid.

35 Ibid.

36 J. Glancey, 'The Tyne it is a changin'', *Guardian* (26 November 2004); G. Engelbrecht, 'The jewel in the region's cultural crown', *Northern Echo* (17 December 2004); P. Johnson, 'All fur coat and no knickers', *Independent on Sunday* (12 December 2005).

37 Recorded interview with Peter Stark, 18 June 2009.

38 R. Willim, 'Looking with new eyes at the old factory: on the rise of industrial cool', in T. O'Dell and P. Billing (eds), *Experiencescapes: tourism culture and economy* (Copenhagen: Copenhagen Business School Press, 2005), pp. 35–50.

39 R. Williams, 'Remembering and forgetting, the industrial gallery space', in M. Crinson (ed.), *Urban memory: history and amnesia in the modern city* (London: Routledge, 2005), pp. 121–44.

40 W. Varley, 'Baltic blunders', *New Statesman*, 134: 5 (2005), pp. 24–5.

41 W. Januszczak, 'Local girls make bad', *Sunday Times* (28 September 2003), pp. 8–9, suggested that the Wilson Twins' exhibition was a 'cynical response to the "regeneration" of Tyneside by local girls who knew the place and its people'. Gordon Burn on the other hand read the show as a call to reflect upon urban change: 'the viewer is invited to note the changes that have taken place … they are fascinated by the corporeal aspects of buildings: by what happens when the newness and cleanness becomes stained and defiled'. G. Burn, *Sex & violence, death and silence: encounters with recent art* (London: Faber and Faber, 2009), p. 462.

42 P. Usherwood, 'B. Opened', *Art Monthly*, 259 (2002), pp. 1–4.

43 Bailey, Miles and Stark provide evidence that the development of these flagships mirrors a growing engagement in the arts and suggest that commensurate levels of 'economic' regeneration, such as in employment, are not necessary to justify a strategy more concerned to engage 'with people who live in a city than it is about regenerating the city itself'. Bailey, Miles and Stark, 'Culture-led regeneration', p. 64.

44 C. Phipps, J. Tobler and S. Smith (eds), *North stars* (London: Zymurgy Publishing, 2005), p. 173.

45 Ibid. 'Andrea Wonfor, dynamic producer and executive who stamped her mark on British television', *Guardian* (11 September 2004). http://www.guardian.co.uk/media/2004/sep/14/guardianobituaries.broadcasting (accessed 28.8.09).

46 I am grateful to Chris Phipps, one of the *Tube*'s producers, for this information.

47 I am grateful to Marshall Hall for this insight.

48 Lancaster, 'As seen on TV', pp. 5–11.

49 M. Bragg, 'Faith of our fathers', *Northern Review*, 3 (1996), p. 82.

50 J. Murphy, 'The ballad of Jamie Allan', *Northern Review*, 15 (2005), p. 97.

51 For a full analysis of the north east folk scene see J. Murphy, 'Folk on Tyne: Tyneside culture and the second folk revival, 1950–75', PhD thesis (Northumbria University, 2007).

Select bibliography

Armstrong, K., 'Whither community arts?', *Northern Review*, 2 (1995).

Armstrong, K., 'Letting the flowers bloom', *Northern Review*, 7 (1998).

Aronsson, P., *Regionernas roll i Sveriges historia* (Fritzes: ERU report, 1995).

Ashton, O. and Hugman, J., 'Letters from America: George Julian Harney, Boston, U.S.A., and Newcastle upon Tyne, England, 1863–1888', *Transactions of the Massachusetts Historical Society*, 107 (1995).

Atkinson, F., *The man who made Beamish: an autobiography* (Gateshead: Northern Books, 1999).

Bailey, C., Miles, S. and Stark, P., 'Culture-led regeneration and the revitalisation of identities in Newcastle, Gateshead and the North East of England', *International Journal of Cultural Policy*, 10: 1 (2004).

BALTIC: the factory (Gateshead: BALTIC, 2002).

Banks, I., 'Art on the front line: a cultural revolution in Sunderland', *Art and Architecture Journal*, 64 (2005–6).

Belchem, J., *Merseypride: essays in Liverpool exceptionalism* (Liverpool: Liverpool University Press, 2000).

Belchem, J. (ed.), *Liverpool 800: culture, character and history* (Liverpool: Liverpool University Press, 2006).

Belfiore, E., 'The methodological challenge of cross-national research: comparing cultural policy in Britain and Italy', Centre for Cultural Policy Studies, University of Warwick, Research paper 8 (2004).

Belfiore, E. and Bennett, O., 'Rethinking the social impact of the arts', *International Journal of Cultural Policy*, 13: 2 (2007).

Belfiore, E. and Bennett, O., *The social impact of the arts: an intellectual history* (Basingstoke: Palgrave Macmillan, 2008).

Benwell Community Development Project, *The making of the ruling class: two centuries of capital development on Tyneside* (Newcastle: Benwell Community Development Project, 1979).

Bianchini, F. and Landry, C., *The creative city* (London: Demos Papers, 1995).

Bianchini, F. and Parkinson, M. (eds), *Cultural policy and urban regeneration: the West European experience* (Manchester: Manchester University Press, 1993).

Black, L., '"Making Britain a gayer and more cultivated country": Wilson, Lee and the creative industries in the 1960s', *Contemporary British History* 20: 3 (2006), pp. 323–342.

Blenkinsop, A., *Enjoying the countryside* (London: Fabian Research Society Series no. 265, 1968).

Bragg, M., 'Faith of our fathers', *Northern Review*, 3 (1996).

Briggs, A., *The history of broadcasting in the United Kingdom volume II. The golden age of wireless* (Oxford: Oxford University Press, 1965).

Briggs, A., *The history of broadcasting in the United Kingdom volume III. The war of words* (Oxford: Oxford University Press, 1970).

Briggs, A., 'Local and regional in northern sound broadcasting', *Northern History*, 10 (1975).

Briggs, A., *The history of broadcasting in the United Kingdom volume IV. Sound and vision* (Oxford: Oxford University Press, 1979).

Briggs, A., *The history of broadcasting in the United Kingdom volume V. Competition 1955–1974* (Oxford: Oxford University Press, 1995).

Briggs, A. and Burke, P., *A social history of the media, from Gutenberg to the Internet* (Cambridge: Polity Press, 2002).

Brighton, A., 'Consumed by the political: the ruination of the Arts Council', *Critical Quarterly*, 1: 48 (2006).

Brighton, A., 'Towards a common culture: New Labour's cultural policy', *Critical Quarterly*, 41: 2 (1991).

Brown, A., *Tyne Tees Television: the first twenty years* (Newcastle: Tyne Tees Television, 1978).

Brunsdon, C., 'Crossroads: notes on soap opera', *Screen*, 22: 4 (1981).

Bunting, B. (ed. R. Cadell) *The complete poems* (Oxford: Oxford University Press, 1994).

Burgess, R., *Babies and broadcasters: the story of 45 New Bridge Street Newcastle upon Tyne 1826–1994* (Newcastle: Newcastle Building Society, 1994).

Burn, G., *The North of England Home Service* (London: Faber, 2004).

Burn, G., *Sex & violence, death & silence: encounters with recent art* (London: Faber and Faber, 2009).

Cameron, S. and Doling, J., 'Housing neighbourhoods and urban regeneration', *Urban Studies*, 31: 7 (1994).

Camporesi, V., 'The BBC and American broadcasting, 1922–55', *Media Culture and Society*, 16 (1994).

Carr, I., 'Novocastrian jazz 1950s and early 1960s', *Northern Review*, 4 (1996).

Casey, B., Dunlop, R. and Selwood, S. (eds), *Culture as commodity? The economics of the arts and built heritage in the UK* (London: Policy Studies Institute, 1996).

Cavanagh, D., 'Buntingology', *Northern Review*, 3 (1996).

Charlton, B., 'Post modernity and regional culture', *Northern Review*, 1 (1995).

Chatterton, P. and Hollands, R., *Urban nightscapes: youth cultures, pleasure spaces and corporate power* (London: Routledge, 2003).

Colls, R., *The colliers rant: song and culture in the industrial village* (London: Croom Helm, 1977).

Colls, R., *Identity of England* (Oxford: Oxford University Press, 2004).

Colls, R. (ed.), *Northumbria. 547–2000* (Chichester: Philimore and Co., Ltd., 2007).

Colls, R. and Lancaster, B., *Geordies: roots of regionalism* (Edinburgh: Edinburgh University Press, 1992).

Colls, R. and Lancaster, B. (eds), *Newcastle: a modern history* (Chichester: Philimore and Co., Ltd., 2001).

Corner, J. (ed.), *Documentary and the mass media* (London: Edward Arnold, 1986).

Corner, J. (ed.), *British popular television* (London: BFI, 1991).

Corner, J., *The art of the record* (Manchester: Manchester University Press, 1996).

Couch, C., *City of change and challenge: urban planning and regeneration in Liverpool* (Aldershot: Ashgate, 2003).

Cox, M. and Giles, M. (eds), *Granada Television: the first generation* (Manchester: Manchester University Press, 2002).

Crinson, M. (ed.), *Urban memory: history and amnesia in the modern city* (London: Routledge, 2005).

Croft, A., *Red letter days: British fiction in the 1930s* (London: Lawrence and Wishart, 1990).

Dagen Bloom, N., *Merchant of illusion: James Rouse: America's salesman of the businessman's utopia* (Columbus, OH: Ohio State University Press, 2004).

Deacon, B., 'Under construction: culture and regional formation in South West England', *European Urban and Regional Studies*, 11 (2004), 213–225.

Dickson, M., *Art with people* (Sunderland: AN Publications, 1995).

Dormer, P., 'The arms length principle', *Marxism Today*, 25: 12 (1982).

Ehland, C. (ed.), *Thinking northern: textures of identity in the north of England* (Amsterdam and New York: Rodopi, 2007).

Ewen, S. and Saunie, P. Y. (eds), *Another global city: historical explorations into the transnational municipal movement 1850–2000* (Basingstoke: Palgrave Macmillan, 2008).

Farrell, T., *Place: a story of modelmaking menageries and paper rounds* (London: Laurence King Publishers Ltd., 2004).

Fawcett, C. B., *Provinces of England: a study of geographical aspects of devolution* (London: Hutchinson, 1961).

Fawcett, H. (ed.), *Looking at Newcastle* (Newcastle: Northumbria University Press, 2007).

Friesner, S., 'Travails of a naked typist: the plays of C.P. Taylor', *New Theatre Quarterly*, 4: 33 (February 1993).

Frith, S., 'The good, the bad, and the indifferent: defending popular culture from the populists', *Diacritics*, 21: 4 (1991).

Fyrth, J. (ed.), *Labour's promised land: culture and society in Labour Britain 1945–51* (London: Lawrence and Wishart, 1995).

Goddard, J. (ed.), *Popular television in Britain* (London: British Film Institute Publishing, 1991).

Goodfellow, D., *Tyneside: the social facts* (Newcastle: Co-operative Printing Society, 1942).

Green, A. and Pollard, A. J. (eds), *Regional identities in North East England 1300–2000* (Woodbridge: Boydell and Brewer, 2007).

Gregson, K., 'The media, regional culture and the Great North Run: Big Bren's human race', *Culture, Sport and Society*, 4: 1 (2001).

Griffiths, B., *North east dialect: survey and wordlist* (Newcastle: Centre for Northern Studies, 2001).

Griffiths, B., *North east dialect: the texts* (Newcastle: Centre for Northern Studies, 2002).

Griffiths, B., *A dictionary of north east dialect* (Newcastle: Northumbria University Press, 2004).

Griffiths, B., *Northern Sinfonia: a magic of its own* (Newcastle: Northumbria University Press, 2004).

Griffiths, B., *The Pitmatic talk of the north east coalfield* (Newcastle: Northumbria University Press, 2007).

Griffiths, B., *Fishing and folk: life and dialect on the north sea coast* (Newcastle: Northumbria University Press, 2008).

Hall, M., *The artists of Northumbria: an illustrated dictionary of Northumberland, Newcastle upon Tyne, Durham and North East Yorkshire painters, illustrators, caricaturists and cartoonists born between 1625 and 1950*, rev. edn (Bristol: Art Dictionaries Ltd., 2005).

Harker, D., *Fakesong: the manufacture of British 'folksong' 1700 to the present day* (Milton Keynes: Open University Press, 1985).

Harrison, J. F. C., *Learning and living 1760–1960: a study in the history of English adult education* (Basingstoke: Macmillan, 1994).

Haynes, J., *Ces't ma vie folks and thanks for coming! An autobiography* (London: Faber, 1982).

Judd, D. and Feinstien, S. (eds), *The tourist city* (New Haven: Yale University Press, 1993).

Katz, V., *Black Mountain College: experiment in art* (Cambridge, MA: MIT Press, 2003).

Kearns, G. and Phil, C. (eds), *Selling places: the city as cultural capital past and present* (London: Pergamon, 1993).

Keating, M., 'Rethinking the region: culture, institutions and economic development in Catalonia and Galicia', *European Urban and Regional Studies*, 8 (July 2001).

Kirk, N. (ed.), *Northern identities: historical interpretations of the north and northerness* (Ashgate: Farnham, 2000).

Lancaster, B. (ed.), *Working class housing on Tyneside* (Bewick Press: Newcastle, 1994).

Lancaster, B., Newton, D. and Vall, N. (eds), *An agenda for regional history* (Newcastle: Northumbria University Press, 2007).

Lee, R., *The Church of England in the Durham Coalfield, 1810–1926: clergymen, capitalists and colliers* (Woodbridge: Boydell and Brewer, 2007).

Leventhal, F. M., ' "The best for the most": CEMA and state sponsorship of the arts in wartime, 1939–1945', *Twentieth Century British History*, 1 (1990).

Leyshon, A., Matless, D. and Revill, G. (eds), *The place of music* (New York: The Guildford Press, 1998).

Lindgren, A., 'Varför inrätta kulturnämnd? Lokal kulturpolitik i två kommuner', *Historisk Tidskrift*, 128: 2 (2008).

Martin, P. J., *Sounds and society: themes in the sociology of music* (Manchester: Manchester University Press, 1995).

Massey, D., *For space* (London: Sage, 2005).

McAllister, A. (ed.), *The Objectivists: an anthology* (Tarset: Bloodaxe Books, 1996).

McCord, N. and R. Thompson, *The northern counties, from AD 1000* (London: Longman, 1998).

McKibbin, R., *Cultures and class* (Oxford: Oxford University Press, 1998).

Metcalf, A., *Leisure and recreation in a Victorian mining community: the social economy of leisure in north east England 1820–1914* (London: Routledge, 2005).

Miles, M., *Art space and the city: public art and urban futures* (London: Routledge, 1997).

Miles, S., '"Our Tyne": iconic regeneration and the revitalisation of identity in NewcastleGateshead', *Urban Studies*, 42: 5–6 (2005).

Milne, G., *North East England 1850–1914: the dynamics of a maritime-industrial region* (Woodbridge: Boydell and Brewer, 2006).

Moore-Gilbert, B. (ed.), *The arts in the 1970s: cultural closure* (London: Routledge, 1994).

Moore-Gilbert, B. and Seed, J. (eds), *Cultural revolution? The challenge of the arts in the 1960s* (New York: Routledge, 1992).

Morris, R. J. and Gunn, S. (eds), *Identities in space: contested terrains in the western city since 1850* (London: Ashgate, 2001).

Murphy, J., 'Folk on Tyne: Tyneside culture and the second folk revival, 1950–75', PhD thesis (Northumbria University, 2007).

Murphy, J., 'Selling coals to Newcastle: the media and publishing in relation to North Eastern folk music, 1945–1975', *Papers in North East History*, 17 (2008).

Myers, A., *Myers' literary guide* (Newcastle: Centre for Northern Studies, 1997).

Myerscough, J., *The economic importance of the arts in Britain* (London: Policy Studies Institute, 1988).

O'Dell, T. and Billing, P. (eds), *Experiencescapes: tourism culture and economy* (Copenhagen: Copenhagen Business School Press, 2005).

Olson, J., *Better places, better lives: a biography of James Rouse* (Washington, DC: The Urban Land Institute, 2003).

Paasi, A., 'Region and place: regional identity in question', *Progress in Human Geography*, 4 (2003), 239–256.

Pegg, M., *Broadcasting and society 1918–1939* (Beckingham: Croom Helm, 1983).

Perkin, H., *The rise of professional society: England since 1880* (London: Routledge, 1990).

Philo, C. and Kearns, G., *Selling places* (Oxford: Pergamon Press, 1993).

Phipps, C., Tobler, J. and Smith, S. (eds), *North stars* (London: Zymurgy Publishing, 2005).

Pickard, T., *High on the walls* (London: Fulcrum Press, 1967).

Pickard, T., 'Work in progress 1', *Northern Review*, 8 (1999).

Pickard, T. and Griffiths, B., *TYNE TXTS* (Newcastle: Amra Imprint and Morden Poets, 2002).

Putnam, R., *Making democracy work: civic traditions in modern Italy* (Princeton, NJ: Princeton University Press, 1993).

Richards, J., *Films and British national identity: from Dickens to Dad's Army* (Manchester: Manchester University Press, 1997).

Robinson, F. (ed.), *Post-industrial Tyneside* (Newcastle upon Tyne: City Libraries and Arts, 1988).

Rowe, W. (ed.), *Salt companion to Bill Griffiths* (Cambridge: Salt Books, 2007).

Russell, D., *Looking north: Northern England in the national imagination* (Manchester: Manchester University Press, 2004).

Scannell, P., 'The stuff of radio', in J. Corner (ed.), *Documentary and the mass media* (London: Edward Arnold, 1986).

Scannell, P., *Radio, television and modern life* (Oxford: Blackwell, 1996).

Scannell, P. and Cardiff, D. (eds), *A social history of British broadcasting volume 1: 1922–1939. Serving the nation* (Oxford: Oxford University Press, 1991).

Scott, M., 'Post-war developments in art in Newcastle: was it a golden age?', *Northern Review*, 4 (1996).

Sendall, B., *Independent Television in Britain, Volume 2, expansion and change, 1958–1968* (London: Macmillan, 1983).

Shaw, K., 'The politics of private public partnerships in Tyne and Wear', *Northern Economic Review*, 19 (1990).

Shields, R., *Places on the margin: alternative geographies of modernity* (London: Routledge, 1991).

Sjohlt, P., 'Culture as a strategic development device: the role of "European Cities of Culture" with particular reference to Bergen', *European Urban and Regional Studies*, 6 (Oct. 1999), 339–347.

Snell, K. (ed.), *The regional novel in Britain and Ireland 1800–1900* (Cambridge: Cambridge University Press, 1998).

Stansfield, K., 'Gateshead Garden Festival strategy', *The Planner* (1 June 1990).

Stead, P., *Film and the working class: the feature film in British and American society* (London: Routledge, 1989).

Stokes, M. (ed.), *Ethnicity identity and music: the musical construction of place* (Oxford: Berg Publishers, 1994).

Thompson, F. M. L. (ed.), *Cambridge social history of Britain Vol.1* (Cambridge: Cambridge University Press, 1990).

Trondman, M., 'Det kulturpolitiska dilemmats forskningscentrum', *KRUT*, 95, 3/99, 11.

Turnock, R. and Johnson, C., *ITV cultures: independent television over fifty years* (Maidenhead: Open University Press, 2005).

Usherwood, P., 'The media success of Antony Gormley's "Angel of the North"', *Visual Culture in Britain*, 2 (2001).

Usherwood, P., Beach, J. and Morris, C. (eds), *Public sculpture of North East England* (Liverpool: Liverpool University Press, 2000).

Vall, N., *Cities in decline? A comparative history of Malmo and Newcastle after 1945* (Malmo: Malmo University Press, 2007).

Vall, N., '"Polishing the pitmen": cultural improvers in North East England 1920–1960', *Northern History*, 41: 1 (2004).

Vall, N., 'Bohemians and "pitmen painters" in North East England 1930–1970', *Visual Culture in Britain*, 5: 1 (2004).

Varley, W., 'Baltic blunders', *New Statesman*, 134: 5 (2005).

Vickery, J., 'The emergence of culture-led regeneration: a policy concept and its discontents', Centre for Cultural Policy Studies, Research Paper 9 (2007).

Wales, K., *Northern English: a social and cultural history* (Cambridge: Cambridge University Press, 2006).

Wallinger, M. and Warnock, M. (eds), *Art for all? Their policies and our culture* (London: Peer, 2000).

Walton, J. and Cross, G. (eds), *The playful crowd: pleasure places in the twentieth century* (New York: Columbia University Press, 2005).

Weight, R. and Beach, A. (eds), *The right to belong: citizenship and national identity in Britain 1930–1960* (London: I. B. Tauris, 1998).

Whetstone, D., *NewcastleGateshead: the making of a cultural capital* (Newcastle: ncj Media, 2009).

White, E. W., *The Arts Council of Great Britain* (London: Davis-Poynter, 1975).

Whyte, I. and Winchester, A. (eds), *Society, landscape and environment in upland Britain*, Special Volume, Society of Landscape Studies (2004).

Wolman, H. L., Cook Ford III, C. and Hill, E., 'Evaluating the success of urban success stories', *Urban Studies*, 31: 6 (1994).

Oral reminiscences

Recorded interviews with the following individuals are all in the author's possession: Leonard Barras, Heather Ging, Val McLane, Michael Mould, Anna Pepperall, Connie Pickard, Alan Plater, Mollie Simmonds, Peter Stark, David Whetstone.

Index